Enclosing Behavior

COMMUNITY DEVELOPMENT SERIES

Series Editor: Richard P. Dober, AIP

URBAN ENVIRONMENTS AND HUMAN BEHAVIOR: An Annotated Bibliography/Edited by Gwen Bell, Edwina Randall, and Judith E. R. Roeder

DESIGNING FOR HUMAN BEHAVIOR: Architecture and the Behavioral Sciences/Edited by Jon Lang, Charles Burnette, Walter Moleski, and David Vachon

ALTERNATIVE LEARNING ENVIRONMENTS/ Edited by Gary J. Coates

BEHAVIORAL RESEARCH METHODS IN ENVIRONMENTAL DESIGN/Edited by William Michelson

ARCHITECTURAL PSYCHOLOGY/Edited by Rikard Küller

MAN'S PERCEPTION OF MAN-MADE ENVIRONMENT/Sven Hesselgren

INSTRUCTIONAL MEDIA AND TECHNOLOGY: A Professional's Resource/Edited by Phillip J. Sleeman and D. M. Rockwell

NEIGHBORHOOD SPACE: User Needs and Design Responsibility/Randolph T. Hester

ENVIRONMENTAL KNOWING: Theories, Research, and Methods/Edited by Gary T. Moore and Reginald G. Golledge

PLANNING BUILDINGS AND FACILITIES FOR HIGHER EDUCATION/UNESCO

THE URBAN NEST/Anne-Marie Pollowy

DESIGNING THE OPEN NURSING HOME/Joseph A. Koncelik

METHODS OF ARCHITECTURAL PROGRAMMING/Henry Sanoff

HOUSING MESSAGES/Franklin D. Becker

BARRIER-FREE ENVIRONMENTS/Edited by Michael J. Bednar

HUMAN RESPONSE TO TALL BUILDINGS/Edited by Don Conway

ENCLOSING BEHAVIOR/Robert B. Bechtel

EDRA Conference Publications

EDRA 1/Edited by Henry Sanoff and Sidney Cohn

EDRA 2/Edited by John Archea and Charles M. Eastman

ENVIRONMENTAL DESIGN RESEARCH, Vol. I: Selected Papers/Edited by Wolfgang F. E. Preiser (EDRA 4)

ENVIRONMENTAL DESIGN RESEARCH, Vol. II: Sumposia and Workshops/Edited by Wolfgang F. E. Preiser (EDRA 4)

MAN-ENVIRONMENT INTERACTIONS: Evaluations and Applications, Parts I, II, and III/Edited by Daniel G. Carson (EDRA 5)

RESPONDING TO SOCIAL CHANGE/Edited by Basil Honikman (EDRA 6)

THE BEHAVIORAL BASIS OF DESIGN, BOOK 1/ Edited by Peter Suedfeld and James A. Russell (EDRA 7)

THE BEHAVIORAL BASIS OF DESIGN, Book 2/ Edited by Peter Suedfeld, James A. Russell Lawrence M. Ward, Francoise Szigeti, and Gerald Davis (EDRA 7)

CDS/31

Enclosing Behavior

Robert B. Bechtel
ENVIRONMENTAL RESEARCH AND
DEVELOPMENT FOUNDATION
TUCSON, ARIZONA

Dowden, Hutchinson & Ross, Inc.
Stroudsburg   Pennsylvania

Copyright © 1977 by **Dowden, Hutchinson & Ross, Inc.**
Community Development Series, Volume 31
Library of Congress Catalog Card Number: 77-2850
ISBN: 0-87933-069-4

79 78 77   5 4 3 2
Manufactured in the United States of America

LIBRARY OF CONGRESS CATALOGING IN PUBLICATION DATA
Bechtel, Robert B
  Enclosing behavior.
  (Community development series; v. 31)
  Includes bibliographical references and index.
  1. Architecture—Human factors. 2. Architecture—Environmental aspects. I. Title.
NA2542.4.B42   720   77-2850
ISBN 0-87933-069-4

Series Editor's Foreword

The idea that architecture and human behavior influence one another is hardly a fresh perception. Both the artists who carved out shadowed spaces for their mystical images in preliterate France and John Portman creating his latest hotel have congruent insights about human nature and its potential response to the built or adapted environment. What is interesting is the growing body of literature about design and behavior relationships, to an extent that this fascinating subject holds promise of becoming a root source for contemporary architecture.

In this context alone, Bob Bechtel's *Enclosing Behavior* comes at an opportune time. It synthesizes the state of the art, offers immediate suggestions about applications, and outlines further topics worth pursuing. In specific terms, it shows how professionals, clients, and users can work together to program and design such typical environments as housing and community facilities. Further, Bechtel demonstrates, through follow-up studies, just what benefits accrue from his suggested approaches, what pitfalls to avoid, and what improvements on methodologies can be made.

Enclosing Behavior is a fundamental book because of Bechtel's knowledge and his enlargement of his mentor's work, the influential Roger Barker. What we have here is more than an interpretation by a disciple, however. Bechtel's experience is a special one, combining as it does theoretical explorations and everyday design practice, experiences that he fluently shares with all in this pioneering work.

Written as a reference book, *Enclosing Behavior* is a welcomed addition to the Community Development Series (CDS), which is intended to facilitate the exchange of information, expert advice, and experience among professionals concerned with the built environment.

CDS publications include state-of-the art books, handbooks, and manuals. They are offered to planners, social scientists, architects, landscape architects, engineers, and those in related disciplines who may find benefits in having such knowledge in a readily convenient format.

Community here is defined in the broadest sense and includes the diverse places that support human activities in all their manifestations. They range in scale from a family room to the metropolis. Obviously, such places vary in size, function, configuration, and detailed attributes, and, accordingly, planning and design methodologies that are used in shaping these places will differ in approach and realization.

In working with community as defined, CDS is neither bounded by traditional theory nor does it presume to establish a philosophic framework for all professional practices. There are, however, some themes that do identify CDS books conceptually. These propositions include: active user and client involvement in problem defining and problem solving; systematic searching out of patterns, relationships and behavioral settings as a prelude to design; a high regard for physical interdependence of communities; ecological ethics; and an interest in not just finding appropriate solutions but also in establishing ways and means for having those solutions implemented.

From time to time, CDS books will appeal to and serve a larger audience than just the related professions. They will do so because the subject matter will help the owner, user, and manager of the built environment become more aware of issues, possibilities, techniques. These books will be organized so that participation and involvement can move from the rhetoric of good intentions to the reality of dealing with substantive matters in comprehensive detail. As the reader will find, *Enclosing Behavior* does much to advance these editorial objectives.

Richard P. Dober, AIP

Preface

This is a book with a single message: there is no such thing as the design of space or spaces. *Behavior*, not space, is enclosed by architecture. No dwelling, building, or city is planned to be empty. In order for the planner or architect to know the purpose of his design, he must know thoroughly the behavior he will enclose. The study of behavior is not a simple, intuitive thing known to everyone. It is complicated and requires long discipline. But once the behavior is understood, the design process that follows is even more creative and satisfying than the design of empty spaces.

Underneath this simple message is the demonstration that behavior for architectural programming is best studied by the techniques of ecological psychology. These techniques are the K-21 scale and the behavior-setting survey, with which the reader will soon become familiar.

While this is a book written by a single author, many persons contributed their work. Clark Achelpohl and Roger Akers spent a great many hours collecting data for the East Side, West Side study. Fred Binding and Rajendra Srivastava supervised observers in the Arrowhead study. Myles Stevens was the architect-collaborator for Arrowhead. Later he assisted John Lawrence Daw and Associates in the final design. Bob Dumouchel was the director of Project Arrowhead.

Burgess Ledbetter of the U.S. Army Cold Regions Research and Engineering Laboratory was the first architect to learn the methods of ecological psychology well enough to incorporate them in his design process. He also prepared the illustrations in this book. Kay Fox labored for many hours typing and retyping the manuscript, which was three years from conception to completion. Last, I owe the greatest debt to Roger Barker, who more than any other person taught me the meaning of the word *behavior.*

Robert B. Bechtel

Contents

Series Editor's Foreword   v
Preface   vii

Introduction: Social Goals Through Design   1
    The Problem   2
    The Uses of Theory   10
    The New Pathway of Design   10
    Conclusion   13
    References   13

1 Client Attitudes toward Social Science   16
    The Monument Syndrome   16
    The Control Syndrome   17
    The Bricks-and-Mortar Syndrome   17
    The "We Already Know That" Syndrome   17
    The "Here Comes That Jargon Again"
    Syndrome   18
    Fees and Prices: The Final Obstacle   19
    References   20

2 Developmental Background   21
    Behavior Specimen Records   21
    An Ecological Perspective   22
    Behavior Settings   22
    The Behavior-Setting Survey   24
    Behavior and Environment   24
    Design and the Behavior-Setting Survey   30
    References   31

3 The Boundaries of Behavior Settings   33
    Boundary Problems   34
    Solutions to Boundary Problems   35
    Conclusions   47
    References   48

4 The Rating Scales   49
    Behavioral Data   49
    Descriptive Aspects of Settings   55
    Quantitative Aspects of Settings   58
    Action Pattern Ratings   59
    Behavior Mechanisms   62
    More Global Scales   64
    References   67

5 The Observational Method: Case 1   68
    Selecting the Observers and the Blocks for
    Study   69
    Recording the Data   69

ix

Description of the Areas   70
Data Collected   71
Conclusion   91
References   92
6 **The Observational Method: Case 2**   93
Background   93
Collection of Data   98
Analysis of Behavior-Setting Data   101
Discussion of Results   106
Final Recommendations   108
Innovative Approaches   115
Applying Innovative Techniques   115
Conclusions   117
References   118
7 **The Interview Method**   119
Random Sampling   120
The Interview   120
The Family Housing Environment of a
Military Base in Alaska   121
Deriving Habitability Guidelines   124
The Results   126
Conclusions and Recommendations   132
Final Comments   136

References   136
8 **The Analysis of Behavior-Setting Data**   137
Types of Analyses   137
Limitations of Behavior-Setting Data   141
References   142
9 **Behavior Focal Points: A Schema for
Community Design**   143
References   153
10 **A Theory of Human Scale**   154
Undermanning Theory   154
The School Studies   156
The City-Town Project   157
The Work of Allan Wicker and His Associates 158
Cost and Undermanning   160
The Problem of Task   160
Undermanning and Design   161
Conclusions   161
Future Research   164
References   164

Appendixes   167
Index   181

Enclosing
Behavior

Introduction: Social Goals Through Design

The design professions should certainly be aware by now that there is a considerable effort from many quarters to incorporate the use of behavioral sciences into professional design practice. The pioneering books of Hall (1966), Proshansky, Ittelson, and Rivlin (1970), Sommer (1969 and 1972b), Michelson (1970), and Wohlwill and Carson (1972) contain pleas for greater utilization of behavioral sciences and are full of illustrations of how this knowledge can be useful. The review articles of Craik (1970 and 1973) are the most comprehensive; journal articles by Winkel (1970), Mann and Hagevick (1971), and Blackman (1966) provide briefer introductions to the field. The journals *Environment and Behavior, Man Environment Systems,* and *Design and Environment* provide articles and references to this field.

Yet, in spite of this growing literature, in spite of conferences held by the American Institute of Architects (AIA) and the Environmental Design and Research Association (EDRA) and recent attempts to require behavioral science evaluations of buildings at the federal level,* this change in design practice has yet to come about (Ferebee, 1972; Pawley, 1971). The reasons for this are several. The process of change takes time, and considering that a short five years ago the field was barely having labor pains, one cannot expect too much to have happened. But more important, perhaps, is that the behavioral scientists and the design professions have not really understood that they are involved in a process of technological revolution. The behavioral scientists are presenting the design profession with a new technology, however imperfect it may be, and much like the first colonial missionary workers, they cannot understand why the "natives" will not instantly accept this obviously superior way of doing things. What is well known and documented among anthropologists (Goodenough, 1963; Spicer,

*For example, see the Housing and Community Development Act of 1974, public law 93–383, 93d Congress, S. 3066, August 1974, which authorizes the Department of Housing and Urban Development to spend up to $10 million on housing research. See also the report of the 1974 HUD Biennial Awards for Design Excellence (Canty, 1974).

1952) and sociologists (Etzioni, 1966) is not applied to the current ferment in the design professions. Technological change among the American Indians or the natives of Thailand is accepted and understood, but technological change among a largely middle-class profession in the Western world is too sacrosanct to be treated on such a level. Yet technological change is clearly what is occurring. Social scientists are intervening in design practice and attempting to produce change, and if there has been any success, it is because some members of the design professions have welcomed and encouraged this intervention. In fact, members of the design professions have played a key role in beginning this new technological change (Lynch, 1960; Alexander, 1964; and Sanoff et al. 1968).

What is important to consider is not the fear that behavioral scientists are going to take over the design professions or overwhelm them but that the new technology being offered has precise benefits for design. Namely, it adds two important stages to the front and terminal points of the design process, and it does not destroy the creative elements of design. The new technology does not harm the creative process any more than celluloid film destroyed writing plays or novels or recording devices destroyed the composing of music. The new technology does, however, regard the largest amount of design that goes on today as a half process—a process without sufficient information to perform optimally and is almost entirely without evaluation. The lack of evaluation is the most devastating criticism that can be made against current design practice. The assumption behind evaluation is that without adequate knowledge of what one has done in the past there is a serious question as to whether one knows what he is doing in the present.

THE PROBLEM

Perhaps none of the requirements for change in the design process would have come about were it not for a basic change in values that has taken place in the

United States and elsewhere. First, there is the environmental movement characterized by such writers as Dubos (1969), McHarg (1969), and others. This movement has revived the conservation ethic and seriously questioned the growth ethic. A second change of values began with Harrington's *The Other America* (1963), which led to the war on poverty, the federal Office of Economic Opportunity programs, and the new democratic ideals of citizen participation. A third influence was the concern for the "economic philistinism" of the United States government (Bauer, 1966), which helped lead to The Panel on Social Indicators and the document *Toward a Social Report* (1969). Still a fourth influence is the consumer protection movement led by Ralph Nader and now being institutionalized at federal, state, and municipal government levels. These movements became popular and forced the middle-class concepts of professional practice to be questioned. The legal profession adapted by inventing Legal Aid storefront operations. The *Miranda* decision brought about changes in police practice. The medical profession developed comprehensive health centers and experienced Medicaid and Medicare laws that changed medical practice. Psychiatry developed the community mental health center and outreach clinics; and, finally, though mixed with the environmental psychology technology movement, the design professions are expected to have social goals: to contribute to the quality of human life without harming the environment, to encourage citizen participation in the design process, and to demonstrate a convincing sense of new social awareness. But exactly how does a design professional go about this? How can the design process be used to accomplish these social goals? There are at least three broad avenues of approach that can be taken: the traditional, the neodemocratic, and the neotechnological.

The Traditional Method

The traditional method is practiced in the majority of architecture and planning offices. The practitioner takes what he has learned from his training and experience and applies it. He offers a service to a client and is paid for that service. The cultural assumptions of this role are so simple and clear that there was previously no need to question them. They were a good way of doing business, and they got things done. The same assumptions undergird the professional practices of law, medicine, engineering, and practically any other group that asserts it is professional. The essence of professionalism is that a person becomes expert in a field through academic study, generally through the graduate level and then others hire his services for a fee. The problem with this practice is that the bulk of information is assumed to flow all one way—from expert to client—and that over the years this has come to mean the professional has adopted a paternalistic attitude, an attitude that he (the professional) is the one who knows best what is good for the client and that it is the client's business to listen only. After all, how could we have professionals without this assumption? If the expert did not know more than the client, he would not be an expert.

It is not just that the expert knows more than the client but more the particular view that the expert takes of his own knowledge and of the competence of his client. The best definition of paternalism comes from a lower-class client in public housing who described a member of the housing board (Bechtel, 1972b): "She can tell you just how you ought to live without even bothering to ask you about it."

Essentially, then, the designer who goes to the drawing board without extensive advocate type consultation with his clients is a practitioner in the paternalistic mode.

What are the reasons for this state of affairs? One of the most salient is the kind of training and the reward system that operate in the schools of design. The architect is educated (as are other professionals) to respond to the criticism and evaluation of his peers, not his clients. Training is based on following successful models of designers who have been rated highly by fellow professionals. The result can be the most-often-referred-to disaster of Pruitt Igoe,* but

*Pruitt Igoe is the most spectacular failure of the U.S. housing system. Built at a cost of over $30 million in 1954, it went through a long series of renovations and was torn down in 1972.

there are other examples ranging from the ape house at the Kansas City Zoo to the city of Chandigarh[†] (Brolin, 1972).

Typical of the paternalistic attitude of the master architect is a statement of Richard Neutra (Dempsey, 1972) that he could build a house in such a way as to guarantee a divorce in one month regardless of whatever couple would inhabit the house. In short, this kind of paternalism assumes the professional knows all he needs to know about human behavior and that it is entirely within his competence to manipulate it. The training, the award system, and accepted professional practices back him up.

The awards given in architecture go back to the tradition of architecture as one of the fine arts. A designer striving to win one of these awards must put into his design what might be called an "artistic swoon" factor that will cause his colleagues to "swoon in ecstasy" at the mere sight of his design. And this is a boost to professional practice as well, for winners of these awards have not been known to go broke *even though their designs may be disasters from the point of view of clients who live in them.*

The paternalistic attitude and the design for artistic merit alone are pathways that have met with considerable financial success. Whether these modes of operation can continue with the financial success they have known in the past is not certain, but it is clear that with the "new awareness" Sommer (1972b) speaks of, there are other pathways and more rewarding ones.

Client-Centered Design: The Neodemocratic Approach

It was Carl Rogers (1951) who originated the concept in psychiatry that rather than have the therapist paternalistically set goals for the patient, the patient should establish his own goals. This notion swept the psychiatric field but has been somewhat modified to-

[†]Chandigarh is a city of 257,000 (1971) designed by Le Corbusier. Unfortunately, it was designed for Western Europeans but the location was India.

day, especially with lower-class clients. From the poverty programs* (Spiegel, 1968; Kramer, 1969) much the same philosophy has crept into design. Many designers embraced this concept as advocacy planning or advocacy design (Davidoff, 1965; Hatch, 1965; *Progressive Architecture*, 1968). Some of these attempts may have been successful. However, the chief problem with advocacy planning is that it needs a scientific basis. Most attempts at citizen participation have failed (Moynihan, 1969). There are many reasons for this, and a few are very pertinent to design practices.

Critical to understanding any advocacy or citizen participation process is the concept that it is essentially an information-gathering operation. However successful the designer may be in establishing a relationship with prospective clients, unless the information he gathers is representative of the persons for whom the design is intended, the exercise is a failure. The citizen advocacy or participation issue frequently is obscured because it is very difficult to tell who represents the people. The poverty workers[†] did not need to be so concerned with representation (cf. Alinsky, 1971) because their purpose was to gain power. Therefore, they would work with any faction that had the motivation to gain power. Unfortunately, the designer is usually unaware of factionalism and thus cannot deal with it (Siegel and Beals, 1960; French, 1962; and Clifton, 1965). Bettleheim (1943) provides the model for the two basic factions—those that ally themselves with the dominant power and those that oppose it—that arise in minority groups. While this generally may hold over large numbers of instances, any one case may vary greatly. For example, in the Arrowhead project (see chapter 6) (Bechtel,

*Kramer (1969) details how the "sleeper" clause of Title II-A, Section 202 (2) (3) of the Economic Opportunity Act of 1964 required citizen participation in the poverty programs and how this requirement became the most distinguished characteristic of all the programs. Moynihan (1969) regards this aspect as a failure.
[†]Alinsky trained his workers to embarrass officials into yielding to demands by use of picket lines and "sit-in" demonstrations.

1972a) there were four identifiable factions. It is imperative to realize that *all* factions do not represent a group. For the kind of information needed for design purposes, there is simply no substitute for scientific sampling procedures; citizen participation alone will not supply this much-needed information.

In Project Arrowhead (Bechtel, 1972a), a questionnaire was administered to a carefully sampled group of 100 residents. One of the purposes of that sample was to discover how many washing machines and dryers would be needed for a new laundromat to be located on the project grounds. About a year later, one of the faction leaders among residents attacked this survey by saying people did not answer correctly; many people had purchased washers and dryers in the meantime and a laundry facility was not needed. It would have been easy to take this "voice of the people" literally and revise plans. However, a second survey with an even larger sample revealed information virtually identical to the first. Suffice it to say that this kind of information is very critical to planning a laundromat in a poor neighborhood, and the process of obtaining it must be as scientific as possible because the risks are far too high to consider other procedures.

Although there are probably many examples of cases where designers have correctly sampled the population being studied, there are overwhelming numbers where sampling is not even mentioned. A good model of how this process should be carried out is Deasy and Bolling's (1969) Hooper Avenue School study. Deasy and Bolling concluded, "One of the clearest lessons is that it is unwise to assume that an individual or group, no matter how conscientious and thoughtful, can accurately predict the complex goals, values and strains of a total school community." In the appendix to this study, the social psychologist Lasswell carefully outlined his sampling procedure.

The usefulness of such a procedure is further illustrated by Deasy and Bolling:

. . . in a project such as this the architect is frequently caught between conflicting groups without any effective means for achieving consensus. As long as decisions are based on personal opinions, it is very difficult to say that the opinions of one group are decisively better than another.

Carefully collected, objective data changes this situation dramatically. Many debates are foreclosed because there is no longer anything to debate. . . .

Thus, while advocacy planning and design may be important in order to involve clients in the design process, it should never supersede the primary need for collecting objective data, and while advocacy procedures are undertaken usually to inform the designer, it more often ends up as the designer informing the clients (in nonpaternalistic fashion, of course) of the facts derived from data collection. Needless to say, Deasy and Bolling found that their conclusions differed widely from traditional concepts of design and the way design decisions are usually arrived at. Their citizen participation effort was disappointing (which is usual), *but this did not interfere with their arrival at sound conclusions.*

One more comment is necessary. When dealing with poor populations (regardless of race), the designer must be aware of one other element besides factionalism. As a result of centuries of the paternalistic attitude, poor people have arrived at a state of dependency (Pareek, 1971; Bechtel, 1972b). This means that the designer is very likely to encounter two mutually contradictory responses from such populations. One is the response: "You are the expert, you tell me." This is the exact complement to paternalism, and it demonstrates how paternalism is fostered by dependency. In fact, each reinforces the other. The second response is something like, "We are tired of you experts coming in here and telling us how to do things." This response is the opposite of the first, but it is not unusual to see it voiced by the same group or even by the same person. There are answers to these responses but the final working out of the relationship often requires the solving of problems beyond the capability of the average designer.

In summary, the designer who attempts to achieve social goals by client-centered design procedures is undertaking an extremely hazardous course. It is not an impossible course, but by far the safest route is the collection of data by strictly scientific procedures. Then, even if the advocacy group is a failure, the basic information for design decisions is not affected. The reason for these difficulties is that both the designer and his clients are now caught in a process of technological change and that a sure citizen participation element has not yet been worked out procedurely that permits simultaneous data-gathering procedures necessary to feed into the design process. The optimal procedure—involving clients in the data-gathering process itself—places the burden of training on the professional.

The Designer-Researcher and Research-Design Teams: The Neotechnological Approach

The research hurdles

The third pathway is to incorporate research components into the design process. This usually means forming a design-research team or having the designer do his own research. It would be less than objective not to say that the social sciences have thrown some formidable obstacles in the way of this path despite the efforts of other social scientists to get designers to accept the new technology.

One of the most severe hurdles to overcome is that most of social science study has not been directed to design-oriented problems. The vast array of social science information has been collected under the strained "publish or perish" motive of career advancement and has been aimed at basic rather than applied answers. Thus, the bulk of social science information takes the form of an untranslated foreign language. It is really worse than that, however, because extrapolating from basic to applied means a whole new series of studies.

Personality-culture research One of the most difficult hurdles for the designer to overcome is the hurdle of personality and personality-culture research. The majority of psychological studies that "filter" over to designers seem to involve some aspect of personality. These studies assume there is a structure of internal being in all persons called the personality and that one who understands personality can predict behavior. Unfortunately, this theory has yet to be demonstrated since clinicians whose work is based on personality theories have yet to predict better than chance (Gough, 1962) and even the very widely used instruments such as the Rorschach Test (Jensen, 1959, 1964) and the TAT test for achievement motivation (McClelland, 1961) have little scientific evidence for reliability (Entwisle, 1972). Small wonder that with so many social scientists using personality-related measures that are not reliable, the designer should be fooled into doing the same.

But if personality measures are valid, what real use could they be to the designer? Aren't the social goals of the design process closely tied with meeting social needs of great numbers of people (cf. Zeisel, 1971)? And how could these needs be appraised by a personality measure? In trying to measure national character, social scientists have found that the modal personality of a culture (that is, the kind of personality assumed to be most typical of that culture) will account for only 35 to 40 percent of the population (Wallace, 1962; Duijker and Frijda, 1960). These disappointing statistical findings have led to more studies in which the statistical basis of inference is dropped altogether; instead one "infers" a "basic" personality for the culture, class, or particular group one is studying without statistical support (Inkeles and Levinson, 1954). Because of a tendency to stereotype social classes, cultures, and groups, the designer may be tempted to base his decisions on such works and then be disappointed at results. Books like Hall's (1966) *The Hidden Dimension* could be misleading in the same way. There remains no safer way than to collect data from the specific population to be served by the design.

The paper-and-pencil tests If the personality-culture research is dangerous to apply uncritically, what

other course can one take? Another frequent mode is the adoption of many tests and measures that have wide use in the social sciences. Included among these are such measures as the semantic differential (Heise, 1969), probably the most widely used of all paper-and-pencil measures in the field of environmental psychology. Good (1963), Sanoff et al. (1971), and Seaton and Collins (1972) are just a few of the many, many examples. What is often not recognized is that no matter how carefully questions are constructed on the semantic differential, no matter how cleverly stated, there are really only three qualitatively distinct bits of information gained: how *good* (or bad) whatever is being considered is; how *strong* (or weak) it seems; and how *active* (or inactive) it is. Now this is fine if all one needs to know is how good, powerful, and active a certain design feature is. But what has that got to do with how people will behave in the design? There is considerable evidence to show that attitudes are very poorly related to how someone would actually behave (Wicker, 1969a), which is what the designer needs to know.

Much the same can be said for many paper-and-pencil questionnaires. Rodman (1963) suggests that most lower-class people very likely hold two sets of value systems: one they would like to hold (or aspire to) and the other they know they have to accept in their restricted circumstances. Which value system is evoked by the questionnaire administered? It is not possible to decide.

Some questionnaires apply strictly to environmental elements and are largely objective. These have been used with some success. Jackson (1969) and Moos (1971) have developed scales for measuring environments of hospital wards. Sommer's (1972b) evaluator's cookbook set of questionnaires is also as good as one could find currently for the purposes of evaluation if one wants to use questionnaires primarily. It is important to keep in mind that despite the tremendous proliferation of paper-and-pencil tests available from social science, very few are readily adaptable to the needs of the designer.

Theory building

It was Kurt Lewin who said that the most practical tool is a theory. And throughout the environmental psychology field, one hears frequent pleas for theory building (Paar, 1970; Rapoport, 1972). This is not to say that some researchers have not tried (Studer, 1970), but the pleas heard generally reflect a consensus that the theory has not been forthcoming or is not yet recognized as viable for most design situations (Mann and Hagevick, 1971). Nevertheless, several fields show promise of someday developing theories useful to the design process.

Pattern analysis One of the most popularly used systems was developed by Alexander (1964; Alexander et al., 1968; Alexander et al., 1970). It is termed *pattern analysis*, and it links specific behavior to specific design features. Alexander compiled these patterns into a programming sequence such that the designer can put them together into a comprehensive design program. Yet the basic problems mentioned earlier remain: how is information obtained to feed into the scheme and how is the final design to be evaluated? For all the usefulness of his system, Alexander has done no more than make the traditional design process more systematic, with an added attempt to link design components to behavior. Certainly this is far from a theory, but it could someday provide the basis to derive a theory when enough data are accumulated.

Chapin and Logan (1969) have provided a system that has curious parallels to Alexander's from the behavioral science point of view. Their system of activity patterns may be the ideal data-collecting system to feed in to Alexander's design procedures. To date this has not been done.

Crowding Crowding behavior has become a popular subject among social scientists (Marsden, 1972; Esser, 1972; Zlutnick and Altman, 1972; Freedman, 1975). The most seminal study on crowding was probably by Calhoun (1962), who discovered the social phenomenon of the *behavioral sink*, a cessation of normal daily patterns of behavior when the number of contacts with other individuals, due to crowding, reaches such a point that it is not possible to perform the ordinary tasks of living.

Crowding behavior has many important consequences for design. Harking back to Neutra's earlier statement (Dempsey, 1972) about design for divorce, the same notion—that of not being free of (or in control of) contact with others—was implied.

Crowding theory, if it can be called such, implies more than a notion of mere density and seems to point to a concept that design must be structured around daily tasks that will be free from interference of too many contacts. Yet as Zlutnick and Altman (1972) conclude, so little has been done for design purposes that the research has not yet evolved to the theory-building stage.

Territoriality Since the publication of Ardrey's *The Territorial Imperative* (1966), the notion of territoriality as a design principle has had a certain popularity. Ardrey's thesis is that people have an instinctive desire to acquire and defend territory. The number of examples from animal studies that demonstrate this phenomenon are limitless. The studies where humans clearly exhibit this drive as a hereditary characteristic can all be challenged from either a methodological or conceptual point of view (Esser et al., 1965). Sundstrom and Altman (1972) provide a typical example of these studies. Their subjects did not consistently occupy specific territories over time because of population shifts, and they did not find a simple relationship between dominance and territorial behavior. Territorial behavior did not seem to be a unitary, temporally stable phenomenon. This is not to say that territoriality may not someday be a useful element (among many others) in the design process; it merely indicates that the concepts are not yet developed enough and supported by research to be useful at present.

Operant learning There is no denying that one of the most promising fields for changing human behavior by manipulating the external environment is the field of operant conditioning (Holland and Skinner, 1961). Although this field has already produced a revolution in teaching with the concepts of programmed learning and teaching machines and remains one of startling success in bits and pieces, it is not a coherent theory that can help design environments, *Walden Two* and *Beyond Freedom and Dignity* to the contrary (Skinner, 1948; 1971).

Unlike many other fields, though, the outlines of a future theory can be clearly seen. Certain elements of the environment, both social and physical-environmental, have been found to reinforce certain behaviors. Other elements have been found to inhibit certain human behaviors. Depending upon what behavior one wants to reinforce or inhibit, the environment can be so constructed. The simplicity of this vision, so enhanced by Skinner's books, will be considerably modified once the complexities of environment behavior and socioenvironment behavior interactions are understood and placed in a viable theoretical structure.

Social modeling A theory of human behavior that may show more promise than those previously mentioned is described by Bandura (1965, 1969) and Bandura and Walters (1963). This theory is based on the deceptively simple notion that people learn appropriate behavior by watching others perform. The cue to having environment control behavior is providing goats for the sheep to follow. Although Bandura and others intend this to be principally a model for childhood learning, presumably adults follow the imitative principle in conditions of uncertainty, such as crowds. This theory has evidence behind many of its hypotheses, but like so many others, it has not been applied to design problems yet. Theories like this suggest that social forces far outweigh physical stimuli of design in the influence of human behavior. If this is the case, then the designer still needs to know what limits there are on how his designs can influence human behavior.

Satisfaction sites Whenever environmental psychology and research akin to it are mentioned, works that deal with centrally motivating forces (such as satisfaction seeking and the quest for happiness) are scarce. Yet, if one considers the human being a unified creature, the seeking of a satisfying environment should be related to general satisfaction. The work of Shelly (1969) and his colleagues shows promise in providing evidence of how satisfaction sites relate to satisfaction seeking in general. Very briefly, Shelly's work demonstrates another way of looking at design problems in terms of social goals. Find those elements of physical design that have been most commonly linked with satisfaction and pleasure, he says, and incorporate them into a design to evoke satisfaction.

This oversimplified explanation does not do justice to Shelly's work, but it reflects the general approach one might take in applying his findings. An added dividend of his work is that it does not depend upon verbal reports of people to obtain data. One observes satisfaction taking place in all its evident signs, and "any behavior which persists or any behavior in which a number of people are involved may be used as an index of satisfaction as well as of the existence of some reinforcement" (Shelly and Adelberg, 1969). Of course, one must make sure that the behavior is not being produced by constraints (jail, for example) rather than by responses to reinforcing elements.

Shelly finds two kinds of satisfaction sites: those that increase arousal and those that decrease arousal. Shopping centers, and in fact most recreational pursuits, seem to increase arousal (an increase in general desires) up to a point where further arousal is unpleasant or exhausting and the person leaves. Arousal sites are chiefly characterized as places where social interaction takes place, while nonarousal or relaxing sites permit relaxation and decreasing levels of arousal. A third type of site is possible: that where one goes because he has nothing better to do. In Jamaica, Shelly and Adelberg (1969) analyzed eighty-two sites. Environmental factors included illumination; size in terms of physical space; presence of food and music; noise level; number of persons; and time spent there. Surprisingly, the amount of activity across all sites was very low. People were relatively stationary.

Shelly further classified his sites into eight types that ranged from a single person sitting on the hood of his car to a large nightclub. His data support the notion of the two general types, the arousing and the relaxing. Shelly's research is similar to that of more formal social theorists such as Thibaut and Kelley (1959).

Behavior settings: theory and problems By no means does the above list of potential theories for environmental psychology exhaust the possibilities or do justice to the positions mentioned. The reader is urged to consult the references in each section in order to learn about these theories in more complete form. But one theory remains that seems to encompass many of those above and to promise more for design practice. Many of the practitioners in the field consider it to be the proper direction (Van der Ryn, 1968; Altman, 1971; Little, 1970). It is the behavior-setting survey technique of Roger Barker and his colleagues (Barker and Wright, 1955; Barker, 1968; and Barker and Gump, 1964).

The advantages of Barker's methods for designers are several. The method assumes that physical environment and behavior are inextricably bound together. The method is observational and makes no hard-to-prove assumptions about motivation or cognition. Also, it is virtually the only method equally applicable to a room or a whole community and in which behavior can be objectively quantified. There are, however, several disadvantages to this method. First, it is a difficult method to learn. The difficulty is not only in the extremely meticulous observations and the seemingly endless calculations of scales and subscales (sixty-three in all), but in the fact that behavior-setting methodology flies in the face of some very cherished traditions in Western society, Western social science, and professional practice. It is very important that the designer recognize the possibility of these traditions in himself and in the social sciences so that he can more objectively evaluate what needs to be done to arrive at a better design process.

Barker and Wright pioneered in the study of ordinary daily behavior—not just bits and pieces of daily behavior but daily behavior in terms of a whole day in the life of an individual (Barker and Wright, 1951; Barker, 1968). Most social scientists have been concerned about the unusual or extraordinary events of life, or they create artificial situations in the laboratory that have no comparable existence in daily life (Barker, 1969). The result, from Barker's point of view, is that a distorted notion of human life has arisen. Freud's *Psychopathology of Everyday Life* (1938) becomes a posture for viewing daily behavior as variations of abnormality.

Another cherished tradition of social science is the prime importance of the individual. Personality research has been mentioned previously. But Barker's unit of behavior, the behavior setting, is supraindividual: it goes on regardless of the individual.

Thus, the designer must accept two premises that are contrary to traditions if he is to see the value of Barker's work: he is designing an environment for ordinary daily behavior about which very little is known outside Barker's work, and his designs are for great numbers of people, not distinct individuals. These two premises are not easy to accept either for social scientists or designers. One designer-researcher expressed to me after a discussion of Barker's techniques a protest based on his own research and design: "But you simply cannot lose sight of the individual!"

There is, however, one advantage of Barker's techniques that has not been mentioned and that needs to be emphasized more than any other: its directness in collecting valid information. It measures what people *do* with design features, not what they *say* they do. This is extremely important in considering whether to use questionnaires or observations. Binding* provided a very apt illustration. He was observing a church choir practice that was held regularly once a week. This was a behavior setting. When asked how much time they spent singing during choir practice, the

*Personal communication to author.

members of the choir made estimates that ranged from a low of thirty minutes in the hour to fifty minutes. Since this was choir practice, what better assumption about the behavior was there except to believe that most of the time was devoted to the central purpose of their gathering—singing? Being already skilled in observing daily behavior, Binding took out his stopwatch and clocked the time spent singing over several periods. The average time was eight minutes out of the hour.

The central lesson of Barker's research cannot be dismissed. When trying to determine what kinds of behavior are connected with particular design features or what kinds of behavior occur in any connection, there is no substitute for measuring behavior as it occurs in its own natural context (Willems and Raush, 1969).

Despite the importance of Barker's work, however, very few studies have been done linking behavior settings to design problems (Bechtel, 1972a, 1972b; Gump, 1972), and the results of these are likely to be slow in being assimilated. Nevertheless, the need for such techniques is so great that they will no doubt be adopted by many more eventually. More promising is the emergence of theoretical beginnings. Barker (1960) first proposed that the size of behavior settings is related to both the size of institutions and the kinds of satisfaction people get out of settings. This theory has important consequences for the design profession. It means simplistically, that smaller settings create greater pressures to participate and generate greater satisfaction. This is in direct contradiction to the assembly-line rooms of huge office buildings and consolidated schools. Wicker (1968, 1969b; Petty, 1975) is continuing research in this area, and some modifications of the theory are being made. Some applications of the theory were demonstrated in the Arrowhead public-housing project (Bechtel, 1972a) by reducing the size of the project to smaller social areas (See chapter 9 for a summary of undermanning research.) As yet, however, much needs to be done to make behavior-setting technology more available to designers. This book is an attempt in that direction.

THE USES OF THEORY

This discussion of various potential theories that may some day be of use to the design professions has revealed a very fragmentary picture. It might be accurate to say that all of them are theories that need to be rather than theories that are. It is well to keep in mind, however, what use can be made of the theories if and when they become available and that the facts they have uncovered provide a pool of resourceful information that is available now.

The chief purpose in developing a theory for designers to use is that it will enable the designer to apply essential elements of behavior to design principles. The elements of behavior will be given and the elements of design should follow. But the theory can never be more than a general guideline, it can never be a substitute for data gathering before design, and it can never be a substitute for evaluation. The accumulation of many evaluation studies will be the final test of any theory.

THE NEW PATHWAY OF DESIGN

Design Teams

It is safe to assume that the design professions will never be the same again. For better or worse, there is a new awareness that the design professions have to include new elements from the behavioral sciences in their process. One of the most informative examples of this new pathway is the firm of Brolin and Zeisel. Zeisel (1971) is a behavioral scientist who teamed up with an architect. He described some of the operations necessary for this new way of working. Significantly, his method lacks the evaluation step stressed above. Lang's article (1971) includes evaluation and lists the contribution of evaluation to theory building for design.* Yet, how can this contribution be made with the state of design practice as it now exists? Each firm, though it may include the essential step of evaluation, is not in the business of broadcasting its results to help competitor firms or to announce its own failures to the world. How can anyone reasonably expect the design profession to perform this kind of data-sharing operation voluntarily? Is it not a great deal like asking the contractor to perform his own building inspections? If evaluation is to have any meaning, it must be done by impartial, outside observers using standard, universally accepted criteria. Clearly, such a facility does not exist, and the forces opposing it would be formidable. What, then, are the new alternatives? Given the lack of a national apparatus for evaluation, the only present solution seems to be design teams of the Brolin-Zeisel caliber or university or nonprofit organizations such as Sanoff's.

Eclecticism versus the New Medievalism

The team approach, however, can only lead to a new kind of medievalism where each team builds its own fortress of data and techniques and then sallies forth in publication crusades trumpeting its own wares in the holy land of competition. How will this state of affairs, nearly upon us, help the profession as a whole? Is it really any different from the old paternalism with a new twist?

First, it is obvious that not enough is known in the current state of the art for any team or firm to be completely self-contained. Cooperation, especially with data, is a necessity for the advancement of any profession. Some external apparatus needs to be set up for evaluation. Don Conway's recent attempts (for

*The most recent and elaborate construction of a model for social science collaboration in the design process is the "coolfont" model (Conway, 1974).

the AIA) to make evaluation a legal requirement for every government building contract are a beginning. This step needs to be accomplished. A national repository for data or a national foundation for design research would be better.

Considering that these steps are not likely to be taken in the near future, however, the designer has no choice but to brave the new medievalism and to attempt to be as eclectic as possible. So little knowledge is available that it is necessary to borrow from whatever study that shows something has worked. Until the time that truly working theories evolve, the only choice is to be eclectic.

The Incremental Model

In the current period, and for some time to come, it does not look as if a usable theory of design and behavior will be forthcoming. Research in environmental psychology and sociology is becoming incremental, accumulating facts largely without theory. This incremental stage may last for some time, and it is similar to the way the practice of medicine works. In this regard, the designer can set up a design process that is deliberately incremental in nature. The following steps in data collection for evaluation are suggested. A firm would do well to begin this process by reviewing several buildings it has constructed and answering the following questions.

What does it communicate? Even though the behavior enclosed by the building is the primary criterion for success, it is still important to know what kind of message the outside of the building communicates. It was Ruesch (Ruesch and Kees, 1956) who first suggested that a building is a form of nonverbal communication. The Mayan temples, by their steep sides, conveyed the impression of a priest ascending into heaven when he disappeared at the top. Hence, the construction was functionally linked to the message of religious awe. Are similar messages conveyed by, say, skyscrapers? This will not be an easy question to answer since such messages are not easy for the average citizen to articulate. It is better for the designer to articulate the message he intends and then to ask people who are looking at the building whether it conveys that message. Seaton and Collins's (1972) work suggests that colored slides might be substituted for the actual building without a great loss of validity. Finally, the designer must ask whether the message he conveys by his external design is consistent with what he intended for behavior inside the building. A black youth took one look at a high-rise building in public housing and decided that it was designed to provide absolute control of the residents by moving a tank to the front where every window could be covered. Are there unintended messages in design?

What behavior does it encourage? A building is designed to encourage a specific group of behaviors. What is the evidence that these behaviors are actually encouraged? A major error of design is not to identify these behaviors precisely before design work begins. The design should at least demonstrate that the office workers, factory workers, tenants, and whoever else occupies the building are better able or at least as able to perform as they were in their former buildings. Of course, even though many criteria for success may not be met in improved performances, other benefits may still add up to a successful design. Generally, however, the specific behavior for which the building was designed should be enhanced in some demonstrable fashion.

What behavior does the design inhibit? Less obvious, but just as important in design, is the knowledge of what behaviors are inhibited by design features. Most obvious of the behaviors to inhibit is breaking and entering. Carman (1972) demonstrates how those behaviors can be suppressed by increasing accessibility under public scrutiny and decreasing it in private

areas. Other factors that may be important are needs to decrease talking in some places (for example, hospital corridors) but to increase it in others. An example of an environment that has become self-defeating is the museum where the need to house great collections has so overstimulated viewers that their opportunity to appreciate fully any one exhibit has been greatly inhibited (Bechtel, 1969).

How successful? Finally, the success of a design can be evaluated only when the goals and objectives of that design have been stated in precise enough terms to be measured and evaluated. The time to formulate these goals is at the very beginning of the project, at what Lang (1971) calls the problem identification phase and Zeisel (1971) calls the choosing of criteria. In any case, the research must be done either by a careful sampling of the population or by a technique like behavior-setting analysis that uses the whole population under consideration. An evaluation should, preferably, test the same population used in the initial research because a repeated measures design is especially powerful (Winer, 1971).

Control groups, that is, measuring similar people not influenced by design features, are sometimes necessary to determine whether the design effect was due to the physical change or due to the fact of people's being in a new building and being measured. The best text showing how to eliminate these confusions is by Campbell and Stanley (1963).

It is incorrect to refer to a "new" design process since the works of Lang (1971) and Zeisel (1971) outline the design process in great detail. However, two critical steps seem to be left out. One is the step of defining the behaviors to be enclosed by the design, and the other is the incorporation of the data into a systematic way of storing and retrieving information across different firms. The latest attempt at building a design process model (Conway, 1974) has incorporated all the necessary steps for architectural practice utilizing social science. It is worth emulating as a new model.

CONCLUSION

It was suggested at the beginning of this introduction that the designer has three pathways to follow in order to achieve social goals through design. The first is to impose these goals paternalistically. This is the method most often followed in practice. The second is to attempt client-centered design by use of the various participation techniques borrowed from the war on poverty programs. The third pathway is by doing research. The chief conclusion is that there is no way to escape doing research if one wants to accomplish social goals by design. The paternalistic method often ends in disaster for the client. The techniques of citizen participation have not proven satisfactory enough.

But research is a mixed blessing. Theories have not yet been satisfactorily formulated. Research must be done correctly to get results; but since the design professions have no way yet to take systematic advantage of the data, each researcher is left on his own. There are no accepted criteria for evaluating success in the design profession other than financial and reputational at the present time. Until such criteria are established and until the design professions organize their own academies of evaluation, the achievement of social goals will remain highly individualistic. There is only hope that with the passage of time, the need for standard research and evaluation procedures will become so accepted that the proper organizations will be formed to develop them. In the meantime, we have only the knights in shining armor riding their white horses—alone. For these few who are constantly increasing in number, this book was written.

REFERENCES

Alexander, C. *Notes on the Synthesis of Form.* Harvard University Press, 1964.

Alexander, C.; Hirshen, S.; Ishikawa, S.; Coffin, C.; and Angel, S. *Houses Generated by Patterns.* Center for Environmental Structure, 1970.

Alexander, C.; Ishikawa, S.; and Silverstein, M. *A Pattern Language Which Generates Multi-Service Centers.* Center for Environmental Structure, 1968.

Alinsky, S. *Rules for Radicals: A Pragmatic Primer for Realistic Radicals.* Vintage Books, 1971.

Altman, I. Remarks commenting on papers at the symposium on Consumer Behavior and Environmental Design at the American Psychological Association Convention. Washington, D.C., September 4, 1971.

Ardrey, R. *The Territorial Imperative.* Atheneum, 1966.

Bandura, A. "Vicarious Processes: A Case of No-Trial Learning." In L. Berkowitz, ed., *Advances in Experimental Social Psychology,* Academic Press, 1965, vol. 2.

——. *Principles of Behavior Modification.* Holt, Rinehart and Winston, 1969.

Bandura, A., and Walters, R. *Social Learning and Personality Development.* Holt, Rinehart and Winston, 1963.

Barker, R. "Ecology and Motivation." In M. Jones, ed., *Nebraska Symposium on Motivation.* University of Nebraska Press, 1960, pp. 1–9.

——. *Ecological Psychology.* Stanford University Press, 1968.

——. "Wanted: An Eco-Behavioral Science." In E. Willems and H. Raush, eds., *Naturalistic Viewpoints in Psychological Research.* Holt Rinehart and Winston, 1969, pp. 31–43.

Barker, R., and Gump, P. *Big School, Small School.* Stanford University Press, 1964.

Barker, R., and Wright, H. *One Boy's Day.* Harper & Row, 1951.

Barker, R., and Wright, H. *Midwest and Its Children.* Row, Peterson, 1955.

Bauer, R., ed. *Social Indicators.* MIT Press, 1966.

Bechtel, R. Remarks at the Smithsonian Conference on Appraising the Museum's Effectiveness as an Educational Institution, November 21, 1968.

——. "The Public Housing Environment: A Few Surprises." In W. Mitchell, ed., *Environmental Design: Research and Practice 1—Proceedings of the EDRA 3/AR8 Conference,* Los Angeles, UCLA, January 1972a, pp. 13-1-1 to 13-1-9.

——. "Dependency: An Unintended Result of Public Housing Policies." Paper delivered at the Conference on Housing and Mental Health, School of Architecture, University of Maryland, College Park, Maryland, March 27, 1972b.

Bettleheim, B. "Individual and Mass Behavior in Extreme Situations." *Journal of Abnormal and Social Psychology* 35 (1943):417–452.

Blackman, A., ed. "Environment and Behavior." *American Behavioral Scientist* 10 (1966).

Brolin, B. "What Went Wrong at Chandigarh?" *Smithsonian* 3 (1972):56–63.

Calhoun, J. "Population Density and Social Pathology." *Scientific American* 206 (1962):139–148.

Campbell, D., and Stanley, J. *Experimental and Quasi-Experimental Designs for Research.* Rand McNally, 1963.

Canty, D. "The 1974 HUD Design Awards: An Interdisciplinary Jury Looks Beyond Appearances." *AIA Journal* 62 (December 1974):23-24.

Carman, J. "To Catch A Thief . . . Wrap Security in a Tight Package." *Buildings* (May 1972):78-81.

Chapin, F., and Logan, T. "Patterns of Time and Space Use." In H. Perloff, ed., *The Quality of the Urban Environment.* Resources for the Future, 1969.

Clifton, J. "Culture Change, Structural Stability and Factionalism in the Prairie Potowatomie Reservation Community." *Midcontinent American Studies Journal* 6 (1965): 101-123.

Conway, D. ed. *Social Science and Design: A Process Model for Architect and Social Scientist Collaboration.* American Institute of Architects, Research Report, 1974.

Craik, K. "Environmental Psychology." In *New Directions in Psychology*, Holt, Rinehart and Winston, 1970, vol. 4.

——. "Environmental Psychology." *Annual Review of Psychology* (1973):403-422.

Davidoff, P. "Advocacy and Pluralism in Planning." *Journal of the American Institute of Planners* 31 (1965):331-338.

Deasy, C., and Bolling, R. *Real Goals Versus Popular Stereotypes in Planning for a Black Community* (pamphlet), 1969.

Dempsey, D. Man's Hidden Environment *Playboy Magazine* (May, 1972).

Dubos, R. *So Human an Animal.* American Museum of Natural History, 1969.

Duijker, H., and Frijda, N. *National Character and National Stereotypes.* North Holland Publishing Company, 1960.

Entwisle, D. "To Dispel Fantasies About Fantasy-Based Measures of Achievement Motivation." *Psychological Bulletin* 77 (1972):377-391.

Esser, A. "A Biosocial Perspective on Crowding." In J. Wohlwill and D. Carson, eds., *Environment and the Social Sciences: Perspectives and Applications.* American Psychological Association, 1972, pp. 15-28.

Esser, A. et al. "Territoriality of Patients on a Research Ward." In J. Wortis, ed., *Recent Advances in Biological Psychiatry.* Plenum, 1965, vol. 8.

Etzioni, A. *Studies in Social Change.* Holt, Rinehart and Winston, 1966.

Ferebee, A. "Design for Human Behavior." *Design and Environment* 2 (1972):23.

Freedman, J. *Crowding and Behavior.* Viking Press, 1975.

French, D. "Ambiguity and Irrelevancy in Factional Conflict." In M. Sherif, ed., *Intergroup Relations and Leadership.* Wiley, 1962.

Freud, S. The Psychopathology of Everyday Life in *The Basic Writings of Sigmund Freud*, Random House, 1938.

Good, L. "Introduction to Research Problems Relating Architectural Environment and Human Behavior." Master's thesis, University of Kansas, 1963.

Goodenough, W. *Cooperation in Change.* Russell Sage Foundation, 1963.

Gough, H. "Clinical Versus Statistical Prediction in Psychology." In L. Postman, *Psychology in the Making.* Alfred A. Knopf, 1962, pp. 526-584.

Gump, P. "Milieu, Environment and Behavior." *Design and Environment* (1972):48-59.

Hall, E. *The Hidden Dimension.* Doubleday, 1966.

Harrington, M. *The Other America.* Macmillan, 1963.

Hatch, C. R. "Some Thoughts on Advocacy Planning." *Architectural Forum* (June 1968):72.

Heise, D. "Some Methodological Issues in Semantic Differential Research." *Psychological Bulletin* 72 (1969):406-422.

Holland, J., and Skinner, B. *The Analysis of Behavior.* McGraw-Hill, 1961.

Inkeles, A., and Levinson, D. "National Character: The Study of Modal Personality and Sociocultural Systems." In G. Lindzey, ed., *Handbook of Social Psychology.* Addison-Wesley, 1954, 2:977-1020.

Jackson, J. "Factors of the Treatment Environment." *Archives of General Psychiatry* 21 (1969):39-45.

Jensen, A. "The Reliability of Projective Techniques: Review of the Literature." *Acta Psychologica* 16 (1959):108-136.

——. "The Rorschach Technique: A Re-evaluation." *Acta Psychologica* 22 (1964), pp. 60-77.

Kramer, R. *Participation of the Poor.* Prentice-Hall, 1969.

Lang, J. "Architecture for Human Behavior: The Nature of the Problem." In *Architecture for Human Behavior:* proceedings of a conference held by the Philadelphia Chapter of the AIA. 1971, pp. 5-14.

Little, K. Address to the Interprofessional Council on Environmental Design, Conference on Application of Behavioral Sciences to Environmental Design, University Park, Maryland, May 1970.

Lynch, K. *The Image of the City.* MIT Press, 1960.

McClelland, D. *The Achieving Society.* Van Nostrand, 1961.

McHarg, I. *Design with Nature.* The Natural History Press, 1969.

Mann, L., and Hagevick, C. "The 'New' Environmentalism: Behaviorism and Design." *American Institute of Planners Journal* (September 1971):344-347.

Marsden, H. "Crowding and Animal Behavior." In J. Wohlwill and D. Carson, eds., *Environment and the Social Sciences: Perspectives and Applications.* American Psychological Association, 1972, pp. 5-14.

Michelson, W. *Man and His Urban Environment: A Sociological Approach.* Addison-Wesley, 1970.

Moos, R. *Revision of the Ward Atmosphere Scales.* Social Ecology Laboratory, Stanford University, June 1971.

Moynihan, D. *Maximum Feasible Misunderstanding: Community Action in the War on Poverty.* Free Press, 1969.

Paar, A. "In Search of Theory." In H. Proshansky, W. Ittelson, and L. Rivlin, *Environmental Psychology*. Holt, Rinehart and Winston, 1970, pp. 11–16.

Pareek, U. "Poverty and Motivation: Figure and Ground." In V. Allen, ed., *Psychological Factors in Poverty*. Markham, 1970, pp. 300–317.

Pawley, M. *Architecture versus Housing*. Praeger, 1971.

Petty, R. "Experimental Investigation of Undermanning Theory." In D. H. Carson, ed., *Man-Environment Interactions, Part II*. Dowden, Hutchinson & Ross, 1975, pp. 259–269.

Petty, R. and Wicker, A. "Degree of Manning and Degree of Success of a Group as Determinants of Members' Subjective Experiences and Their Acceptance of A New Group Member: A Laboratory Study of Barker's Theory." In press.

"Progressive Architecture." *Advocacy Planning* (September 1968):102–115.

Proshansky, H.; Ittelson, W.; and Rivlin, L. *Environmental Psychology*. Holt, Rinehart and Winston, 1970.

Rapoport, A., EDRA Three, *Design and Environment* 3 (1972):52–53.

Rodman, H. "The Lower Class Value Stretch." *Social Forces* 42 (1963):205–215.

Rogers, C. *Client-Centered Therapy*. Houghton Mifflin, 1951.

Ruesch, J., and Kees, W. *Nonverbal Communication*. University of California Press, 1956.

Sanoff, H. et al. *Techniques of Evaluation for Designers*. Design Research Laboratory, North Carolina University, 1968.

Sanoff, H.; Burgwyn, H.; Adams, J.; and McNamara, M. *Housing Research and Development*. Community Development Group School of Design, 1971.

Seaton, R., and Collins, J. "Validity and Reliability of Ratings and Simulated Buildings." In W. Mitchell, ed., *Environmental Design: Research and Practice 1—Proceedings of the EDRA 3/AR8 Conference*, Los Angeles, UCLA, January, 1972b, pp. 6-10-1-6-10-12.

Shelly, M., ed. *Analyses of Satisfaction*. MSS Educational Publishing Company, 1969, vol. 1.

Shelly, M., and Adelberg, T. "Satisfaction Sites in Jamaica: Empirical Analysis." In M. Shelly, ed., *Analyses of Satisfaction*. MSS Educational Publishing Company, 1969, 1:221–266.

Siegel, B., and Beals, A. "Pervasive Factionalism." *American Anthropologist* 42 (1960):394–417.

Skinner, B. *Walden Two*. Macmillan, 1948.

———. *Beyond Freedom and Dignity*. Alfred A. Knopf, 1971.

Sommer, R. *Personal Space*. Prentice Hall, 1969.

———. "The New Evaluator Cookbook." *Design and Environment* 2 (1972a):34–37.

———. *Design Awareness*. Rinehart Press, 1972b.

Spicer, E., ed. *Human Problems in Technological Change*. Russell Sage Foundation, 1952.

Spiegal, H. *Citizen Participation in Urban Development*. NTL Institute for Applied Behavioral Science, 1968, vols. 1–2.

Studer, R. "The Dynamics of Behavior-Contingent Physical Systems." In H. Proshansky, W. Ittelson, and L. Rivlin, *Environmental Psychology*. Holt, Rinehart and Winston, 1970, pp. 56–75.

Sundstrom, E., and Altman, I. "Relationships between Dominance and Territorial Behavior: A Field Study in a Youth Rehabilitation Setting." University of Utah, 1972.

Thibaut, J., and Kelley, H. *The Social Psychology of Groups*. Wiley, 1959.

"Toward A Social Report," U.S. Department of Health, Education, and Welfare, 1969.

Van der Ryn, S. Remarks at the AIA Conference on Socio-Physical Technology, Washington, D.C., November 14–15, 1968.

Wallace, A. *Culture and Personality*. Random House, 1962.

Wicker, A. "Undermanning, Performances, and Students' Subjective Experiences in Behavior Settings of Large and Small Schools." *Journal of Personality and Social Psychology* 10 (1968):255–261.

———. "Attitudes Versus Actions: The Relationship of Verbal and Overt Behavioral Response to Attitude Objects." *Journal of Social Issues* 25 (1969a):41–78.

———. "Size of Church Membership and Members' Support of Church Behavior Settings." *Journal of Personality and Social Psychology* 13 (1969b):278–288.

Willems, E., and Raush H., eds. *Naturalistic Viewpoints in Psychological Research*. Holt, Rinehart and Winston, 1969.

Winer, B. *Statistical Principles in Experimental Design*. 2d ed. McGraw-Hill, 1971.

Winkel, G. "The Nervous Affair Between Behavior Scientists and Designers." *Psychology Today* 3 (1970):31–35.

Wohlwill, J., and Carson, D., eds. *Environment and the Social Sciences: Perspectives and Applications*. American Psychological Association, 1972.

Zeisel, J. "Fundamental Values in Planning with the Non-paying Client." In *Architecture for Human Behavior: proceedings of a conference held by the Philadelphia Chapter of the AIA*, 1971, pp. 23–30.

Zlutnick, S., and Altman, I. "Crowding and Human Behavior." In J. Wohlwill and D. Carson, eds., *Environment and the Social Sciences: Perspectives and Applications*. American Psychological Association, 1972, pp. 44–60.

1

Client Attitudes Toward Social Science

After reading the introduction, the reader may have come to his own conclusion that the burden of social change in the design professions is not entirely with the designer. In an increasing number of instances, the designer has been willing to incorporate social science in his programming only to find that his client balks at the notion. The process of education and social change is equally difficult in the world of clients the design profession must serve. Before going on to the intricacies of ecological psychology, it is well to examine the kinds of attitudes that clients may have that are resistant to the notion of designing for people, or enclosing behavior. The reader must keep in mind also that many of these attitudes are held by designers as well as by clients.

THE MONUMENT SYNDROME

Syndrome is a psychiatric term for a collection of symptoms that go together and center around a specific problem. The problem may not surface immediately, and the designer may be aware only that nothing he proposes is accepted by his client or clients. A good example concerns a large institute of psychiatry a few years ago. The prospective clients were the director of the institute and the member of the board. At first, everyone seemed to be in agreement; they needed a first-class, functional, mental-health facility that would suit the needs of patients and psychiatrists in training.

Gradually it became apparent that something was wrong. The director, especially, did not find any of the concepts or drawings that the architect proposed as satisfactory. Another architect was chosen. Then followed a series of architects that covered the roster of the most famous in the United States. All, somehow, in the end were unsatisfactory. Eventually it became apparent that the director wanted a monument to himself and his achievements, something that would be an enduring commemorative to what he had accomplished. The board, by contrast, wanted a functional unit tailored to the needs of patients and trainees. The situation became polarized, the board and directors could not agree, and the building was never designed and built. Thus were many thousands of hours of design work wasted.

Not always does the monument syndrome take so long to surface. Many designers report encountering a straightforward request on the part of politician clients, bureaucratic officials, and industrial leaders. The most obvious cue is when the client wants the building named after himself. The aware designer will try to solicit from the client what he wants the building to reflect, what image the client wants to present. The degree to which that image is personally related to the client is often the degree to which that building is to be a monument.

THE CONTROL SYNDROME

Sometimes as part of the monument syndrome and sometimes entirely on its own, another attitude will emerge in which it becomes clear that the client seeks to control the inhabitants of the building. Although every building "controls" inhabitants to some degree—signs send males to the men's room, corridors channel traffic away from busy offices, doors keep the uninvited out—this syndrome goes beyond these conventional ways of channeling behavior. A classic example exists in a New York City skyscraper office building built for a soap manufacturer. The building was constructed and manged so that no individual (with the exception of the president of the company) could put up even so much as a picture of his own in the assigned offices or work spaces. In short, the building was entirely under control of management, and the inhabitants had nothing to say about personalizing their own spaces. Within a short time, the inhabitants began to sabotage the building by "accidentally" breaking fixtures they did not like. But the struggle goes on, and management has design on its side of the issue.

Often, the control syndrome will express itself in the stated result the client wants to have on the behavior of the building occupants. A good example is wanting open office spaces so no one can loaf behind a partition.

THE BRICKS-AND-MORTAR SYNDROME

Perhaps no attitude is as common and unyielding as the attitude that buildings are just bricks and mortar, and the whole business is best left to those who know how to work in that medium. This attitude is reflected in the rhetoric a public-housing authority board member once used on a prospective architect: "If you had to choose between putting toilets in the houses and using a sociologist, which would you pick?" And so it is that an architect who might have otherwise felt social science was a selling point realized the client did not agree.

This very basic attitude is one that prevails from the Congress of the United States to the smallest business concern. It is the attitude responsible for stripping buildings of social amenities, which was done in the now-infamous Pruitt Igoe, but it is commonly done in buildings everywhere. Zeisel and Griffin (1975) provide a good example. In the housing project they describe, the architect intended the open-space area of a housing complex to be landscaped for public use. When it came time to make the final cuts from the budget, the client simply eliminated these "fringes." The result is that the central open space is now virtually unused.

It is this kind of attitude that is responsible for most of the shortcomings in the built environment today. Buildings are seen as simple structures, and social and design amenities alike are merely tolerated if the budget allows. The bricks-and-mortar client is equally resistant to design innovations. His requirements are strictly traditional.

THE "WE ALREADY KNOW THAT" SYNDROME

The resistances to social science are not really a great many, but there is one hardy strain that can be found almost everywhere. The holder of this attitude possesses a great advantage because he can express himself with almost no effort in thought or speech. He will commonly wait until a social scientist (or designer) has finished revealing a finding that has taken years and considerable funds, and then he will stand up and recite the one sentence that is his answer to all that social science has ever produced: "We already know that." And then he may add, "Why are social scientists always telling us what we already know?" And, as though this is perfectly self-evident to all concerned, he sits down, having very little else to say.

A good example of this attitude occurred after a recent survey the author made of a community that had an acute housing shortage. The findings pointed overwhelmingly toward adding greater space to nearly every dwelling. The findings also revealed which rooms in the house were in greater need of expansion and which house types should be expanded or eliminated. When one of the designer-clients heard this report, his immediate response was: "Everyone wants more space. We already know that."

Upon careful reflection, however, it was not something he really knew at all because there was no way to apply the vague notion that people wanted just more space. He did not know *where* they wanted more space, or *what kind* of space they wanted more of, or that in this particular case *most of the housing problems would be solved by adding more interior space.* More space was needed for interior storage and in the bathroom as first priority. No more outdoor space was needed.

This example is fairly typical of the "we already knew it school," and a careful examination of a problem usually shows that what was assumed to be known is not really known in a way that it could be applied and that it is usually not known in any kind of useful detail.

THE "HERE COMES THAT JARGON AGAIN" SYNDROME

It has already been mentioned that much of what social science has done is in the form of foreign language. There is no denying that social scientists have been to blame for creating an obscure jargon that sometimes is not clear even to themselves. Yet there is another side to the jargon accusation. In some cases it is unavoidable. When a physicist discovers a new element he must give it a name. Thus we have such oddities as yttrium, californium, and berkelium. When a drug company develops a new product, they give it a catchy name like Thorazine or Serpasil. Few accuse physicists or drug companies of creating unnecessary jargon. In fact, many of the drug names are simpler than the scientific names of the drugs; for example, the generic name for Thorazine is chlorpromazine hydrochloride. But when a social scientist must do the same he is often accused of creating jargon.

The problem is with the English language. There are not enough words to apply to these new discoveries, and, in many cases, the ordinary English words are inadequate or misleading to describe a situation. A good example of this is supplied by Dashiell's (1935) experiments. Dashiell wanted to investigate whether people work better alone or with coworkers. The problem was that the English word *alone* did not describe the degrees of aloneness that made a difference. One could be working alone in a room with workers in the near vicinity that could be seen and heard. One could also be alone in a room with no other persons present but with other workers in the next room or some other part of the building. And, finally, one could be alone in a building with no one else present. The English word *alone* does not describe any of these subtleties, which can influence behavior. New terms like *social facilitation* and *social reinforcement* need to be created because they describe specific new conditions discovered by social scientists, and the easiest way to refer to these conditions is by the use of carefully defined new terms.

There is some element of resistance to new knowledge in the "here comes that jargon" syndrome, but there is no escaping the fact that a person who wants to know about the discoveries of social science must learn some new terms and some new ways of looking at things. It cannot be done without effort.

FEES AND PRICES: THE FINAL OBSTACLE

By no means have the client (or designer) attitudes against the use of social science been exhausted, but there is one that is final—and fatal. It goes something like this: "We agree and are in sympathy with the use of social science on this project. The budget simply does not allow it." There is a resemblance here to the bricks-and-mortar syndrome. Whatever the attitude, it is a convincing one, and it places the designer who wants to use the social scientist in a double bind. If he uses the social scientist, he must cut into his own fee, and in these days of competition based on fees, the profit margin is cut very thin. On the other hand, if he does not use the social scientist, he must program his work with insufficient information.

The problem is really one of social, not economic, values. There was a time when buildings were not constructed with internal plumbing. So when plumbing first came along, it, too, was an unnecessary frill. Gradually plumbing became an accepted part of the design and building process. When the use of social science is valued as much as plumbing, then there will be no difficulties about including it in the building process.

The reason social science is not valued as highly in the building process today is not necessarily because social science has not yet been convincing but because the cost of a building to the client is figured incorrectly. Social custom dictates that the cost of a building not be the *total* cost but only the initial cost. That way the client is easily fooled into thinking he gets a bargain without social science. The game becomes one of keeping the initial construction cost as low as possible with no thought to what this might mean to the total cost. In fact, "total" cost of a building is never mentioned. Social custom dictates that accounting procedures, construction, and design perform their functions as though the total cost of a building does not exist.

What is meant by "total" cost? Let us say the average building lasts forty years. The total cost, then, is the amount it takes to build, operate, and tear down the building during its entire existence. For example, if a factory building is constructed to house 300 workers and the workers have 100 square feet of work space, the building has 30,000 square feet. Most buildings also have hallways, toilets, and other spaces, but we will ignore these for the moment and consider the total cost of the building. If initial construction is very cheap, let's say $25 per square foot, then the initial construction cost is $750,000. But that accounts for only a very small fraction of the building's life. Let us say the building exists for forty years and the 300 workmen in the building make a very low wage of $5,000 each per year. This means the workers cost $1.5 million to maintain every year, or more than twice the initial cost of construction. And in forty years, this wage cost will amount to $60 million. Needless to say, this is a great deal more than the initial cost.

Let us say that the designer of this building made a mistake because he did not employ a social scientist and that this mistake meant that the overall work force wasted one-half of 1 percent of their time. The total cost of this mistake over the life of the building is $300,000, or 40 percent of the initial cost.

How much would it have cost the client and the designer to avoid this $300,000 mistake? If the architect's fees were 5 percent of $37,500, then the social scientist would cost at most ten percent of that, or $3,750. And this cost of the social scientist is probably the greatest exaggeration so far. Williams and Ostrander (1975) report on a project where the total cost was only a few hundred dollars. But if the exaggeration remains, then the cost of the social scientist could have produced a return of eightyfold over his fee. Much of this exercise has been based on supposition, but the point is that when the entire life of the building is considered, the cost of a social scientist is very minimal and one of the best bargains available in the building and design professions.

Trites and his associates (1970) did a study of hospital corridor designs that illustrate how much can be saved by properly researching employees' behavior. They found the radial corridor to be superior to the single or double corridor designs most common for hospitals. On the basis of average salaries for 1968, the radial design cost $77 per bed less than the other two designs in extra travel time. In a 100-bed hospital, that would amount to $7,700 per year, or $308,000 over the life of the hospital (assuming wages remained at the 1968 level). There were also benefits in reduced absences and sick time so these savings were really much greater.

Perhaps one more argument might be made while considering the total cost over the lifetime of a building, and that is the cost of the money to build it. The average house at $30,000 building cost will cost the owner $46,808 in interest alone at 8 percent over thirty years with a $28,500 loan. Therefore, the cost of money can easily exceed the initial building cost itself, and this may be a good reason to keep the initial cost down. Yet this argument assumes that the social scientist will somehow raise the initial building cost when, in fact, he may even find ways to reduce it. Certainly, undermanning theory research discussed in chapter 9 reports consistent findings that most organizations could have fewer people, especially in the higher pay brackets. Therefore, if it ever becomes the custom to look at total cost of a building, the social scientist can be the most profitable member of any team in terms of cutting *real* cost to the client.

REFERENCES

Dashiell, J. F. "Experimental Studies of the Influence of Social Situations on the Behavior of Individual Human Adults." In C. C. Murchison, ed., *Handbook of Social Psychology*. Clark University Press, 1935, pp. 1097–1158.

Trites, D.; Galbraith, F.; Sturdavant, M.; and Leckwart, J. "Influence of Nursing-Unit Design on the Activities and Subjective Feelings of Nursing Personnel." *Environment and Behavior* 2 (1970):303–334.

Williams, Sandra, and Ostrander, Edward. "Maximizing Behavioral Inputs and Minimizing Time and Dollar Costs: A Case Study in Collaboration." Paper delivered in the workshop session on Social Science in Architectural Design, EDRA 6, April 1975.

Zeisel, John, and Griffin, Mary. *Charlesview Housing.* Architecture Research Office, Graduate School of Design, Harvard University, 1975.

2

Developmental Background

The history of behavior-setting methodology is more than twenty-five years old. In 1947, two psychologists, Roger Barker and Herbert Wright, moved from the University of Kansas in Lawrence to a small town about twenty miles to the northeast—code named Midwest. Both had been pupils of the great social psychologist Kurt Lewin, and both were determined to search out the structure of behavior in a total human environment. At that time, Midwest had a population of about 700, ideal for their purposes, because Barker and Wright wanted to be able to study the process of children growing up in the context of a total community that was small enough for them to observe. At the town site, they set up the Midwest Psychological Field Station as a base of operations from which to observe the residents. As time went on, the psychologists and their staff became part of the community.

BEHAVIOR SPECIMEN RECORDS

The first efforts of Barker and Wright were published in the book *One Boy's Day* (1951), which detailed the complete behavior record of one eight-year old boy from the time he got up in the morning until he went to bed at night. The technique that evolved from this study became known as the collection of *behavior specimen records*. Barker and Wright eventually accumulated eighteen such records for the use of social scientists. This was the first archive of complete daily behavior records of children and remains the sole archive of such material up to the present.*

The specimen record technique was developed largely by Herbert Wright. A description of this method is contained in the first chapters of *Midwest and Its Children* by Barker and Wright (1955) and is reprinted in Wright's book, *Recording and Analyzing Child Behavior* (1967). This technique consists in hav-

*Other researchers, however, like Schoggen and Schoggen (1971), using the specimen record technique have cataloged behavior of children over periods of time of less than a total day.

ing a team of observers record the total behavior of an individual by writing down all that occurs. So intensive is this experience that observers can work for only about twenty minutes at a time; hence, a team is necessary if any length of time is involved.

The recordings are largely common sense, and they involve the most ordinary observations about what the person being observed is doing. Table 2-1 gives a description of specimen records of four persons in a family watching television. Each behavior specimen can be divided into discrete units called *behavior episodes* (Barker and Wright, 1955).

The behavior specimen record can have great utility if one wants to show detailed use of a given environment by individuals. Unfortunately, unless specific aspects of the environment need to be studied intensively, the behavior specimen technique is too time-consuming to be of general use to the designer.* The best use of this technique is in gaining insight into detailed use of a behavior object, such as a vending machine, a television, or a couch. For the evaluation of an entire house or office building, its use would be too time-consuming in both observations and analysis of data. The detailed technology of behavior specimen records is fully explained in Barker and Wright (1955) and in Wright (1967).

AN ECOLOGICAL PERSPECTIVE

Long before the term *ecology* became popular, Barker and Wright had described their work as *psychological ecology*. This was later changed to *ecological psychology* in the 1968 book.

Soon after moving to Midwest, it became apparent to Barker and Wright that the methods of psychological investigation they had used up to that point were not only inappropriate but in many cases misleading. The cornerstone of all psychological investigation was (and still is) the psychological experiment. Barker had

*For example, the 119 children of Oskaloosa engaged in about 100,000 episodes of behavior each day, or over 36 million a year (Barker and Wright, 1955).

been especially skilled at setting up such experiments to discover factors in children's behavior. One of his most famous experiments was a demonstration that children, when frustrated, regress in their behavior—that is, when confronted with a frustrating experience, their level of behavior regresses from a normal maturity level to one below a level they are capable of (cf. Barker, Dembo, and Lewine, 1941). In short, the child *acts* younger.

The problem with this conclusion was that it had no evidence for reality in the ecological environment. Barker's students observed that children in the natural environment were not frustrated in the way they were frustrated in his laboratory experiment, and even when frustrations did occur in the natural environment, the children did not regress in the way they seemed to in the experiment. Thus, there must be ecological validity to any laboratory conclusion about human behavior; it must be shown to occur also in the natural setting.

From this perspective, Barker eventually evolved the notion of the naturally occurring unit of human behavior: the behavior setting.

BEHAVIOR SETTINGS

Barker (Barker and Wright, 1955; Barker, 1968) has defined the behavior setting as "a standing pattern of behavior and a part of the milieu which are synomorphic and in which the milieu is circumjacent to the behavior" (Barker and Wright, 1955). In simpler terms:

1. A behavior setting is a standing pattern of behavior that occurs over and over again in a given place and at a given time. You can go to the *place* where it occurs at the *time* it occurs and see the behavior repeated each time the setting happens.
2. Yet behavior settings, even though they are defined as separate entities, are a part of the flow of behavior in a community. People move in

TABLE 2–1
Two Minutes of Family Viewing

Time	Tommie	Jamie	Mother	Father
28′	He is watching TV with close attention.	Out	Out	He turns his head to ask a question. He moves the newspaper and looks back at it.
28′30″	Rests his hand on his leg. He wipes his nose with his arm and looks at his brother and father.	Returns and sits on couch. He sits all the way back with his feet stretched straight out and his hands between his thighs. He watches TV.	Enters living room carrying an article of clothing on a hanger. She glances at TV.	Looks up as Mrs. Barker passes through. At the same time TV says, "Hey look over there." He watches TV set for ten seconds, then turns back to newspaper. He looks up at set again. (There is marching music on TV.)
29′	Says something to Jamie and something to his father. He leaves the room after looking at them.	Watches TV intently. Answers his father's question and looks at him for a few seconds.	Carries article of clothing on hanger into another room.	Takes his hand off his head and looks at the boys. He asks something about what is on television. He then moves his legs slightly.
29′30″	Returns and sits on couch. He places one leg out and tucks the other underneath him. Wiggles his foot a little.	Flutters his feet as a swimmer does and then stops. Still watching TV.	Returns to the living room, stands in the doorway and pays no attention to TV. She seems to be clearing something from the table.	He holds the newspaper up; hard to tell if he is looking at it or at the television set.

From Surgeon General's Scientific Advisory Committee on Television and Social Behavior, *Television and Growing Up: The Impact of Televised Violence*, p. 89, which was borrowed from R. Bechtel, C. Achelpohl, and R. Akers. Correlates between observed behavior and questionnaire responses on television viewing in E. A. Rubinstein, G. A. Comstock, and J. P. Murray, eds. *Television and Social Behavior*, vol. 4: *Television in Day-to-Day Life: Patterns of Use* (Washington: Government Printing Office, 1971). This specimen record differs from those collected by Barker and Wright in that it was recorded on television tape, thus permitting the observer to go back over parts he missed and to "stop" the behavior when he got tired.

and out of settings but the settings do not disappear when different people arrive; they have a life of their own. Yet when the community changes, settings change also.

While most persons can easily identify settings, there comes a time when the observer is confronted with the need to determine when two behavior patterns are two settings or only one. It is then that the highly technical aspects of the behavior setting come forth to enable such a determination.

Barker (1968) defines the behavior setting as having seven measurable dimensions. These include: (1) people who enter into both settings, (2) leaders common to both settings, (3) space common to both settings, (4) objects common to both settings, (5) behavior in one setting influenced by behavior in the other setting, (6) time common to both settings, and (7) behavior common to both settings. Figure 2-1 shows the arbitrary scale used to measure whether two behavior patterns are separate settings. This scale may seem complicated at first, but generally when overlap in each of the areas is below 50 percent, the settings are separate, and a score of twenty-one is obtained. Thus, with this scale to measure the separateness of settings, Barker and Wright were able to count 2,030 behavior settings in their small town during the year that lasted from July 1, 1951, to June 30, 1952. This encompassed an enormous amount of behavior, virtually accounting for an estimated 95 percent of the behavior of all persons in the community (Barker and Wright, 1955).

THE BEHAVIOR-SETTING SURVEY

Behavior settings as discrete units of behavior are easily recognized. They are the football games, the grocery stores, the church services, the streets and sidewalks—in short, the catalog of all the behavior that takes place in a community. Yet the settings are not scattered about like stones thrown at random; they have definite relationships to one another, to the physical environment, and to the social structure in a community. The systematic way to collect data on behavior settings and their relationships is known as the behavior-setting survey. This is not a survey in the ordinary sense of interviewing persons to determine some facts about them; this is a survey of *behavior*.

A behavior-setting survey is begun in what may seem a most unscientific, even gossipy, manner. Newspapers, high-school yearbooks, telephone directories, and other public media are scanned to make a preliminary list of settings. Each telephone number indicates at least one setting. Newspapers give announcements of meetings, weddings, funerals, demonstrations, sales, and sports events. These are all settings. High-school yearbooks list the extra curricu-

lar events, the classes, the sports schedules, and special events. These are also settings.

But much of the behavior that goes on in a community is not reported publicly, and for this reason field workers and informants are necessary. The field workers go into the community to observe settings, and informants relate many settings that the field workers might miss. When all these sources of information are culled, a final setting list can be made.

Generally a setting survey requires one year. The twelve-month period is necessary because many settings, such as holidays and seasonal celebrations, occur only once a year. However, for many specialized purposes, setting surveys can be done for much shorter periods of time (Bechtel, Binding, and Achelpohl, 1970; Bechtel, 1970).

Concurrent with the gathering of settings are the various scales used to quantify behavior within and across settings. These scales provide no fewer than sixty-three separate bits of information about each setting.

When completed, the behavior-setting survey data are the raw material around which the designer can give form to his structures. The survey can be tapped for information about a room, a building, streets and sidewalks, or any other aspect of the community in part or in whole. The behavior-setting survey is a complete catalog of behavior indexed to locations, times, frequencies, populations, age groups, intensities, and a complex of other details. Its use is not easy to master, but it provides the only known comprehensive way to master design elements of behavior.

BEHAVIOR AND ENVIRONMENT

One of the most pervasive questions posed to the practitioners of ecological psychology is that of just how the environment influences behavior. The anthropologist Birdsell (1970) posits an ecological model for primitive groups that forces a direct relationship between the amount of food available and the composi-

A behavior setting has been defined as a standing pattern of behavior and a part of the milieu which are synomorphic and in which the milieu is circumjacent to the behavior.

The K-test of interdependency of two behavior settings is based upon ratings of the degree to which:

1. The same people enter both settings;
2. The same power figure or leaders are active in both settings;
3. Both settings use the same physical space or spaces that are near together;
4. Both settings use the same or similar behavior objects;
5. The same molar action units span the two settings;
6. Both settings occur at the same time or at times that are near together; and
7. The same kinds of behavior mechanisms occur in the settings.

These criteria of interdependence assume that, in general, the greater the degree to which behavior settings involve the same people, the same place or contiguous places, the same time or contiguous times, the same or similar behavior objects, the same molar actions and similar behavior mechanisms, the greater their interdependence. To estimate the degree of interdependence of a pair of behavior settings, both were judged with respect to each of these criteria on a 7-point scale.

A K-value of 21 was set as the cutting point for differentiating the behavior settings of Midwest. Pairs of unit settings with a K-value of less than 21 were considered as belonging to the same setting and those with a K-value of 21 or greater as belonging to separate settings.

Pairs of behavior settings with K-values below 21; each of these pairs of settings was combined into a single setting.

	K-value
First grade Music Class vs. Second Grade Music Class	16
Clifford's Drug Fountain vs. Cigar and Candy Counter	19
February Meeting Women's Club I vs. March Meeting Women's Club I	19
Vacant Lot B vs. Vacant Lot C	20

Pairs of behavior settings with K-values greater than 21; each member of these pairs of settings was identified as a separate setting.

	K-value
First Grade Academic Activities vs. Second Grade Academic Activities	28
County Engineer's Office vs. County Registrar of Deeds Office	28
Presbyterian Worship Service vs. Presbyterian Sunday School Exercises	22
Rotary Club Regular Meeting vs. Rotary Club Farmer's Night	22

Figure 2-1
The identification of K21 behavior settings.

THE INTERDEPENDENCE SCALE FOR
JUDGING VALUE OF K

Scale for judging the degree of interdependence of any pair of behavior settings A and B. On all criteria, a low rating indicates interdependence, and a high rating indicates independence of setting A and setting B.

1. Rating of population interdependence, i.e., of the degree to which the people who enter setting $A(P_B)$ are the same as those who enter setting $B(P_B)$. The percent overlap is judged by the following formula:

$$\text{Percent Overlap} = \frac{2\,P_{AB}}{P_A + P_B}$$

Where P_A = Number of people who enter setting A,
P_B = Number of people who enter setting B,
P_{AB} = Number of people who enter both setting A and setting B.

This percent overlap is converted to an interdependency rating by the following scale:

Rating	Per Cent Overlap
1	95–100
2	67–94
3	33–66
4	6–32
5	2–5
6	trace–1
7	none

2. Rating of leadership interdependence, i.e., of the degree to which the leaders of setting A are also the leaders of setting B.

This is judged in the same way as population interdependence for persons who penetrate to Zones 4, 5, or 6 settings A and B.

3. Rating of spatial interdependence, i.e., the degree to which settings A and B use the same or proximate spatial areas.

Rate on the following scale. In the case of scale points with two definitions, the most appropriate one applies; if more than one applies, give the lowest scale rating.

Rating	Per Cent of Space Common to A and B	
1	95 to 100	
2	50 to 94	
3	10 to 49	or A and B use different parts of same room or small area.
4	5 to 9	or A and B use different parts of same building or lot.

Figure 2-1 (Continued)

Rating	Per Cent of Space Common to A and B	
5	2 to 4	or A and B use areas in same part of town.*
6	trace to 1	or A and B use areas in same town but different parts of the town.*
7	none	or A in town, B out of town.

4. Rating of interdependence based on behavior objects, i.e., the extent to which behavior setting A and behavior setting B use identical or similar behavior objects.

Rate on the following scale. In the case of scale points with two definitions, the most appropriate one applies; if more than one applies, give the lowest rating.

Rating		
1	Identical objects used in setting A and setting B; i.e., all behavior objects shared.	
2	More than half of the objects shared by A and B	or Virtually all objects in A and B of same kind.**
3	Half of the objects shared by A and B	or More than half of the objects in A and B of same kind.**
4	Less than half the objects shared by A and B	or Half the objects in A and B of same kind.**
5	Few behavior objects in A and B identical	or Less than half the objects of A and B of same kind.**
6	Almost no objects shared by A and B	or Few behavior objects of same kind** in A and B.
7	No objects shared	or Almost no similarity between objects in A and B.

5. Rating of interdependence based on molar action units, i.e., degree to which molar behavior units are continuous between setting A and setting B.

The molar behavior in behavior settings A and B may be integrated in two ways. The inhabitants of setting A may interact across the boundary with the inhabitants of B, e.g., the person

*Three parts of Midwest were identified: (a) south of the square (approximately 15 square blocks); (b) area of town square (approximately 5 blocks); (c) north of the square (approximately 15 blocks).
**Objects of the same kind are different instances of objects that have the same dictionary definition; e.g., spoons are used in the behavior setting School Lunch Room and the setting Clifford's Drug Store Fountain, but they are different spoons.

Figure 2-1 (Continued)

in the cytosetting Preacher interacts directly with the members of the cytosetting Congregation in the Church Service. On the other hand, behavior begun in one behavior setting may be completed in the other, e.g., delivering lumber for a construction project starts at the setting Lumber Yard and is completed at the setting House Construction. Scales are provided for both kinds of behavior integration. For each kind of behavior integration, use the highest per cent which applies. The average of the two ratings is the final rating.

Rating	Per Cent of Behavior in A Having Direct Effects in B, or Vice Versa. (Highest Per Cent Counts)	Per Cent of Behavior Actions Beginning in A Which are Completed in B, or Vice Versa. (Highest Per Cent Counts)
1	95–100	95–100
2	67–94	67–94
3	34–66	34–66
4	5–33	5–33
5	2–4	2–4
6	trace–1	trace–1
7	none	none

6. Rating of interdependence based on temporal contiguity, i.e., the degree to which settings A and B occur at the same time, or at proximate times.

Most behavior settings recur at intervals. Any pair of settings, therefore, may occur close together on some occasions and be temporally separated at other times. For example, the American Legion meets monthly, while the Boy Scout Troop meets weekly; once a month their meetings occur during the same week. The closest temporal proximity of setting A and setting B determine the column to enter in the table below. The per cent of contact at the point of closest proximity determines the interdependence rating in the column at the right. The per cent of contact is computed as the ratio between the number of occurrences of both settings at this closest point of contact divided by the total number of occurrences of both behavior settings.

Scales for Rating Temporal Interdependence

Interdependence Rating	(Closest Temporal Proximity Per Cent of Contact)					
	Simultaneous	Same Part of Day	Same Day	Same Week	Same Month	Same Year
1	0.75–1.00					
2	0.50–0.74	0.75–1.00				
3	0.25–0.49	0.50–0.74	0.75–1.00			
4	0.05–0.24	0.25–0.49	0.50–0.74	0.75–1.00		
5	0–0.04	0.05–0.24	0.25–0.49	0.50–0.74	0.75–1.00	
6		0–0.04	0.05–0.24	0.25–0.49	0.50–0.74	0.50–1.00
7			0–0.04	0.05–0.24	0.25–0.49	0–0.49

Figure 2–1 (Continued)

Example: The Boy Scout Troop met every Monday night during the survey year. The American Legion met the first Wednesday of every month. The closest temporal proximity of these settings was "Same Week." Enter column headed "Same Week." The 12 Scout and the 12 Legion meetings which occurred in this close contact were added and the sum divided by the sum of the 12 Legion meetings and the 52 Scout meetings, as follows:

$$\frac{\text{12 Scout Meetings} \quad \text{12 Legion Meetings} \quad 24}{\text{52 Scout Meetings} \quad \text{12 Legion Meetings} \quad 64} = .37$$

In column "Same Week," .37 falls at scale point 6. The temporal interdependence score, then, is 6.

7. Interdependence based on similarity of behavior mechanisms, i.e., the degree to which behavior mechanisms are similar in setting A and setting B.

Ratings are based on the following 12 behavior mechanisms:

Gross Motor	Writing	Eating
Manipulation	Observing	Reading
Verbalization	Listening	Emoting
Singing	Thinking	Tactual Feeling

The interdependence score is determined by the number of behavior mechanisms present in one setting and absent in the other as indicated in the following table;

Interdependence Rating	Number of Mechanisms Present in One Setting and Absent in the Other
1	0–1
2	2–3
3	4–5–6
4	7–8
5	9–10
6	11
7	12

The total interdependence score K is the sum of the separate interdependency ratings; the value of K can vary between 7 and 49.

Source: From R. Barker and H. Wright, Midwest and Its Children (Row, Peterson, 1955). Reprinted by permission of R. Barker and H. Wright.

tion of the hunting gathering band in Australia. But most human habitations are a far cry from this direct relationship between man and the environment. A whole host of physical structures, social systems, roles, and other paraphernalia of society stand between the direct effects of nature and the urban or rural citizen of the United States so that these elements operate on the individual to influence behavior and become part of the ecological input operating on persons within settings.

Barker (1968, p. 147) states that his first expectation was to be able to predict behavioral outputs successfully once he had correctly ascribed the ecological inputs. It did not work out. Considering inputs from the social environment, only about half were found to elicit congruent behavior episodes (Barker 1968, p. 149).

Even more discouraging for design enthusiasts who believe that design can influence behavior, Barker concedes "that the nonsocial, ecological environment does not demand behavior, that it enters psychology only as permissive, supportive, or resistive circumstances" (Barker, 1968). Predictions of behavior from the nonsocial environment were assumed to be much lower than those from the social environment.

It is assumed in Barker's theories that the most predictable influence on behavior exerts itself via the behavior setting. Each setting has its own schedule of behavior, and the complete schedule is usually kept in the heads of the people who lead the settings—the shopkeepers, teachers, policemen, and others who direct or help direct behavior. The schedule of behavior can be thought to contain two types of what Barker calls *circuits* to maintain behavior in the setting and, hence, the integrity of the setting. These are *deviation-countering circuits* and *vetoing circuits*. The deviation-countering circuits generally force people to correct things or change behavior when some deviation from normal behavior is perceived, for example, when the clock stops, when a window is broken, when a student makes an error on a test, when a car goes up a one-way street the wrong way. Vetoing circuits are a little stronger in the force they exert on

the behavior. They do not redirect the behavior; they eliminate the one who behaves from the setting itself —the clerk stealing from the cash register is fired, the broken radiator is replaced, the student who fails all his courses has to leave college. Generally the vetoing circuit operates when the entire setting program is threatened.

This brief discussion, of course, does not do justice to Barker's intentions. The important features to keep in mind, however, are that each setting has resources, both social and nonsocial, to preserve the integrity of its behavior programs by either directing deviations to be corrected or expelling those who threaten it. The deviation countering or the vetoing can be done by social or nonsocial means.

DESIGN AND THE BEHAVIOR-SETTING SURVEY

An overwhelming question remains for the designer, planner, or researcher confronted with the need for data about human behavior: why do a behavior-setting survey? Aren't there many easier ways to do such research? For example, wouldn't the set of questionnaires Sommer recommended (1972) do well for evaluating a building environment, and why not use Moos's questionnaire (1971) for institutional environments or Chapin's (1969) time activity systems for a more general environment? More to the point, why not use Alexander's (1968) pattern sequences as a basis for constructing an environment? Certainly all of these techniques have their merits, not the least of which is that they are easier to do and better known than the behavior-setting survey. Why bother learning the complicated process of a behavior-setting survey?

There are two principal reasons why the behavior-setting survey is especially suited to answer questions about the relationship between behavior and the physical environment. The first is that the observable events of behavior are those most easily influenced by the physical environment (Barker, 1968). Consider that the unobserved events, the feelings, attitudes, and other internal processes generally give way to the environmental presses of the setting. The chairman may not feel well, but he will preside over the meeting because he is chairman; the driver may be young and capricious, but he stops at nearly every stop sign because the setting demands it. In short, the observable elements of behavior are those most closely linked to the physical environment. Yet in contrast to this principle, most of the research on the relationship of behavior to environment has been done on the *nonobservable* aspects of human behavior.

The second reason why behavior-setting surveys are so well suited to measuring the effects of the physical environment lies in what Barker (1968) calls the researcher as *operator* versus the researcher as *transducer*. When the researcher is an operator on the scene, he imposes his own view on the data both in a selective and a confining way. As an operator he has a specific question in mind, and he selects only the data that he thinks are related to that question. Preferably he will take a very limited portion of the environment and subject it to highly controlled variables. In short, the operator manipulates the environment in such a way that either it was not the same as it was before he came on the scene or he obtains a segment of it that is not representative of the whole.

The transducer, on the other hand, makes every effort to study the data as they exist without his presumptions. He is merely a transmitter or coder, not a manipulator. For this reason, most questionnaires, experiments, interviews, and similar methods are manipulators of the environment. They reflect (and *must* reflect) only a limited funneling of data from the natural environment as it exists.

The researcher as transducer is a universe away from the research methods most commonly in use today. The transducer attempts to receive and organize *all* behavior and not just his preconceived categories. The consequences of this view are profound. If a researcher attempts to be merely a transducer, he flies in the face of most of the accepted ways of doing research that are known today. He may have

hypotheses and preconceptions, but he tries to measure virtually everything in molecular behavior. Nothing could be more disturbing to the academic behavioral scientist. The very foundation of behavioral science is the hypothesis-testing reductionism copied from the physical sciences (Marx and Hillix, 1963), and the very thought of the researcher as transducer is anathema to such thinking.

There is no reason, however, for such a reaction to the behavior-setting survey. Doing a behavior-setting survey does not necessarily imply that the researcher does not have hypotheses of specific interest in certain parts of the data. The survey merely guarantees that as nearly as possible the whole environment will be measured so that the researcher, admitting his fallibility, will not lose essential elements that might bear on the influence of that environment on behavior. This is especially important for designers and planners who are not generally as astute at generating hypotheses as behavioral scientists and who are really interested in the effect of the physical environment on the *whole* of behavior. The behavior-setting survey is then adaptable to any kind of environment without imposing the assumptions of most questionnaires or other instruments, and it is comprehensive enough to catch many diverse elements that even the most careful researcher might have missed. In short, with the state of the art in environmental psychology being what it is, the behavior-setting survey is the best way of making sure that most contingencies are provided for. The illustrations that form the bulk of this book will demonstrate the greater wisdom of that approach.

REFERENCES

Alexander, C.; Ishikawa, S.; and Silverstein, M. *A Pattern Language Which Generates Multi-Service Centers.* Center for Environmental Structure, 1968.

Barker, R. G. *Ecological Psychology.* Stanford University Press, 1968.

Barker, R.; Dembo, T.; and Lewin, K. "Frustration and Regression: An Experiment with Young Children." *University of Iowa Studies in Child Welfare*, 18 (1941).

Barker, R., and Wright, H. *One Boy's Day.* Harper & Row, 1951.

———. *Midwest and Its Children.* Row, Peterson, 1955.

Bechtel, R. "A Behavioral Comparison of Urban and Small Town Environments." In John Archea and Charles Eastman, eds., *EDRA 2: Proceedings of the Second Annual Environmental Design Research Association Conference,* Pittsburgh, Pa., October 1970, pp. 347–353.

Bechtel, R.; Achelpohl, C.; and Binding, F. *East Side, West Side and Midwest: A Behavioral Comparison of Three Environments.* Epidemiological Field Station, 1970.

Birdsell, J. B. "Local Group Composition Among Australian Aborigines: A Critique of the Evidence from Fieldwork Conducted Since 1930." *Current Anthropology* 2 (April 1970):115–130.

Chapin, F. S., and Logan, Thomas H. "Patterns of Time and Space Use." In H. Perloff, ed., *The Quality of the Urban Environment.* Resources for the future, 1969.

Marx, M., and Hillix, W. *Systems and Theories in Psychology.* McGraw-Hill, 1963.

Moos, R. *Revision of the Ward Atmosphere Scales.* Social Ecology Laboratory, Stanford University, June 1971.

Schoggen, M., and Schoggen, P. "Environmental Forces in the Home Lives of Three Year Old Children in Three Population Subgroups." *DARCEE Papers and Reports,* Vol. 5, No. 2., 1971.

Sommer, R. "The New Evaluator Cookbook." *Design and Environment* 2 (1972):34–37.

Wright, H. *Recording and Analyzing Child Behavior.* Harper & Row, 1967.

3

The Boundaries of Behavior Settings

Try to imagine how behavior would appear on a long time-exposed film if we could photograph the earth from above and all the roofs of buildings were removed. On the streets we would see transparent streams of color and grey paralleled by similar streams on the sidewalks. But within buildings, the streams would congeal into round clusters in rooms and at specific points would appear quite opaque. Some of these clusters would appear isolated and discrete while others would appear merged together in clusters on top of clusters.

This fanciful time-exposure follows a concept that Roger Barker introduced in his book *Stream of Behavior* (1963). Behavior occurs in a stream, and it flows lightly in some places and more densely and in loops and pools in other places. When the dense patterns become relatively permanent, they are behavior settings.

But to return to our time exposure, how can we make any sense out of the permanent loops and pools that occur along the various streams? They are associated with particular places, especially in buildings, and the fact that they show up opaque on the time exposure indicates they take place frequently. The first distinction that could be made from the photograph is that some of the clusters are clear while others seem to merge together and overlap. The definition of boundaries of behavior settings is one of the most critical areas in the study of behavior and architecture because both architects and people in behavior settings are conscious of and are constantly striving to erect or tear down boundaries as the behavior and the architecture demand.

A behavior-setting boundary is the place where the behavior stops. An ideal boundary is a wall, which stops behavior from getting out or in. Such obvious qualities as opacity to sight and sound are important requirements in setting boundaries. Yet it is when setting boundaries are not so obvious that the problems of boundary definition occur.

BOUNDARY PROBLEMS

Unclear Definition

Some environments foster boundary problems. LeCompte and Willems (1970, p. 236) describe a boundary problem in a rehabilitation hospital (figure 3-1):

The prevocational skills area is interesting because it provides a need for one of the defining characteristics: To the left . . . is a fragile white screen that marks the boundary of this setting. Its function is to inform one that he is entering a different place. As a boundary, its function is more symbolic than real. That is, it does not filter out auditory stimuli, and it is too low to effectively stop all visual cues. But the inhabitants of the prevocational skills area need it to define their territory.

LeCompte and Willems go on to describe large settings, such as laboratories and hospital wards, where boundaries are maintained—sometimes by talking in whispers, other times by movable screens around beds. The same prevocational skills area, shown in figure 3-2, illustrates how the inhabitants of the setting attempted to make their boundaries more physical. This is an example of one solution to the boundary problem when architects have failed to provide the physical barriers needed to enclose behavior. This solution cannot always be effected by the inhabitants of settings, however; more often, the coercive quality of the architecture forces people to tolerate setting boundary conflicts.

Deliberately Overlapped Areas

Many places of work maintain deliberate boundary problems as a way of doing business. Figure 3-3 shows the city room of the *Kansas City Star*, which is typical of large newspapers. Some employees constantly complain about not being able to get any work done because of the intrusions of sounds, sights, and smells. Others seem to relish the high load of

Figure 3-1
Prevocational skills area before physical boundaries were erected. Courtesy of W. Ayhan LeCompte.

stimulation. It remains to be proven whether this is actually the best environment for getting newspaper work done.

Still another environment that preserves merging boundaries is the city market. The city market of Kansas City (figure 3-4) and the bazaar of Tehran, Iran (figure 3-5), are places where sights, sounds, and smells overlap and merge to advantage.

Figure 3-2
Prevocational skills area after physical boundaries were erected to protect setting functions. Courtesy of W. Ayhan LeCompte.

Figure 3-3
City room of the *Kansas City Star.*

SOLUTIONS TO BOUNDARY PROBLEMS

Limited Access

Not all boundary problems are solved by the complete barrier of a wall. Sometimes the nature of the behavior is such that it need be only partially enclosed. For example, the nursing station design of a new mental hospital posed a dilemma for architects; it needed to be modified so that maximum therapy

Figure 3-5
Bazaar, Tehran, Iran.

could be effected. The newest nursing stations at that time were entirely glass encased and did not permit any but visual contact between nurses and mental patients (figure 3-6). It was deemed unsatisfactory by psychiatrists because it inhibited patient contacts. On the other hand, the nursing stations in the old Kirkbride* day hall were deemed unsatisfactory by

Figure 3-4
City market, Kansas City, Missouri.

*Thomas Kirkbride developed a mental hospital plan that involved large, rectangular day rooms. These became the standard for state mental hospitals throughout the U.S. and to this day constitute the majority of such buildings. The Philadelphia Mental Hospital of 1856 was the prototype.

Figure 3-6
Glass-enclosed nursing station. Courtesy of ERDF.

Figure 3-7
Old nursing office. Courtesy of ERDF.

the nurses because the patients could walk in anytime through the open door if the station were left unguarded (figure 3-7). This left the nurses highly vulnerable. In behavior-setting terms, it left their penetration and autonomy levels too low for privacy.

New therapeutic modes dictated having nurses mix with patients on wards without any nurses' stations. When this was tried briefly with a few nurses, observations revealed that the nurses were not able to sustain continuous prolonged contact with patients and had to retreat periodically. Without a nursing station, this often meant leaving the ward entirely or going to the broom closet "for a smoke." After a period of time, it became very evident that the nurses needed a place of their own outside the completely boundaryless quality of the open ward. Yet at the same time, the boundary of their place of retreat had to be semipermeable, permitting the patients to have optimum contact with the nurses.

The architectural solution to this boundary problem was a nursing station that projected into the ward with a three-sided counter about waist height. The interior of the station contained rooms for retreat of nurses and the safety of medicines. The station seemed to be a satisfactory solution (figures 3-8 and

3-9) to the boundaries for a behavior setting that permitted both overlap with the ward and yet the security of physical boundaries for the nurses.

Behavioral Principle

The nursing station problem points up an example of what LeCompte (1972) calls *querencia.* According to LeCompte:

The querencia is the exact spot which every Spanish fighting bull chooses to return to, between his charges, in the arena. It is his invisible fortress, or camp. . . . The nearer the bull is to his querencia, or stamping station, the more formidable he is, the more full of confidence, and the more difficult to lure abroad into the territory of the bullfighters. . . .*

To return to the nurses in the mental hospital, who exactly parallel the professionals in LeCompte's rehabilitation hospital, there was *no querencia* in the situation of the open ward, and the nurses felt uncomfortable, threatened, and unable to carry out

*Quoted from the biographer of Lorca: R. Campbell, *Lorca* (Yale University Press, 1959), p. 3.

Figure 3–8
Proposed design for new nursing station. Courtesy of ERDF.

their professional duties. In the glass-enclosed station, on the other hand, the querencia was so forbidding that no patient dared approach; in the Kirkbride nurses' office, it was too easily threatened. Only when the territory was well defined by setting boundaries that were neither impermeable nor too

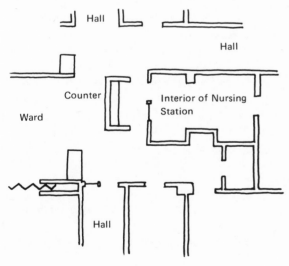

Figure 3–9
Floor plan of new nursing station.

permeable did both nurses and patients achieve a satisfactory overlapping of boundaries.

Creating Boundaries

Another solution, at the opposite end of the scale, is to create many boundaries where there were none before. This is often a solution for a group of people with a large, ill-defined territory. For the astute architect designing a mental hospital ward, an important question can be raised: where are the querencias of the patients? A partial answer comes from one of the most decisive and interesting research projects ever undertaken in the mental hospital. (For full details of this complex project, the reader should turn to *Ward H* by Colarelli and Siegel [1966].)

One important part of the research was to assign definite boundaries to a large psychiatric ward for thirty-six patients. Actual boundaries were painted on the floor. These became the querencias for groups of nine patients and three attendants. The boundaries became a way to change the amorphous setting of patients and aides into well-defined groups with aides responsible to specific patients, and all responsive to a given territory. Although the main purpose of the project was not to test the effects of the boundaries, one of the results was that the patients jealously guarded their areas as their own territories.

The success of this project points up how effective even the faintest boundaries can be in helping to define social groups. It points up even more severely the possible detrimental effect of a lack of querencias for patients in mental hospital wards that continues today. Osmond (1959) has coined a term to describe the large open ward: *sociofugal space.* It resists human intimacy and conversation. Breaking up any of these sociofugal spaces into smaller settings changes the area into a *sociopetal space,* tending to increase human intimacy and conversation. The amount of space defined by boundaries, then, tends to influence the kinds of behaviors that will take place. Large spaces foster a "waiting room" atmosphere while smaller spaces foster more intimate conversation.

The K-21 Scale

While some boundary problems in the manmade environment may be obvious to a casual onlooker, there is a need to quantify the problems in order to determine how settings can be made more secure in their boundaries and which settings need to be restructured.

A research laboratory in Fairbanks, Alaska, provides a somewhat exotic atmosphere. The various jobs handled inside the offices may entail measuring soil samples collected at Point Barrow, planning flood control measures on the Chena River, conducting visitors through the permafrost tunnel, or doing behavior setting surveys around the office.

The office configurations of the laboratory are quite similar to those found in offices throughout the world. The spaces were designed to be fairly flexible, and not the greatest attention was paid to possible boundary problems. In figure 3-10 there are two desks with such obvious overlapping boundaries that the question arose with the researchers as to whether they could indeed be separate settings at all.

In the first potential setting, a sergeant, a military career man, handles the dispatching of vehicles and the administration of army personnel. He is, in army jargon, the NCOIC, the noncommissioned officer in command. Opposite him sits a secretary who acts as the receptionist and secretary for the laboratory. The room they occupy has three doors, a main one leading from the entrance hallway into their office and two doors on either side leading into other offices. This means that anyone coming to visit any other person in the organization must go past them. In more behavioral terms, their office is a junction in the mainstream of behavior. The seargeant cannot make a telephone call that is not overheard by the secretary, and she cannot make one out of his earshot. Most of the persons coming to her as a receptionist will also

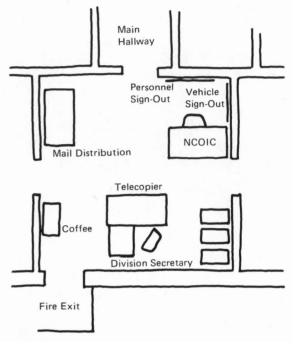

Figure 3-10
Floor plan of the secretary and sargeant's overlapping behavior settings.

glance at him. When she is not present, he will answer her calls, and when he is absent, she answers his (figure 3-11). Furthermore, the coffee urn sits beside the secretary's desk, and other personnel who come to get coffee feel some obligation to speak with both the sergeant and the secretary. Thus, there is considerable overlap of function, behavior, and space.

The author and Burgess Ledbetter, research architect and project officer for Army contract DAAG-17-73-C-0104, under which these data were collected, did K-21 scales of the two settings.* The results appear in table 3-1.

The scoring of the K-21 scale is explained as follows:

1. Population interdependence was given a rating

*See figure 2-2 above for the K-21 scale. The reader may want to follow the scoring using the scale.

Figure 3-11
Secretary and sergeant's overlapping behavior settings.

TABLE 3-1
K-21 Scale Scores for the Sergeant and the Secretary

Bechtel's Scores	Ledbetter's Scores
1	1
6	6
3	3
5	6
4	4
1	1
1	1
21	22

of 1, indicating a 95–100 percent overlap. It was observed that both the sergeant and the secretary had populations overlapping both settings nearly 100 percent.

2. Leadership interdependence was found not to be overlapping as much as it might seem at first. The sergeant leaves his setting more often than the secretary does, and she will answer more of his calls than he answers hers. However, both cannot act in a leadership capacity in the other's setting. The sergeant does not have knowledge of the secretary's business nor does she know about his. Only the sergeant can handle military matters, and only the secretary knows the location of files and how to run the telecopier. They are both reduced to being an answering service for the other, which is not a leadership role. Therefore, each observer rated the leadership interdependence as 6, which is only a trace to 1 percent of occupancy time.

3. Rating of spatial interdependence is easy in this case because it closely fits Barker's designation of "different parts of same room or small area." The rating is 3. This was also calculated in terms of actual square feet of floor space and found to be less than 49 percent overlap.

4. Interdependence of behavior objects is slight. No objects, or virtually none, are actually shared since both have their own telephones, pencils, paper, desks, and so forth. Furthermore, many of the objects used by one are not used by the other, such as files, the telecopier, and the typewriter. This is the only rating on which the observers disagreed, one scoring a 5 and the other a 6.

5. Interdependence of molar actions is obvious from the observations of telephone calls answered across boundaries. Yet considering the occupancy time of both settings, this only occurs up to but not exceeding 33 percent of the total and is rated 4 by both observers.

6. The interdependence on temporal contiguity is nearly total and is rated 1 by both observers. The

hours of work are the same in both settings. Only if one of the leaders were out a great deal would time overlap be less.

7. Interdependence based on similarity of behavior mechanisms is also nearly total. There is little activity (telephoning, talking) the sergeant does that is not also done by the secretary and vice versa. Both observers rated the interdependence as 1.

The K-21 scale reveals in what kinds of behavior and physical aspects there is overlap. In population, time, and behavior mechanisms, the overlap is almost total. Both the secretary and the sergeant work at the same time, are visited by the same people, and do the same things. But in leadership, the objects they use, and molar behavior they differ enough to be considered separate settings. Consider that if each knew more about the other's job, that would be enough to lower the leadership rating and make the score less than 21. Also, if the sergeant were to learn to use the typewriter and telecopier better, this would also cause the settings to merge into one. Thus, only knowledge seems to keep the settings separate. But why doesn't the sergeant learn more about secretarial work and the secretary more about military matters? In the course of time, one would expect some of the details to rub off on the other. The reason, of course, is that each has a separate role. The sergeant cares for military matters, and the secretary cares for the files and similar tasks. Each guards the province of his duties as important to keep separate. The sheer force of the roles in this case is what finally keeps the two settings separate.

But consider what this means in terms of work and performance. A psychological effort must be put forth to sustain boundaries that exist only psychologically. In some ways, this makes all of the work of each setting more difficult, and it makes some of the work nearly impossible. To counsel military men, the sergeant must physically leave his setting, and the secretary must trust to the honor or others while typing confidential memos or making confidential calls.

This setting was chosen for study for two reasons: to illustrate that in the absence of physical boundaries, psychological ones must be erected, and to provide an example of a setting that is just at the cutting point of the K-21 scale. Barker (1968) advises that when K-21 scores ranging between 18 and 23 are obtained, the scales should be carefully done over with more detailed observational data to ensure that the ratings are reliable. Once this is done, however, it is well to bear in mind that settings with a range of scores from 18 to 23 are likely to be standing patterns of behavior with boundary problems. Just because two potential settings score below 21 does not mean each is a smoothly functioning single setting. Similarly, settings in the 21 to 23 category are also likely to have boundary problems.

Barker and Schoggen (1973) propose doing K-21 scales for all possible behavior settings in an environment. The scores then will define as hierarchies of settings those with lowest K-21 scores among them. This would be an exhaustive process for an entire community, but in a building it would be of great assistance in redesigning or rearranging the offices to provide less permeable boundaries.

Ledbetter has taken the original office layout of the laboratory (figures 3–12 and 3–13) and suggested a reassignment of space according to the need for more secure boundaries (figures 3–14 and 3–15). His commentary follows:

Conditions and Limits
The organization is the center of operations for research projects conducted mostly in the field. It hosts visiting researchers from its parent organization outside Alaska. Although called a research laboratory, little laboratory work takes place in the building. Most such research is performed in the field while writing, reducing data, reading, and other desk related tasks occur in the building. Likewise, the administrative staff perform only desk related tasks in the building.

For the nine resident research and technical personnel there are fifteen administrative and support employees. However, only seven of the fifteen people are located in this building. The remaining eight are in satellite locations and may only enter this building once a day for thirty minutes.

The building contains three stories, one being a basement. At the center of the building are two entrances, one to the front and one to the rear. A portion of the first and second

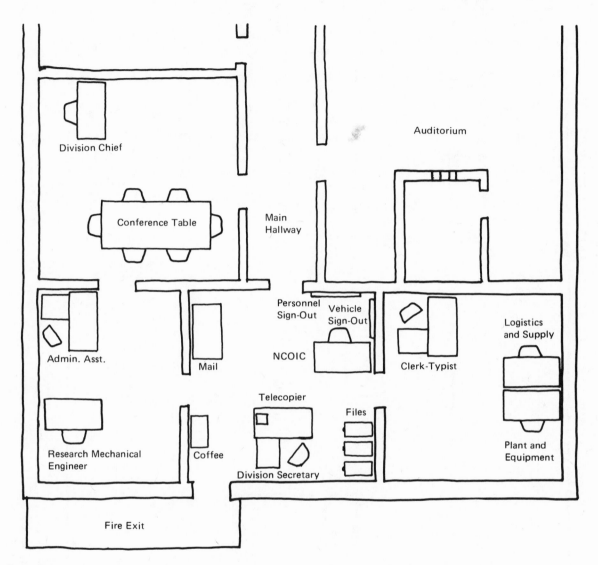

Figure 3-12.
Simplified existing first floor of research laboratory.

floor is occupied by the research organization being discussed. In this demonstration it is assumed that the organization must remain split between two floors rather than merge into one. This restraint is imposed by the owners of the building.

Informal relations between the researchers on the second floor and the administrative staff on the first floor are good. The scores for the Social Contact Action Pattern and Talking Behavior Mechanism for this organization are one of the highest for work organizations on the Army Post. Ironically, a shortcoming common to many work organizations is the absence of this informality.

In the organization, the social contact, which is extensive, is often the source of conflict among the work settings. As a result, productivity suffers. For example, people gather in the

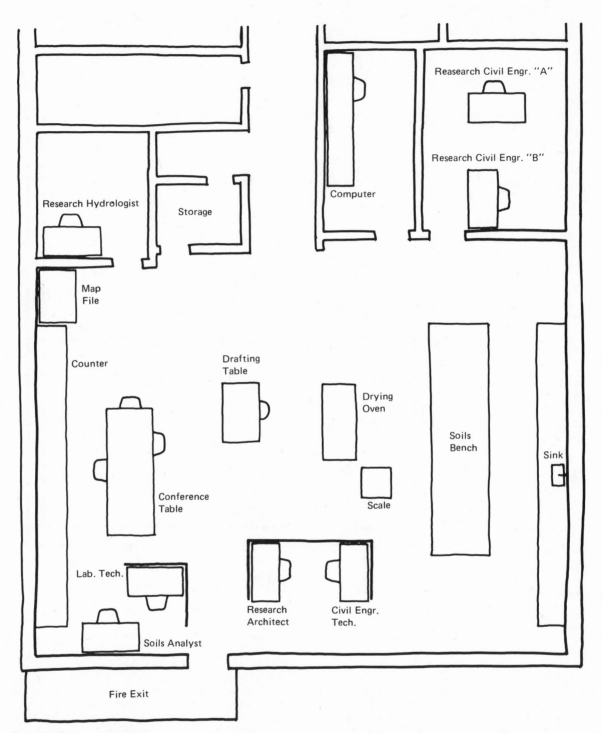

Figure 3-13
Simplified existing second floor of research laboratory.

The labeled areas in the floor plan:

Research Hydrologist

Storage

Research Civil Engr. "A"

Research Civil Engr. "B"

Computer

Map File

Counter

Drafting Table

Drying Oven

Soils Bench

Sink

Scale

Conference Table

Lab. Tech.

Research Architect

Civil Engr. Tech.

Soils Analyst

Fire Exit

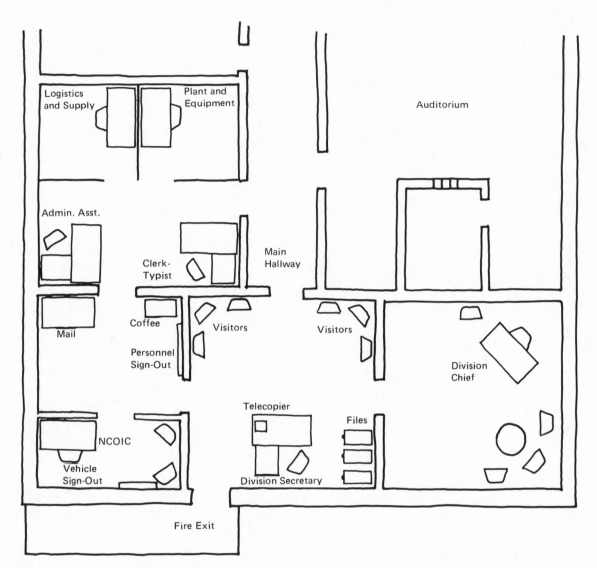

Figure 3-14
Proposed change to first floor of research laboratory.

centrally located division secretary and NCOIC office for coffee. Most of the time they linger to talk with others in the space which interrupts the NCOIC and division secretary. To be sociable, those interrupted always respond kindly.

Changing the First Floor
The most pronounced boundary conflicts in this organization are among the division secretary, NCOIC, and coffee break settings. As shown in [figure 3-12], these three settings are located within one small space at the intersection of two offices, the main hallway and an emergency fire escape used as a shortcut between the first and second floor.

The K-21 scores comparing these settings reveal the extent of the boundary overlap. They are shown in Table 1.

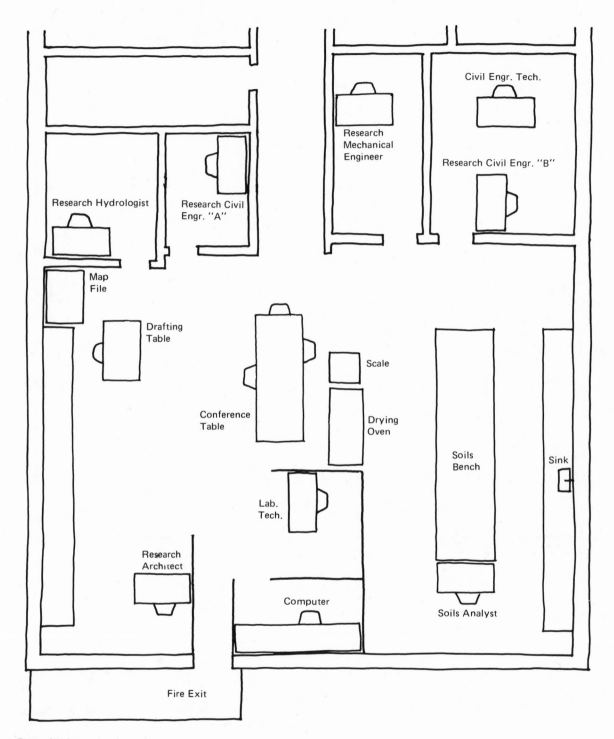

Figure 3-15
Proposed change to second floor of research laboratory.

TABLE 1
Comparing Settings

NCOIC-Division Section	NCOIC-Coffee	Division Section-Coffee
1	1	1
4	4	3
2	2	2
6	6	6
4	4	4
3	3	3
2	2	2
22	22	21

The division secretary receives a lower score on leadership interdependence than the NCOIC for the secretary is responsible for preparing the coffee more often than the NCOIC.

It is not difficult to recognize the conflict created among these settings or in this room. Observation of the occupants' behavior reveals interruptions and annoyance. The occupants readily emphasize the problems in interviews. What should the work areas be like to more closely match the behavior normal to the job? Taking into account moderate space and remodeling limitations, the following descriptions of the physical environment for each setting are suggested.

The NCOIC functions as a personnel coordinator. He assigns jobs and maintains the keys to vehicles and other equipment. These activities require him to be easily accessible since he is often needed by many people. Actually, the more exposure he has to the people the better he can perform his job. However, this occasionally conflicts with his need to counsel the military employees in privacy.

The preferred office for the NCOIC would have the following characteristics. Upon closing a door, the office would allow acoustical privacy for counseling. With the door open, a direct view is available to the coffee break setting and mail distribution (a synomorph of the division secretary). These latter serve as a focal point attracting people who benefit from contact with each other and with the NCOIC.

The division secretary is often interrupted. Currently she is some distance from her supervisor, the division chief. However, her position in the office is excellent for receiving visitors. Yet the visitors have no place to sit and wait. The division secretary must often prepare documents considered private, such as personnel records. She can achieve only limited privacy with the coffee break setting and NCOIC setting in the same area.

Characteristics of an office preferred for the secretary would include the following. She should be highly visible to

visitors and be the first person they encounter. In this way there would be no confusion on the part of the visitor and the secretary could function easily as a receptionist. However the visitor would require seats which can be observed by the secretary. It might also be best if the visitor not directly view the coffee break area lest he make premature judgments of the organization's productivity.

The secretary's position relative to her supervisor, the division chief, is of greatest importance. She should be able to act as a buffer for him by screening visitors, making appointments, etc. To do this effectively, she should be located adjacent to his office and adjacent to the traffic flow in and out of this office.

These preceding characteristics for placement of the NCOIC, coffee break, and division secretary settings are based upon requirements for the job, no matter who fills them. However, there is a setting in this organization that experiences conflict because of the particular person filling the role and setting of administrative assistant. This person was formerly the division secretary for many years. Several years ago she was promoted to administrative assistant. As the reader will see in [figure 3-12], she sits at the entrance to the division chief's office.

After several years, she is still approached as the secretary to the division chief. She is asked "Is the chief in?" "When can I see him?" "Can I go in?"

The K-21 score comparing the administrative assistant and division chief is shown in Table 2.

The boundary conflict is reflected in the low score for these two settings. There is no requirement for the jobs that dictates such a close relationship between these two settings. Actually the administrative assistant shares work with the plant and equipment chief and supply and logistics chief located several offices away.

The administrative assistant setting is at a disadvantage for

TABLE 2

K-21 Scores for Administrative Assistant and Division Chief

3
4
4
5
2
2
1
21

several reasons. Her physical placement at the entrance to the chief communicates that she is his secretary. The memory of her former role as the division secretary lingers. And the stereotype of a woman as a secretary all combine to cause conflict for this setting.

In the same office with the administrative assistant is a research mechanical engineer. He is located here because of a lack of space on the second floor. He and the administrative assistant manage a workable boundary, their K-21 score being 24. He does, however, express concern at being away from his professional peers on the second floor and dislikes the interruptions to his work.

Now that all the settings on the first floor have been covered, [figure 3–14] shows how this space might be rearranged. The research mechanical engineer can be relocated to the second floor since space is found there in this proposed change.

The division chief seldom uses the large conference table in his office. Chairs around a desk or coffee table would suffice. By moving him to the office adjacent to the division secretary, she can keep her prominent position for visitors. In addition the visitors can have a place to wait.

The administrative assistant can now join the plant and equipment chief and logistics and supply chief. Room is also available for the clerk-typist who is occasionally hired to assist them.

The NCOIC is provided a partitioned office with direct access to the coffee break setting and mail distribution synomorph. He has only to close his door for privacy during counsel sessions. In this way the administrative portion of the organization is better arranged to reduce boundary conflicts.

Changing the Second Floor

Although called a laboratory, only one part of the second floor is used for laboratory work. The majority of people use desks (see [figure 3–13]).

The part of the second floor operation that is used as a laboratory consists of one person using the drying oven, scales, bench, and sink for soil analysis. This equipment is permanently affixed so no change is considered other than locating the soils analyst's desk in this area.

TABLE 3

K-21 Scores for Technician and Architect

1
6
3
6
4
1
1
22

The remainder of the open lab space and offices are to be changed. [Figure 3–15] shows the proposed alterations.

In the office areas, the following changes are made. The research mechanical engineer takes over the computer room. The research civil engineer "A" moves to an enlarged room formerly used for storage. His move makes room for the civil engineer technician to move into the office with the research civil engineer "B." These two people work most often with each other. This move solves two problems for the technician.

The technician shared a partitioned area with a visiting research architect. The K-21 score comparing their settings is shown in Table 3.

The technician and architect do not work together. These settings share the same conflict the NCOIC and division secretary experience with their highly permeable boundaries. The phone must be answered for the other person. Visitors to one interrupt the other. Idle conversation easily begins. What might the K-21 score comparing the architect and technician be if they are separated? This is shown in Table 4.

By changing the physical location of people the settings have been altered. Boundary problems caused by physical closeness of settings unrelated in an organization are ameliorated. Unrelated work and low K-21 score suggests problems. Changes that increase the K-21 score improve those problems.

TABLE 4

Proposed K-21 Scores for Technician and Architect

4
6
4
6
4
1
1
26

TABLE 5
K-21 Scores for Technician and Civil Engineer "B"

4
3
4
4
4
1
1
—
21

The technician and civil engineer "B" who work together but sit apart have the following K-21 score shown in Table 5.

This shows a close relation, yet still separate setting. However, they work on the same projects and have a need to be close. By putting them into the same office we might expect the K-21 score comparing the two settings to be that shown in Table 6.

What would result then is the two people join to make one setting. The setting might then be called civil engineering research "x," comprised of two performers each at a penetration level of 5.

Boundary problems can be the conflict between unlike settings being too close or like settings being too far apart. In some cases settings exist only because they are distant from each other. If close, they would naturally merge into one.

Other changes on the second floor simply reflect best use of available space for the settings. The visiting research architect is located near the counter where forms used in his research can be assorted. The conference table, drafting table, and counter are clustered near the map file, since these tables are used mostly as layout spaces.

Conclusion
Most investigations in organizational behavior attempt to correlate a multiple of diverse aspects such as the formal structure, informal structure, and work flow with vague analyses of employee perceptions, including worker and supervisor relations, management styles, etc. Seldom can these be reduced to simply understood guidelines for change, especially by the unskilled office manager or office designer.

The information gained during the behavior setting survey and used in calculating the K-21 scores comparing potential settings can yield an easily mastered framework. This framework can be used for diagnosing problems and determining changes that should improve those problems. By having a score based upon data of the actual use of the environment, the result of the changes can be measured against predicted outcomes. These serve not only to improve the skill of those monitoring the changes but provide a logical approach to changes, often required to convince the participants to support or even allow the changes to be made.

TABLE 6
Proposed K-21 Scores for Technician and Engineer "B"

1
2
3
2
3
1
1
—
13

CONCLUSIONS

This exploration of boundaries of settings suggests a group of principles around which the design of settings can be organized. First, however, more general data needs to be considered.

Wicker (1973) said that the population of settings is divided into performers and nonperformers. These are really labels for leaders and nonleaders, in a sense, but the proper definition is given in the penetration scale. For the present, if one merely thinks of them as performers and nonperformers, he can get enough of a grasp of the two populations to consider the next distinction.

Most settings can be divided into two types: the task or product oriented and the service oriented. In task- or product-oriented settings, the performers and nonperformers work together to get a common task done. These are the offices, assembly lines, and other settings where nonperformers are a regular part of the setting. The same nonperformers work with performers on a daily basis. The service-type settings, by contrast, call the nonperformers customers, patients, clients, or an audience. They serve revolving numbers of people.

Getting back to the notion of the querencia, then, there is a distinction that needs to be made between the task- and service-oriented settings. In the task-oriented settings, both performers and nonperformers can operate without physical barriers between them as groups. Their spaces are defined by task function and may or may not be physically isolated from other settings. In the service-oriented settings, there must be at least a permeable physical barrier between performers and nonperformers. The barrier may be the counter of the nursing station discussed previously, or it may be the grocery counter, the ticket booth, the professional desk, the stage, the platform, or the fruit stand. It may take any form, so long as it serves to preserve the querencia of the performer, the area in which he has his final retreat and into which the non-performers cannot go without invitation.

Therefore, whenever considering the design of service-oriented settings, the designer should consider the location of the semipermeable boundary as the chief focus of the setting. If there are several performers, these may need to be separated by their own nonpermeable boundaries, but the nonperformers seem not to require boundaries. In task-oriented settings, the boundaries are less permeable and chiefly between performers, such as the office or factory setting.

In general, one can observe boundary problems when circumstances permit setting occupants to erect physical boundaries. But for most settings the K-21 scale is necessary to define the extent of boundary problems.

REFERENCES

Barker, Roger. *Stream of Behavior.* Appleton-Century-Crofts, 1963.

———. *Ecological Psychology.* Stanford University Press, 1968.

Barker, Roger, and Schoggen, Phil. *Qualities of Community Life.* Jossey-Bass, 1973.

Colarelli, Nick, and Siegel, Saul. *Ward H.* Van Nostrand, 1966.

LeCompte, William. "Behavior Settings: The Structure of the Treatment Environment." Pages 4-2-1–4-2-5 in William J. Mitchell, ed., *Environmental Design: Research and Practice,* Vol. One. UCLA, 1972.

LeCompte, William, and Willems, Edwin. "Ecological Analysis of a Hospital." In John Archea and Charles Eastman, eds., *EDRA 2: Proceedings of the Second Annual Environmental Design Research Association Conference,* Pittsburgh, Pa., October 1970, pp. 236–245.

Osmond, Humphrey. "The Relationship Between Architect and Psychiatrist." In C. Goshen, ed., *Psychiatric Treatment.* American Psychiatric Association, 1959.

Wicker, Allan. "Undermanning Theory and Research: Implications for the Study of Psychological and Behavioral Effects of Excess Populations." *Research in Social Psychology* 4 (1973):185–206.

4

The Rating Scales

Once the behavior settings have been identified*, the next step of the behavior setting survey is to rate them on the sets of scales created by Barker. The rating scales are the most mysterious and foreboding aspect of the behavior setting survey. M. Brewster Smith (1974) even accused Barker of never having revealed how one can arrive at final scores.

There is no mystery to the scales. They operate chiefly on a basis of *occupancy time* (man-hours). Once the total occupancy time of a setting is calculated, *each scale is rated in terms of the percentage of total occupancy time*. This enables the researcher to construct a profile of the different kinds of behavior that go on in an environment according to how much time each one takes. Another way to look at it is to consider constructing a time hierarchy of behavior. The crude assumption is that behavior which takes the most time needs the most design consideration.

Since each behavior setting must be rated on the scales, this chapter will take the reader through the entire sequence from raw observational data to the final scores on the rating scales. The setting chosen for this example is the sidewalks of a public housing project in Cleveland, Ohio called "Arrowhead". Approximately 1,716 residents and countless visitors have access to these sidewalks so that it is a very large setting with a great variety of behavior. Sidewalks and streets are usually among the largest settings of a community and contain large amounts of occupancy time. They are often the least considered in the design process and given little more than pro forma attention.

BEHAVIORAL DATA

The data were collected by observers who posted themselves at six stations around the sidewalks and reported the events they saw in simple, direct statements on the number of persons involved, the age of

---

*Of course, the identification of settings continues beyond the original list because new settings are discovered as a result of observations and the statements of informants.

the persons, how long the incident took, and a brief description of the behavior. These observations were written down on a tablet. The tablet was then photocopied, and the information on each observation was cut out and placed in a folder corresponding to a particular setting (in this case, sidewalks).

One of the differences discovered between city streets and small-town streets is that city streets are more often separate settings from the sidewalks as opposed to the small town where streets and sidewalks are often one setting. The reason for this is the greater number of people on city streets who do not interact with or overlap the population on the sidewalks. This may be an artifact of choosing a small segment of the city rather than being true of the entire community. In any case, using the K-21 scale, the sidewalks and streets become separate settings.

Once all the observations for sidewalks were collected together, they read something like this:

Observer: MS

Date: 12/21/70   Time: 6:00 P.M.

Five teenage males walk East on Quincy singing (30 seconds)

Observer: CB

Date: 01/26/71   Time: 4:00 P.M.

Man, aged 26, is chasing his hat that has blown off his head by the wind. Lasted three minutes.

Observer: DJ

Date: 01/25/71   Time: 12:38 P.M.

Seven year old school boys going to school. On the way, two boys, aged nine and ten, started a fire at the incinerator (two minutes).

Observer: WS

Date: 01/10/71   Time: 4:25 P.M.

Adult female swept her walkway at row houses 2362 and 2364. (one minute).

The observer's descriptions contain an enormous amount of data that is sorted according to chronology and behavior. A summary of some of the material by behavioral categories is listed below.

Sidewalks and Paths (General)

The amount of activity on the sidewalks was voluminous. During thirty-nine days of observation, 58,137 persons were counted moving on the sidewalks. Of this number, the largest group was schoolchildren, accounting for 47,612. 930 preteens and 950 teens of both sexes went to school every day, accounting for 1,888 persons per school day. These counts do not refer to different individuals but to trips on the sidewalk. A schoolchild, for example, may make eight trips per day: going to school in the morning, coming home for lunch, going back to school, coming home from school in the afternoon, going out to play, coming home for supper, going out to play after supper, and then coming home again.

Despite the fact that 60 percent of the population in Arrowhead was female, 54 percent of the traffic was by males. Arrowhead residents spent about 73.56 hours per day on their sidewalks. For each person, this meant 2.4 minutes per day on the average. A disproportionate share of this was used by maintenance workers and schoolchildren; thus, the average adult resident probably spent much less time on the sidewalks per day. Although much of the time spent under observation was in winter, the weather was unusually warm about half the time, and everyone seemed to get outside. Thus these figures are probably typical for warmer times of the year.

Trips to the Grocery Store

Five hundred eighty-seven persons were observed in 409 trips that clearly indicated walks to the grocery store. The average time on the sidewalk was

1.78 minutes, and the average trip to the store and back took 29.7 minutes. In addition, 93 people were seen pushing or pulling shopping carts in 76 trips, and 252 people were seen carrying bags on 194 trips. This makes a total of 932 persons on 679 trips to the grocery store, or 17.41 trips to the store per day for all of Arrowhead. Considering 636 households in the Arrowhead area, this means only 0.2 trips per week, which is probably too low. The reason for this underreporting is that a large number of persons were seen carrying boxes, and it could not be determined whether these were Christmas gifts. Still, with a minimum of 17 trips for groceries per day from Arrowhead, it would be possible to make estimates of the size any new grocery facility should be.

The L and B Store was the most popular store mentioned (47 times). The A&P was mentioned only 6 times. Residents divided between stores on Central and 55th and those near Quincy and 55th to 40th. More business went to the 55th and Central complex. (See the map of Arrowhead, figure 4-1, for streets.)

Falls on the Sidewalk

Thirty-two persons were reported falling down on the sidewalk for various reasons. The majority were women (11). Fourteen of the falls were due to icy conditions. One girl cut her wrist badly on the broken glass. These reports indicate the sidewalk has its own hazards and cannot be neglected in terms of safety measures.

Use of the Chain Fences

Related to the use of the sidewalks are reports of 51 persons using the chain fences [figure 4-2]. They were used to swing on (6), to sit on (8), to hold on to (3), to jump over (2), to bang something against (3), and to hang rugs on for drying (2). The holding on seems to be a critical use for elderly, especially in winter. The chains, however, are not rigid and serve poorly to steady anyone walking on ice. There is a

clear need for more substantial support during winter. Instances of holding onto the fence and falling would probably be greater except that many older persons do not venture out when conditions are icy.

Sliding or Skating on Sidewalks

Forty-eight persons were reported sliding or skating on the sidewalk. Sixteen were using roller skates, and the remainder were sliding on ice or using sleds or cardboard. Of these 98 persons, 77 or (79 percent) were preteens of both sexes. The remainder were teenagers and one preschooler. The popularity of sliding is an indication of how snowfall increases the activity of children compared to when there is no snow and, apparently, little to do.

Trips to the Laundry

Three hundred forty-nine persons were reported in 226 trips to the laundry. Of these persons, 241 (69 percent) were female. The average trip to the laundry and back took 65 minutes; time spent on the sidewalk carrying laundry was 5.33 minutes. These figures show about 9 trips to the laundry per day or 63 trips per week. The small number of trips in addition to the large carts carried indicate residents make as few trips as possible.

Trips to the Dry Cleaner

Sixty-two persons were observed going to the dry cleaners on 47 trips. The average time on the sidewalk was 3 minutes. Dry cleaning had the fewest trips of all compared to laundry and grocery trips and was dominated by males (61 percent).

Canes and Crutches

Ten aged (65 and over) and 8 adults (18-64) were observed with canes and crutches. During the long

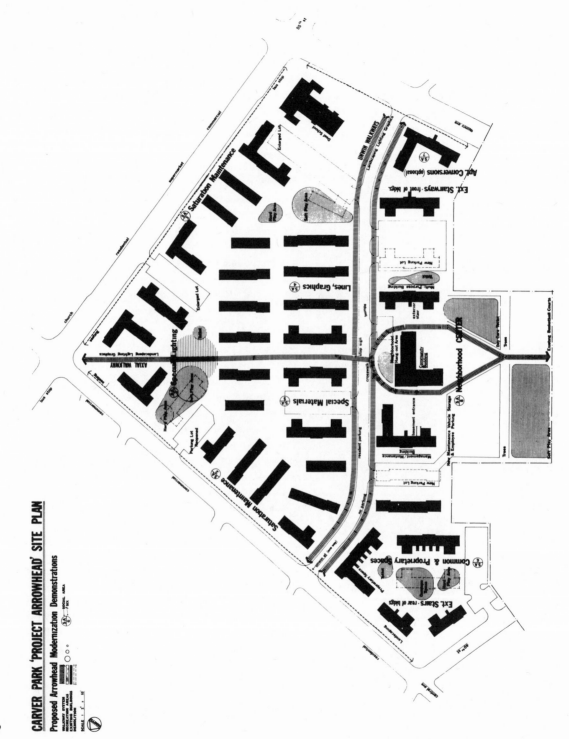

52

Figure 4-1
Paths and sidewalks of the Carver Park Project Arrowhead site plan.

Figure 4-2
Chain fences.

periods when sidewalks are covered with snow and ice, these people are even more handicapped.

Looking for Addresses

On 21 occasions, 34 persons were observed having difficulty in locating addresses in Arrowhead. In purely quantitative terms, this means more than 300 persons a year are ill served by the lack of signs or clear address numbers on the housing estate. Two people were reported completely unsuccessful. Most of the remainder found the address only by asking residents.

Traffic Problems

Unwin Road is both a traffic and congestion problem. It is repeatedly overparked by residents, management personnel, and maintenance workers during the day. Drivers are reported going up Unwin the wrong way. When both sides of the street are parked, the narrow passageway creates accident conditions, two of which happened in the presence of the researchers. Traffic tickets are constantly handed out for parking on Unwin, on the sidewalks, and on the grass. One

woman was nearly hit as she stepped from between the parked cars that make crossing Unwin hazardous. Children were observed making a game of dashing in front of cars as they came down Unwin. Eleven incidents of cars parked on sidewalks near Unwin were reported. Twenty-four times the parking lot made into a play area on Central was reported with cars parked in it. It is clear that residents regularly used this area by driving up over the sidewalk and lawns to find parking space in the play area.

Conversations

One hundred sixty-four persons were reported in conversation on the sidewalks during the observation period. Of these 71 events, 9 (13 percent) were arguments, 4 (6 percent) involved chasing or scolding someone, and 5 (7 percent) were conversations from an individual in a window to one on the sidewalk.

Maintenance workers alone used up 13 percent of the reported conversation time, contributing some data to support the residents' notion that maintenance workers are not conscientious.

Fighting

Twenty-six incidents of fighting, three of which drew crowds, could be considered separate settings in themselves. Of the 53 persons involved, only 10 (19 percent) were adults. Incidents between males and females were more numerous among adults than between males. The average fight lasted 17.5 minutes. There were two incidents of boxing for recreation in addition to the fights.

Intoxication

Nine male adults and three female adults were reported intoxicated on the sidewalks. No serious consequences were reported from these incidents except a bottle was reported smashed on the sidewalk and one intoxicated female was reported lifting her dress for all to see.

Lockouts

Incidence of lockouts was reported by security men as the next to the most troublesome problem in Arrowhead. Four incidents of lockout were observed, during three of which the residents tried to break into their own dwellings. In all three cases, the people breaking in were teenagers or preteenagers indicating that probably a fair percentage of lockouts are not reported and that some of the damage to dwellings occurs when an individual tries to get in after a lockout. It is also possible that since adults were not involved in these incidents, many residents attribute some of the damage to outsiders rather than to their own children.

Running

The use of the sidewalk was by no means restricted to walking in a sedate fashion from one place to another; 551 persons were reported running in 257 incidents. Children and teenagers predominated, of course, but 38 (7 percent) were adult males and females. Sixty-six percent of the persons running were males, and the average incident lasted 4.52 minutes.

Dogs

The use of dogs as playmates was especially popular among preteen males. Of 79 persons reported playing with dogs, 32 (41 percent) were preteen males. Of 49 incidents of dogs and humans, 4 occasions were reported when a dog was chasing someone not in play and only one occasion when an adult chased a dog. On two occasions observers reported nonresidents bringing large dogs onto the housing estates. Although from these figures dogs do not seem to be a large problem, a few residents complained they were afraid of them.

Playing on Roof

Although a roof is not part of sidewalks and paths, two incidents of three preteen boys playing ball on a roof were reported. The incidents lasted about 30 minutes each.

Shootings

Shooting complaints were reported prior to the observation period. However, observers reported 10 shooting incidents during the 39-day observation period. Four of these incidents were connected with celebrating New Years Eve. In another incident, someone came out of his house and shot in the air. In another an adult woman shot at some teenagers for cutting through her backyard, and a man shot at a boy for an unknown reason. The remaining incidents were shots in the air. There were two occasions where boys were shooting out street lights with BB guns and shooting out a resident's window with a BB gun.

Gunshots were not an entirely uncommon occurrence at Arrowhead and many residents carried guns, sometimes openly showing them. While most of the incidents are clearly high spirits and it is true that adults deliberately missed the children they shot at, the effects that gunshots had on the feelings of safety among residents were said to be as shattering as their loud reports and were observable in the incidents witnessed firsthand by the researchers. In one case people close to the incident could not finish lunch; in another, workers were so disturbed they left the job and went home.

Going to Church

One hundred forty-three persons were reported going to church during the five Sundays under observation. Since some of these were cold winter days, it was expected that numbers would be few. The average trip to church and back was 75 minutes since many went to Sunday school also. Seventy-seven percent of the church goers were female.

Littering and Destructiveness

During the rent and maintenance strike, there were countless incidents of people throwing their trash and garbage on the lawn, in the basements, on the sidewalks, on other peoples' steps, and anywhere they could get rid of it. These occasions were not counted because it was felt they were not typical of the usual situation when trash and garbage was collected and burned. Other incidents not connected to the overfull incinerators were reported. These involved deliberate incidents of breakage, intent to harm, or destruction. In 5 incidents, teenagers, preteens, and adults deliberately broke bottles in public places, such as playgrounds, or in other places where people walk. Teenagers broke soft-drink bottles while adults broke liquor bottles. The result was a virtual carpet of glass so that the large playground had to be swept whenever a game was to be played there.

Snowballs were responsible for window breakage on many occasions. A preteen boy was seen throwing one at his little sister while she watched from behind the glass. An older thirteen-year-old deliberately tried to break windows. Still another teenager bombarded the outside apartment door "with all his might." Two preteen males also tried to break windows with snowballs.

Snowballs are among the softer objects thrown, however. One teenager threw a large screw through a window. Throwing rocks at cars was another problem. Four incidents of throwing rocks at cars in the various parking lots were observed. On other occasions, preteen males were seen throwing tin cans from the trash piles at each other.

One adult woman, in apparent pique at the modernization program, threw all the floor tiles from her third-floor apartment onto the macadam space between buildings.

Riding Bikes, Crazy Cars, Wagons

Two hundred five children or teenagers and two adults were observed riding bikes, crazy cars, and other vehicles on the sidewalks and playgrounds. Eighty-seven percent of these were male. The average incident lasted 9.38 minutes.

Note that these behavioral categories were those most often mentioned by the observers. Other categories, such as washing windows (for which one must walk on the sidewalk) or sweeping and cleaning up, were too few to be mentioned.

For a clearer picture of all the details to follow, the reader should consult the behavior-setting information sheet in appendix A which contains spaces for all the descriptive aspects listed, sections for all the population data, and instructions for using each of the rating scales. Once calculations are made on the information sheet, they are transferred to the behavior setting code sheet (Table 4-1).

DESCRIPTIVE ASPECTS OF SETTINGS

Each setting has a name, a class, a genotype, a unit, a locus, soma, narrative, and data. These are usually recorded on the setting information sheet (appendix A).

The *name* refers to the common name given to the setting by local population (history class, Boy Scout meeting, church picnic, sidewalks and paths, and so forth). In coding for computer analysis, the setting is also given a number.

TABLE 4-1
Behavior Setting Code Sheet

Name:

Genotype Number	1-4:	Authority System	8-9:	Number of Occurrences	11-13:
Behavior-Setting Number 5-7:		Class of Authority Systems	10:		

Occupancy Time of Base Subgroups				Maximum Penetration of Subgroups		Action Pattern	
On Base	No. P Hours	OT Code		Group		Rate	
On Base							
Inf	ML* / C	14-15:		Inf	57:	Aes:	1:
Presch	ML / C	16-17:		Presch	58:	Bus:	2:
Y S	ML / C	18-19:		Y S	59:	Prof:	3:
O S	ML / C	20-21:		O S	60:	Educ:	4:
On Base Child	ML / C	22-23:				Govt:	5:
Adol	ML / C	24-25:		Adol	61:	Nutr:	6:
Adult	ML / C	26-27:		Adult	62:	PersAp:	7:
Aged		28-29:		Aged	63:	Phil:	8:
On Base Total	ML / C	30-31:		Grand Max	64:	PhysH:	9:
Males	ML / C	32-33:		Males	65:	Rec:	10:
Females	ML / C	34-35:		Females	66:	Rel:	11:
Population (number)				Performers (number)			

*ML and C refer to military and civilian population breakdowns only used on military bases.

TABLE 4-1 (Continued)

On Base Total	$\dfrac{\text{ML}}{\text{C}}$	36–38:	On Base Total	$\dfrac{\text{ML}}{\text{C}}$	67–68:	Soc: 12:
Off Base Total	$\dfrac{\text{ML}}{\text{C}}$	39–41:	Off Base Total	$\dfrac{\text{ML}}{\text{C}}$	69–71:	Mechanism Rate AffB: 13:
Grand Total		42–45:	Grand Total		72–74:	GroMot: 14:
Grand OT (code)		46: Blank 47–49:	Perf/Pop		75–76	Manip. 15:
Total Duration		50–53:	Aver. No.		77–78:	Talk: 16:
Average Attendance		54–56:				Think: 17:
						GRI 18:
						Pressure Rating Children: 19:
						Adolesc: 20:
						Welfare Rating Children: 21:
						Adolesc: 22:
						Autonomy Rating Wtd: 23:
						Social C. OT I
						II
						III
						IV 24–40:
						Social C. Pen.L. I
						II
						III
						IV 41–45:

The *class* indicates whether it is a business, church, government, school, or voluntary association. In the case of the sidewalk example, the class is government since it is a government housing project.

Genotypes is a general classification of settings according to their similarity of standing patterns of behavior. Common genotypes are listed in Barker (1968, appendix 2). They include a description of the behavior program, and penetration classes of the inhabitants. For example:

Attorneys Offices. Lawyers (penetration levels 5 or 6) initiate legal actions, prepare legal defense in civil and criminal cases, give legal advice, draw up contracts, prepare wills, prepare federal and state income tax returns, manage office; secretary (penetration level 4) carries out office routines; clients (penetration level 3) seek and pay for advice and service.*

Genotypes are those settings whose leaders at penetration level 5 (see page 64) could be interchanged without interruption of the setting program. In the above example of attorney's offices, most attorneys could be interchanged with minimal interruption (although in highly specialized law practices, this would not be the case). In our example of sidewalks, there are no other sidewalk settings, so the setting and the genotypes are the same. Genotypes are listed by number on the information sheet.

Unit of the setting refers to the setting that controls all others within an authority system of settings; for example, one setting (the manager's office) controls many other settings in the public-housing environment in Arrowhead (Bechtel, 1972b).

Locus of the setting refers to whether it is in the specific geographical area being studied. (See second and pages following of the information sheet in appendix A) In Barker's (1968) study it was (a) in town; (b) in town, rotating; (c) in town, but no town occupants; or (d) out of town. In the residential area study (Bechtel, Achelpohl, and Binding, 1970) it was (a) in block; (b) in block, rotating; (c) in block but no block participants; or (d) out of block. This could have been extended to (e) out of block, in city, and

*Roger Barker, *Ecological Psychology* (Stanford University Press, 1968), p. 212.

(f) out of block, out of city, if these measures were desired on residents who worked outside the residency area. In the Arrowhead study, the locus designations were (a) on project, (b) on project, rotating, (c) on project but no project participants, (d) off project. (The behavior setting information sheet in appendix A uses an in-block, out-of-block designation.)

Soma is a term used to describe the physical aspects of a setting and is especially critical for design-oriented professionals. Ordinarily these descriptions are made in an informal manner by social scientists but for design research a design professional might want a highly technical description with schematic drawings. A drawing of the paths and sidewalks is shown in figure 4-1. Soma descriptions are not recorded on the code sheet but are kept in the form of written or typed notes, sometimes accompanied by photographs on the first page of the behavior-setting information sheet (appendix A).

Journalistic description is a narrative of what goes on in the program of the setting. Its abstraction is the genotype program across several similar settings. Once again, these are not marked on the coding sheet and are usually kept in the form of written or typed notes. The expanded description on the preceding pages goes far in describing the flavor of life on the sidewalks and paths of Arrowhead. Many design aspects could be concluded from the description alone—for example, the inadequacy of the chain fences for the elderly.

Further descriptive aspects can be added or increased in detail as needed. It is a common practice to photograph each setting so the relationship of occupants and environment is clearer. The use of behavior objects may require extensive observation if they are of concern.

QUANTITATIVE ASPECTS OF SETTINGS

Frequency is the number of times a setting occurs within a given time reference, usually a year.

Duration is the number of hours a setting uses. The maximum for any one year (except leap year) is 8,760, for all 24 hours of each day. Usually homes will have such a duration, but so will sidewalks and paths. See columns 50-53 in table 4-1.

Population is the total number of persons who enter the setting. These are divided further into town and out-of-town persons (or block and out of block) and into age categories (see columns 14-45 in table 4-1).

Occupancy time is the man-hours spent in each setting by each population group.

Occurrence is the number of days in which a setting operates. The maximum is 365 (366 for a leap year). See columns 11-13 in table 4-1.

ACTION PATTERN RATINGS

The standing behavior patterns in behavior settings are rated according to eleven categories of molar behavior: aesthetics, business, education, government, nutrition, personal appearance, physical health, professionalism, recreation, religion, and social contact.* These are among the most difficult aspects of a behavior-setting survey, and they must be measured with great care. Often the researcher or an observer will have to watch a number of setting occurrences with stopwatch in hand to get accurate and reliable ratings. Each of the action patterns is rated on a scale ranging from 0 to 14. The total score is arrived at by adding the subscales: participation, supply, evaluation and appreciation, teaching, and learning. Ratings on the subscales are based on the percentage of occupancy time devoted to the particular action pattern.

Subscales

Participation is the amount of the behavior devoted to the action pattern rated according to:

0   Action pattern does not occur
1   Occurs 1 to 20 percent of occupancy time

*Barker and Wright (1955) originally had thirteen patterns, including orientation and philanthropy in addition to the eleven cited above. These two were dropped by the time Barker's 1968 book was published.

2   21-40 percent
3   41-60 percent
4   61-80 percent
5   81-100 percent

Most classrooms would be rated 5 on participation in education since education occurs there more than 81 percent of the occupancy time. In our example of the sidewalks, since there were 32 incidents of sweeping or cleaning the walks in some fashion, the rating is clearly not 0, but the occupancy time involved (less than 10 hours) is well below 1 percent and thus receives a rating of 1. Most settings are rather easy to rate in that they either involve no trace of the action pattern, in which case they rate 0, or only a trace to 20 percent, and therefore rate 1. The settings where there are large amounts of an action pattern are the ones that require a great deal of observation. It can be difficult to measure 60 percent as opposed to 80 percent of occupancy time. A time sampling procedure is sometimes useful, perhaps five minutes of every two hours after the main behavior traffic pattern is known.

To rate on the *supply* subscale, it must be observed that either a product or a person is prepared in the setting being measured for another setting. Obviously manufacturing would be high in this subscale but so would any form of rehearsal for a performance. Supply is rated the same as participation, but supply and participation ratings are exclusive. One action pattern cannot be rated on both except additively, for example, education 4, supply 2, total 6. (A six total is possible because of overlapping percentages.)

Evaluation and appreciation subscale refers to behavior that shows an appreciation or evaluation of the general behavior or some part of the behavior that occurs in the setting. Obvious examples are clapping, but less obvious are giving tests in school. The behavior must be open and explicit to be rated on this scale. Compliments, encouragement, and other spontaneous acts are not rated. The behavior is usually a scheduled part of the behavior pattern. The scubscale is:

0   No explicit evaluation or appreciation

1 Less than half of occupancy time
2 More than half.

Teaching and learning includes the obvious behavior in classrooms but excludes learning that is not formal. Teaching and learning are rated on the same scale as evaluation (0, 1, 2).

All action patterns are rated by summing the scores for the four subscales listed above. Very seldom does the researcher have any use for the data on subscales separately. Only the total score was used for comparisons in Bechtel (1970, 1972a, 1972b).

Action Pattern Definitions

The definitions given here sometimes do not seem to fit field situations and may require an exercise of judgment on the part of the researcher. The best way to resolve such problems is by observation, often by consulting informants, and more often by a combination of the two. The stopwatch is the final arbiter in judging percentages of occupancy time.

Barker (1968, p. 55) defines *aesthetics* as "any artistic activity; any behavior aimed at making the environment more beautiful, as this is locally defined."

In the participation subscale he adds "removing the unsightly." This is an important aspect of many recent activities having to do with cleaning up the environment. Also, urban areas are more likely to have demolition settings, which are scored high for aesthetics.

Any kind of minimal effort to make a setting attractive usually rates a 1 (1–20 percent of occupancy time). The settings most commonly having to do with aesthetics are usually art classes, art supply stores, rehearsals, trash or garbage removal, and floral shops (see table 4–2). Beauty shops are not usually included under aesthetics because the customers are beautifying themselves, an action pattern called *personal appearance*. But *teaching* personal appearance (as in the setting charm class) does rate high on aesthetics.

Sidewalks and paths, for example, rate a 2 (total) on aesthetics; there were a few incidents observed of residents' sweeping and cleaning up the area but not enough to be considered more than a trace. Hence, a score of 1 is given on the participation subscale. Similarly, residents regularly gathered to criticize the appearance of sidewalks and porches; this meeting rates a 1 on the evaluation subscale.

Barker (1968, p. 56) defines the *business action pattern* as "the exchange of goods, services, or privileges where *payment is obligatory*." Exclusive of gifts

TABLE 4–2
Settings Rated High in Aesthetics

East Side	West Side	Arrowhead
Around the house	Florist delivery (6)	African drums class (8)
	Trash collection (5)	Charm class (7)
	Garbage collection (5)	Creativity unlimited (7)
	Demolition (5)	Arts and crafts (adults) (7)
		Arts and crafts (boys) (7)
		Arts and crafts (girls) (7)
		Adult sewing class (6)
		Marching (6)
		Maintenance office (6)
		Puppetry class (6)
		Incinerators (5)
		Modernization program (5)
		Christmas caroling (5)

or hiring for wages, this is the professionalism action pattern. In the residential areas studies in Bechtel, Achelpohl, and Binding (1970) and in Bechtel (1972a, 1972b) there were few business settings originating in the areas measured, but several settings rating high in business reached into the areas from other parts of the city. These were the delivery routes, repairmen, and so on. Business can usually be rated by observing the actual time spent selling and transacting business versus the time spent socializing, daydreaming, or on other personal matters. Many stores can rate surprisingly low on this action pattern.

There was a 1 rating for the sidewalks on business because it was observed that some illegal business was going on, but this was only a trace.

Education is easily defined by the formal educational roles of teacher and pupil. The informal teaching and learning that goes on in many settings, as for example among children, is not included. Public lectures do not rate on this action pattern. Home study courses where there is a formal communication with someone who serves as a teacher is rated. No formal education took place on the sidewalks; therefore the rating was zero.

The *government* action pattern has to do with any form of government—local, county, state, or federal. Barker (1968, p. 58) defines this pattern as strictly having to do with "law making, law interpretation, and law execution." This does not include paying at parking meters but it does include giving tickets for overtime, police patrols, and working in the post office (but not buying stamps or mailing letters).

Settings that involve evaluation or appreciation of government (like Fourth of July picnic speeches) will have a government rating. Usually government ratings will be very minimal as in the case of a church service offering a prayer to government, or maximal as in the mayor's office. Lawyers' offices are also very high. In the case of these particular sidewalks, the participation rating was 3 because a strike was going on which involved a great deal of police activity and the surveillance of government officials and union pickets. The evaluation was 1 and the teaching and learning

was 1, since residents were informally taught to picket on the sidewalks. The total rating was 5.

Any behavior that involves eating or drinking or the preparation of food or drinks is rated on *nutrition*. Any setting in which a person consumes food or drink is rated. The sidewalks were rated 1 because there was a noticeable amount of eating or drinking but not more than 20 percent of occupancy time. There was also no supply or teaching and learning rating.

Personal appearance is not a functional classification; it has to do with trying to look good rather than dressing for environmental conditions. Thus, dressed up for a party would get a rating but dressing for the cold would not. Many differences exist among geographical areas as to what constitutes dressing up. For example, at a local Kansas City high school students took a great deal of care to dress up in the "hoboist looking clothes." They would go to such lengths as to tear holes in the clothing, wrinkle it through an old-fashioned set of washer rollers, and paint stain it. This was followed by the tie-dying fad later. The important thing to keep in mind is the current local definition of what is dressed up and what is house wear. Informants and observers are especially critical here. Personal appearance also includes such items as make-up, hair style, and general grooming. The lowest end of the scale is what would be expected in the home rather than the public environment, for example, hair curlers and robes. Barker (1968, p. 61) suggests the following scale:

0 House clothing and adornment
1 Street, school, and work clothes
2 Dressing for church or Sunday school
3 Dressing for a semiformal party
4 Formal dress affairs
5 Fancy dress balls, ceremonial dress.

Uniforms count only as work clothes unless they are dress uniforms or are in out-of-contact settings, (for example, police uniforms at school, army uniforms in church). The sidewalks rated the usual 1 for street, school, or work clothes worn by most people. There was no supply rating or teaching and learning.

The *physical health* action pattern concerns all behavior directed at preserving physical (not mental) health. It includes clinics, doctors' offices, the school nurse, physical examinations, classes in first aid, and so on. Physical health on the sidewalks was rated 2 because of the trace amount in occupancy time and the evaluation component of many visiting nurses, parents, and health officials to the nearby settlement house. There was no teaching and learning rating.

Professionalism is a very narrowly defined behavior pattern having only to do with the payment of wages. The following scale is from Barker (1968):

0   Performers receive no pay
1   1–20 percent of occupancy time of performers is paid
2   21–40 percent
3   41–60 percent
4   61–80 percent
5   81–100 percent.

Since maintenance workers who patrolled the sidewalks and raked leaves were paid, the rating was 1. There was no supply, teaching, or learning rating. It is conceivable that some maintenance workers at other times would be learning on the job, in which case the rating would be 1, for a total of 2.

Barker (1968, p. 64) defines the *recreational action pattern* as "behavior that gives immediate gratification: consumatory behavior; play, sport, games." Settings range from those that are entirely devoted to recreation, such as parties, movies, dances, and swimming pools, to those that are flexible, such as drug stores or restaurants, to those that are never rated, such as banks, attorneys' offices, courts, or places of religious worship. Recreation took up to 61 to 80 percent of the occupancy time on the sidewalks, for a rating of 4. There was no rating given for supply, teaching, or learning. It is true that much informal learning of games took place on the sidewalk, but the reader will recall this is not *formal* learning and so was not rated.

Religion is closely tied to a worship service. When prayers are offered at banquets or sports events, these are rated as 1. No religious behavior took place on the sidewalks nor did they "supply" people to religious settings since the people were only in transit on the sidewalks. The rating was 0.

The *social contact* action pattern is defined by Barker (1968, p. 66) as "having interpersonal relations of any kind." There is no setting that will not have some rating on this action pattern. Even a play in which there is absolute silence in the audience will be rated because the players are communicating to the audience. Low ratings are in settings where people work alone and hence have no one to interact with. There was a high degree of social contact on the sidewalks, given a rating of 4.

BEHAVIOR MECHANISMS

Action patterns classify the type of global behavior going on in the setting, such as aesthetics, business, or religious, while behavior mechanisms classify the personal units of behavior, such as crying, walking, talking, or thinking.

Subscales

There are three subscales for behavior mechanisms. *Participation* is rated similarly to the action patterns:

0 Occurs less than 10 percent of occupancy time
1 10–33 percent
2 34–66 percent
3 67–90 percent
4 More than 90 percent.

Tempo is the maximum speed at which the behavior is performed normally. The pace of walking on the sidewalk is much brisker than the walking in a cafeteria line. The rating is given to the average pace, not the unusual. For example, of 58,137 persons observed on the sidewalk at Arrowhead (Bechtel, 1972a), 551 were seen running. The running was not averaged with the walking, but only the walking was considered in the rating at its maximum speed.

Barker's (1968, p. 67) scale is as follows:

0 When the mechanism occurs, its maximal normal speed is slow; reaction times are long.
1 The maximal normal speed of the mechanism is in the median range, neither fast nor slow.
2 The maximal normal speed of the mechanism is above the median range.
3 The maximal normal speed of the mechanism is near the physio-logical limit.

Usually athletic events such as basketball, football, and track are rated as 3 because of the performers. Most other settings are at 1, with only a few at 2 when it is seen that the performers are constantly in a hurry.

Intensity is rated according to the maximum rate of energy expended (Barker, 1968, p. 68):

0 When the mechanism occurs, the maximum normal rate of expenditure is very low.
1 Maximal normal energy expenditure is in the median range.
2 Maximal normal energy expenditure is above the median range.
3 Maximal normal energy exerted is near the physiological limit.

Athletic events usually rate a 3, although teenage dances will also rate 3 in the 1970s era. Behavior setting mechanisms are rated for each setting by adding the sum of the scores for each subscale. The possible range for each mechanism is 0 to 10.

Definitions of Behavior Mechanisms

Affective behavior is another term for emotional behavior. Any of the visible signs of emotion are scored for affective behavior mechanism, among them, strong outward signs such as yelling, screaming, crying, and normal activities with an emotional tone such as singing with strong feeling, cheering at a football game, or quiet reverence in a church. Since the amount of observed affective behavior was rather high (61–80 percent) with so many children present, the rating was 4 for participation on the sidewalks and paths, but 1 for tempo and for intensity.

The *gross motor activity* behavior mechanism involves the use of the large muscles of the body and includes such activities as walking, running, swimming, in fact, almost any activity except sitting. An odd exception to this in the late 1960s was the custom of teenagers to swing their arms widely to music while sitting at tables. On the sidewalks gross motor behavior involved 100 percent of the occupancy time (4), which was above the median range (2) but within the median intensity range (1) for a total score of 7.

The *Manipulation* behavior mechanism involves the use of the hands. It may be accompanied by gross motor activity. Use of the hands includes clapping and tapping of fingers, as well as pushing, pulling, using any kind of hard tool, holding books, turning pages, and so on. Since some people were carrying packages, bicycling, and so forth, the participation scale was 1 and intensity and tempo at 1 each, for a total of 3.

Talking includes any form of verbal expression whether words are articulated or not and may overlap with affective behavior. Virtually all the children on the sidewalks were observed talking in the incidents reported, many talking to themselves while in play fantasy. The total rating was 4.

It is difficult to observe the *thinking* behavior mechanism so it is scored almost always as a result of having to solve a problem or make a decision. Barker (1968, p. 69) scores it entirely on a basis of how much occupancy time of a setting is concerned with problem solving or decision making. Only a trace of thinking behavior was scored, and this was largely because of the lockout incidents when people had to figure how to get inside.

Considering the action patterns and behavior

mechanisms, there are three important judgments to be made in terms of occupancy time. First, does the behavior occur *at all* in the setting? If there is *no trace* of the behavior, the rating is 0. Next, is the decision of whether the behavior occurs more than just a trace? A trace is usually scaled up to 20 percent of occupancy time and is scored 1. The final judgment involves whether more than just a trace is present. Usually, if a behavior is *prominent* it will be more than 50 percent of occupancy time. Here one must fall back on careful observation of the setting rather than informants.

MORE GLOBAL SCALES

In addition to the action patterns and behavior mechanisms, which can largely be observed by the actions of people in the settings, there are several more global measures that are inferred from rules of the setting or calculated by combining other measures. These measures include penetration levels, richness, pressure, welfare, and autonomy.

Penetration levels are one of the most important measures of behavior-setting surveys. The penetration level is a measure of how central the person's performance is to the setting. The higher the penetration level, the greater the involvement and importance of the person in a setting. There are six zones of penetration (1) onlooker, (2) invited guests, (3) members, (4) performers, (5) joint leaders, and (6) single leaders. Onlookers are the least involved. They are like the sidewalk superintendents at a construction job, that is, they are there but add nothing to the setting and have no influence on it. Invited guests are like the fans at a football game or the audience at a play. They are necessary to the setting but have the lowest participation level in its functioning. Level 3 persons are the bona-fide members, the persons who have membership cards and who have certain rights as members. Level 4 persons are active functionaries or officers in the organization. They have some power in directing the course of

events but are not the leaders (for example, sergeants at arms and secretaries in offices). Level 5 are joint leaders. These are presidents and vice-presidents and other central officers who run organizations. In less formal settings, they are the leaders with the most social power. Level 6 are single leaders, without whom the setting could not function. An example would be a one-person radio station but also teachers in a one-room schoolhouse. If there is a level 6 leader, no other persons can be rated at level 5.

Penetration levels were used by Binding (1969) to study leadership in a small community. They are also the critical measures of participation in Barker and Gump's (1964) school study and in churches (Wicker, 1969). Measurement of penetration levels in any environment can determine the leadership levels available to residents of that environment and will also tell whether the residents are taking advantage of them (Bechtel, 1970, 1972a, 1972b).

Penetration levels have been only indirectly related to physical design aspects through the size of the setting. Wicker (1969), Willems (1967), Gump and Frisen (1964), and Barker (1968) have shown that larger organizations tend to have larger settings and smaller organizations smaller settings, meaning that the average penetration level per person is higher for smaller settings. Since the penetration level is higher, the participation level is correspondingly so. Thus, forces toward higher participation levels are controlled through setting size, and in many cases this can translate into room size.

Penetration levels are among the easiest of the rating scales to measure. Membership lists or organizations have officers listed, newspapers will often describe leading roles, and informants are likely to know who leads in most settings. In the case of the sidewalks, for example, the leaders were clearly the maintenance workers, who received a penetration rating of 4, and the maintenance supervisor, who received a rating of 5. Since penetration levels are marked only on the code sheet (table 4-1), the markings would be as follow in the columns 57-66: infants, 3; preschool, 3; young school, 3; old school,

3; adolescents, 3; adults, 5; aged, 3; males, 5; and females, 3.

Richness of a setting is a calculation of exposure of range of occupants' ages and leadership to varieties of behavior. The greater the range of occupant groups of all ages, the higher the penetration levels, and the greater the behavior mechanisms and action patterns, the higher will be the richness index. The general richness index is calculated by summing the penetration ratings of the fourteen population subgroups (see Table 4–1), the ratings of all the action patterns, and the ratings of all the behavior mechanisms and weighting the sum for the occupancy time of the setting.

The occupancy time is coded by ranking occupancy times from the lowest to the highest and coding by intervals. Each interval is then ranked, and the rank number is the code used. (See Barker's appendix 1 [1968].)

The general richness index (GRI) is then calculated by the following formula (Barker, 1968, p. 70):

$$GRI = \frac{(\Sigma\ PenR + \Sigma\ ApR + \Sigma\ Bmr)\ cOT}{100}$$

PenR: Penetration ratings of the setting
ApR: Action pattern ratings of the setting
BmR: Behavior mechanism rating of the setting
cOT: Code number of occupancy time

General richness indexes of settings vary from location to location. Barker (1968) reported a GRI range of from 57 to 1. Barker does not use a mean GRI for all settings. In the Kansas City study (Bechtel, Achelpohl, and Binding, 1970), the GRI range extended from 19.7 to 0.7 for East Side and 24.5 to 1.6 for West Side. Mean GRI index for East Side (N = 23 settings) was 5.19 and for West Side (N = 46 settings) 7.88. At Arrowhead, the range was from 24 to 0.51, with a mean of 8.54 for 67 settings. Thus, the outdoor residential areas of the public-housing environment in Cleveland provided a richer behavioral environment

than either of the two outdoor residential areas studies in Kansas City, but all of these were less rich than the small town outdoor environment. If richness of behavior is the goal of design then the small-town environment is the one to emulate. The GRI for sidewalks and paths was 29.82, indicating a fairly rich environment.

Pressure is the degree to which forces outside the setting act to bring a person into a setting or tend to make him avoid it. This implies nothing about the attractive or repulsive qualities of the setting itself. Barker (1968, p. 71) developed the following scale to rate pressure of behavior settings on children, but it could just as well be adapted for adolescents or elderly or middle-aged people:

1. Required: Children are required to enter the setting: They have no choice. An example is school classes, but they are rated only for children of school age.
2. Urged: Eligible children are pressured but not required to attend. They have some choice, e.g., cub scouts.
3. Invited: Eligible children are welcomed to the setting: They are asked to attend.
4. Neutral: Children are free to enter this setting equally with others; there is no positive or negative discrimination with respect to children.
5. Tolerated: Children are not welcomed to the setting: others can enter more freely than children; there is resistance to children but not strong.
6. Resisted: Children are pressured not to enter the setting, but they are not forbidden. There must be strong reasons (counterpressures) to allow a child to enter.
7. Prohibited: Children are excluded, e.g., an organization meeting like the Masonic Lodge.

Children and adolescents' pressure ratings were given a 4 since the sidewalks and paths did not discriminate against or favor them in any way.

Welfare rates whether a setting exists for a certain age group. Barker (1968, p. 75) used this rating to test whether the setting exists for children, but it could just as well be used for other age groups. His scale of welfare rating for children follows (Barker, 1968, p. 75):

0. The setting is not concerned with Children
1. Serves child members: The setting serves the welfare of its child inhabitants; its product of output is children processed in a particular way, educated, recreated, strengthened, fed, bathed, etc. The processing must be exclusively children, not people in general.
2. Serves children in other settings: The setting instigates and supports *other* settings that are primarily for the welfare of children; it has no child members itself. The setting fosters other settings that are rated 1 on child welfare. This rating is only given if the setting would itself cease, if the setting it fosters ceases. An example is the elementary school board meeting.
3. Children serve other members: The setting has child performers who operate the setting for the benefit of the members of other age groups. For example, PTA meetings where children sometimes provide the program. The welfare rating for sidewalks and paths was zero for children and zero for adolescents.

Barker (1968, p. 76) refers to the *autonomy* scale as *local* autonomy, that is, it must be adapted to the locale. In Barker's studies the town was the unit of autonomy. In *East Side, West Side* (Bechtel, Achelpohl, and Binding, 1970) it was the city block, and in Arrowhead (Bechtel, 1972a, 1972b) it was the arbitrarily chosen sector of a public-housing estate. Ratings are made according to whether decisions on the appointment of performers, admittance of members, determination of fees and prices, and establishment of programs and schedules occur within five geographical areas according to an ever-decreasing proximity to the setting as follows: within the town (block, project, estate), outside the town but within the school district, outside the district but within the county, outside the county but within the state, and

outside the state but within the nation. The highest autonomy rating is 9; it indicates that the four decisions are made entirely within the unit of study (town, block, project, etc.) and thus that the setting has maximum autonomy. A rating of 1 means that the four decisions are made at the national level. Rating 3 means state level, 5 county, and 7 school district.

Many times the four decisions will be made at different levels. In these cases, the relative weight is scored by multiplying the percentage times the rating. For example, if 25 percent of the decisions are made at the unit of study (most local), this is multiplied times nine for a score of 2.25, and if 75 percent are made at the county level, this is multiplied times five for a score of 3.85 with a total autonomy score of 6.10.

Autonomy levels were found to be extremely critical measures in the Arrowhead project (Bechtel, 1972b). This scale relates directly to design in the sense that it is a measure of how closely the building, town, or block population is controlled by outside forces. Other things being equal, the more they are controlled, the less chance there is to influence or be influenced by the physical environment.

The prime example of management interference with the physical environment is the management dictum that no part of the physical environment can be interfered with by the occupants. While Barker's autonomy scale does not directly measure such management practices, its measures pick up a general management tone of strictness, dependence, or similar interferences by its measure of *amount* of autonomy left to the local residents. For example, Bechtel (1972b) found that the percentage of the four decisions made by the Public Housing Authority amounted to 68 percent in all the public settings of the Arrowhead residential area. The result was a dependent environment where so few decisions were left to the residents that they became dependent on management.

Many beginners have trouble with autonomy ratings because of a tendency to try to rate settings isolated from the rest of the community. The rating applies to what level the decision is made within (or outside) the community, *not* within the setting itself. More research is needed to explore the ramifications of autonomy, but it is already clear that without high autonomy levels of residents, design intentions can be overwhelmed.

The autonomy rating for sidewalks and paths was 7.5 because of the amount of restrictions placed on movements by the management of the housing project *not* at the local level. For example, performers' selection (maintenance workers, supervisors) was done at the county level and partly by the local maintenance foreman, for a score of 7; members (public-housing residents) were selected partly by the county, for a score of 8; plans and programs were jointly made by the local management and the county authority, for a score of 8; and financial arrangements were also a combination of local and county authority, for a score of 7. Thus the average score was 7.5.

The reader is now urged to go back over the rating scales and tally them for all the areas covered, using the sidewalks and paths. The following chapter will illustrate the entire process for two city blocks involving many settings.

REFERENCES

Barker, Roger G. *Ecological Psychology*. Stanford University Press, 1968.

Bechtel, Robert B. "A Behavioral Comparison of Urban and Small Town Environments." In John Archea and Charles Eastman, eds., *EDRA 2: Proceedings of the Second Annual Environmental Design Research Association Conference*, Pittsburgh, Pa., October 1970, pp. 347–353.
———. "The Public Housing Environment: A Few Surprises." In W. Mitchell, ed., *Environmental Design: Research and Practice 1—Proceedings of the EDRA 31AR8 Conference*, Los Angeles, UCLA, January 1972a, 13-1-1 to 13-1-9.
———. "Dependency: An Unintended Result of Public Housing Policies." Paper delivered at the Conference on Housing and Mental Health, School of Architecture, University of Maryland, College Park, Maryland, March 27, 1972b.
Bechtel, R. B.; Achelpohl, C.; and Binding, F., *East Side, West Side, and Midwest: A Behavioral Comparison of Three Environments*. Epidemiological Field Station, 1970.
Binding, F. R. S. "Leadership in an American Community." Ph.D. dissertation, University of Kansas, 1969.
Gump, Paul, and Friesen, W. "Participation in Nonclass Settings." In R. Barker and P. Gump, eds., *Big School, Small School*. Stanford University Press, 1964, pp. 175–193.
Smith, M. "Psychology in Two Small Towns." *Science*, 184 (1974):671–673.
Wicker, Allan, "Size of Church Membership and Members' Support of Church Behavior Settings." *Journal of Personality and Social Psychology* 13 (1969):278–288.
Willems, Edwin. "Sense of Obligation to High School Activities as Related to School Size and Marginality of Students." *Child Development* 38 (1967):1246–1260.

5

Observational Method: Case 1

When a designer or researcher wants to find out about a certain housing project or a building, there are several ways he can go about it. One way is to interview persons living in the building or project. A second method is to mail a questionnaire without interviewing. A third is to live in the surroundings for a while to experience the kind of life that goes on there. Each of these methods is commonly used, but they involve introducing elements that interfere with data gathering and may change the kind of information sought in unintended ways.

Interviewing people is a scientific method in its own right, and it involves skills and techniques of establishing rapport, questioning, and the ability to evaluate answers. Questionnaire construction is even more precise. It involves pretesting, sampling respondents, coding responses, and analyzing and interpretating data that are not only beyond the resources of most designers but are often not part of the training of many social scientists. Furthermore, evidence is gathering that urban residents across the United States are becoming less and less willing to respond to interviews and questionnaires.

Barker (1968) maintains that trying to find out about peoples' activities in any of the above way interferes with the activities themselves. There are two ways this interference occurs. The person conducting the interview or sending the questionnaire imposes his own concepts and views on the respondent through the very questions he asks. The questions direct the respondents' answers to occur in areas that the questioner chooses. The really important areas may be those the questioner never thinks to ask.

Asking questions to persons living in an environment cuts and slices up the environment in ways the questioner feels are necessary. The questioner does not know if his way of dissecting the environment is the most usual way, and even with the best intentions, a researcher can influence his results by giving forth hidden cues to the respondent of the kinds of data he wants (Rosenthal, 1966). How can the designer or researcher who wants to know about a given environment gather information without interfering in such a way as to thwart his own purpose?

Observation of behavior is one way, although even this method has some element of intrusion. In addition, the observer cannot be all places at once and may miss a great deal of the things he needs to know. Many environments are so constructed that an observer must be able to view events at several levels before he can understand how everything fits together. For example, in the mental hospital, one can get contrasting views of the environment by observing patients, aides, nurses, doctors, or administrators, and living in any of these roles can give contradicting views of the environment (Bechtel, 1965).

One of the best methods to obtain information about a total environment is to have teams of observers from each element in the environment report on events as they take place. Since the observers are already persons living in the environment, they can report on events as they take place, and their interference will be at a minimum. Another advantage of selecting observers who live in the area to be studied is that they are experts in the area and can serve as consultants to any questions the researcher has about what goes on there.

What follows is an example of the observational method of behavior setting surveys that is considerably shorter than the traditional one year of the Barker studies. In this case the data collection lasted one month. Two blocks were selected for study; one block was called East Side, the other West Side, describing these locales in relation to the areas of Kansas City, Missouri.

SELECTING THE OBSERVERS AND THE BLOCKS FOR STUDY*

The first contacts with potential observers were made through young black militants who knew the East Side and some white intermediaries who knew the West Side. The East Side was the ghetto area of

*Work on this project was done at the Greater Kansas City Mental Health Foundation's Epidemiological Field Station under contract with the Center for Epidemiological Studies, National Institute of Mental Health.

Kansas City, Missouri. The West Side was the poor white and Mexican-American area.

Training took place in the research offices, which at that time consisted of a mobile home in the parking lot of the Western Missouri Mental Health Center. The two full-time observers and their two part-time assistants were picked up and brought to the offices for training sessions. The two full-time observers were an elderly black woman from the East Side and a retired waitress who was living on welfare on the West Side. The part-time observers included an elderly black man who did not believe we would ever pay him and a Mexican-American mother who was the quietest member of the group. After two weeks of practicing with behavior-setting information sheets and discussing behavior the observers knew about, they were asked to begin writing down observations on legal-sized yellow pads. Observations were made in their own neighborhoods and the written descriptions on the pad were checked by the researchers until, after about a week, they felt the observations had reached sufficient quality. At first, the temptation to interpret behavior was irresistible, and the yellow pads had almost a soap opera quality of rejected lovers and mysterious visitors. However, as it became clearer that objectivity was necessary, the quality changed to more crisp descriptions of numbers, ages, and simple activities.

The data collection then began and lasted from October 15, 1969, to November 15, 1969.

RECORDING THE DATA

The observers' notes were collected about every other day by the researchers and taken to the office. There the handwritten sheets were duplicated, and the various descriptions cut up and placed in folders. One folder was assigned to each potential setting.

More of the burden of the behavior-setting survey was placed on informants and observers in the city than is true of the small town studies. In the small town many settings are reported in local newspapers, school newspapers, and other public areas. In the city this was virtually impossible, since public media (with the possible exception of the irregularly published *West Chapel Press*) did not concern themselves with the behavior of residents in the blocks studied.

Some concern was felt that most of the observers were older people (over fifty) and therefore might not have access to the behavior of young people. To a great extent this was mediated by the fact that they had children and grandchildren, and these younger people acted as informants to their elders. We saw no evidence of a generation gap among our observers and informants.

Once the observation period of October 15–November 15, 1969, was completed, the data in each of the folders were analyzed, and questions of clarification and elaboration were asked of the observers and informants.

Because the researchers so closely monitored the observers, no systematic exercises were conducted to achieve reliability, but this was a necessity for further studies. Generally when two observers agreed on

numbers of people, age breakdowns, and behavioral descriptions, it was felt reliability had been obtained.

DESCRIPTION OF THE AREAS

West Side

West Side is a block-long section of West Side Street with thirty houses, about fifteen on each side of the street. It is a lower-income neighborhood with some people receiving welfare and disability payments. There are forty dwelling units among the thirty houses. Some houses, as is common in lower-class neighborhoods, had been converted into apartments. Figure 5–2 shows a map of the block, and figure 5–2 shows views of the area.

The West Side is in the extreme western portion of Kansas City, Missouri. Its location is on top of limestone bluffs that overlook the stockyards and the

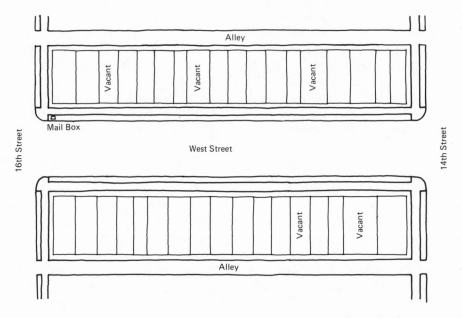

Figure 5–1
Map of West Side.

TABLE 5-1
West Side Population, by Age

Number of Persons	Age	
	Years	*Years/Months*
2	0	1:11
2	2	5:11
8	6	8:11
6	9	11:11
22	12	17:11
7	18	24:11
3	25	34:11
9	35	44:11
17	45	54:11
8	55	64:11
7	65 and up	
Total 91		

TABLE 5-2
East Side Population, by Age

Number of Persons	Age	
	Years	*Years/Months*
0	1	1:11
2	2	5:11
1	6	8:11
1	9	11:11
6	12	17:11
2	18	24:11
3	25	34:11
1	35	44:11
8	45	54:11
2	55	64:11
13	65 and up	
Total 39		

Kaw River. This is the oldest section of town where the first buildings were put up in the early 1900s; cowboys once climbed up the bluffs to visit saloons, but in the late 1800s the saloons gave way to wealthy homes, and these eventually became the rundown apartment houses of the West Side. The large lots were split up, and smaller, cheaper homes were erected. The population is divided into forty-eight males and forty-three females; 30 percent are Mexican-American. (See table 5-1 for a population breakdown.)

East Side

The section known as the East Side was developed in the 1920s and 1930s as a middle-class residential area. Blacks began moving in after a 1953 court decision, and the East Side became the Negro ghetto in Kansas City, not without its violence in the form of bombings and vandalism.

The block selected is composed of small, single-family dwelling units constructed in the 1920s and 1930s. Many of these have been converted into apartments for several families. There are fourteen houses and twenty-two dwelling units. See figure 5-3 for a map and figure 5-4 for views of the area. The population is divided into sixteen males and twenty-three females. (See table 5-2 for a population breakdown.)

DATA COLLECTED

A technical description of the behavior settings found in East Side and West Side will be used as an example of data collected by the observation method. In all cases, the reader must keep in mind that three environments are being compared: the small-town white environment investigated by Roger Barker and his colleagues and frequently referenced in Barker and Wright (1955) and Barker (1968), and East Side, and West Side, the two blocks studied by the observation method.

Behavior Settings

East side

Twenty-three behavior settings with their totals on penetration levels, action patterns, behavior mecha-

Looking south

Looking north

Figure 5-2
Four views of West Side.

Looking farther south

Alley

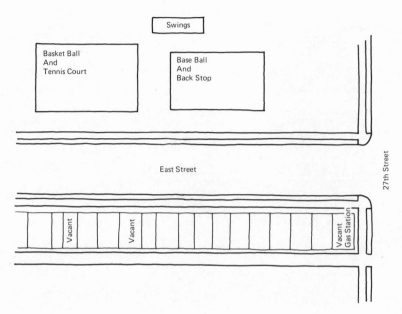

Figure 5-3
Map of East Side.

nisms, occupancy time, and general richness indexes are listed in table 5-3. (These data will be discussed and compared in later sections. The reader should recall that the listing of settings and these calculations is the first task of a behavior setting survey.)

West side

West Side had forty-six settings that were observed; they are listed with their data in table 5-4.

Zones of Maximal Penetration

Definition

Barker (1968, pp. 49-52) defines six zones of penetration for every behavior setting that range from zone 6 (the single leader without which the setting

would dissolve) to zone 1 (th onlooker who adds virtually nothing to the setting and has no voice in its affairs).

Comparison of the three environments

Figure 5-5 makes clear the striking differences between the three environments. Midwest has the highest level of maximal penetration because more than half of its settings (54 percent) have single leaders. West Side has the next lowest level of maximal penetration with 37 percent at level 5, and East Side is a poor third with 30 percent of its behavior settings at level 3.

Important aspects

Perhaps no element of Barker's methods is more powerful in appraising behavior opportunities in an

Looking north

East Side Park

Figure 5-4
Four views of East Side.

North end

Looking west across park

Figure 5-4 (Continued)

TABLE 5-3
Behavior Settings and Data for East Side

Behavior Settings	Penetration Totals	Action Pattern	Behavior Mechanism	Occupancy Time	General Richness Index
Postman's route	6	24	17	12	5.6
Produce man	3	16	9	10	2.8
Men working in park	0	17	28	24	10.8
City street work crew	0	12	23	4	1.4
Car on fire	2	21	31	12	5.4
Power and light	0	10	20	8	2.2
Garbage collection	0	16	20	5	1.8
Kids in park	8	25	35	29	19.7
Newspaper delivery	0	11	26	9	3.3
Bus stop	12	23	10	17	7.7
Sidewalk	4	18	20	27	11.3
Road	4	7	21	27	8.6
Work on car	4	3	13	6	1.2
A house	5	24	31	17	10.2
Insurance man	3	6	11	4	.8
Mrs. B	3	3	6	6	.7
Mrs. C	10	3	6	7	1.3
Police check	3	25	23	9	4.6
Milkman	3	16	13	9	2.8
Water meter reader	6	18	11	8	2.8
Water work crew	0	16	14	14	4.2
Accident	2	15	17	25	8.5

environment than the penetration level measure. Essentially this is at once a measure of depth of participation and leadership. Research (Barker and Gump, 1964; Willems, 1967; Wicker, 1969) has shown that behavior-setting size and penetration levels are related generally in terms of satisfaction and other elements (like sense of obligation). The smaller the setting size, the greater the penetration level, the greater the pressure to participate, and usually the greater the satisfaction with the experience. In this regard, Midwest would seem to be an environment providing much more participation opportunity and satisfaction potential than either West Side or East Side. And, of the two city blocks, West Side seems to have greater potential for participation and satisfaction than East Side.

Action Pattern Profiles

Action patterns are the standing behavior patterns of settings. Eleven action patterns were scored for each setting. The degree to which each occurs in a setting is rated on a scale made up of four subscales. Ratings are made in the framework of local perceptions and values although field workers may sometimes interpret the ratings.

Figure 5-6 shows the action patterns of East Side, West Side, and Midwest. Under each set of bars, the letters N, O, D stand for number of settings, number of occurences, and duration, respectively. Often these three scores are averaged for comparison across different environments. Barker (1968) calls this average an Ecological Resource Index (ERI). This average

TABLE 5-4
Behavior Settings and Data for West Side

Behavior Settings*	Penetration Totals	Action Pattern	Behavior Mechanism	Occupancy Time	General Richness Index
Around the house	28	15	27	35	24.5
Family gathering	22	25	24	8	5.8
West Chapel Press	13	30	26	15	10.4
Wedding preparation	18	18	22	5	2.9
Garage sale	12	31	20	23	14.5
Beer party	6	13	21	11	4.4
Working on car	6	9	28	20	8.6
Dress delivery	5	9	24	5	1.9
R.K.	10	20	20	12	6.0
Joe H.	11	25	21	16	9.1
L.B.	14	25	26	9	5.9
R. & A.R.	5	28	15	18	8.6
J.E.	12	22	15	12	5.9
J. & W.B.	20	26	22	19	12.9
E.B.	5	22	17	8	3.5
B.	6	19	18	7	3.0
M.	14	27	15	11	6.2
1,420 people	11	15	19	14	6.3
C.	14	11	19	11	4.8
Horace C.	12	13	16	33	13.5
Y.	15	14	18	6	2.8
Delbert C.	15	14	13	14	5.9
H. (1)	8	20	14	9	3.8
Power and light	1	18	20	9	3.5
Robbery	5	13	24	5	2.1
Sidewalk	25	21	30	26	19.8
Bike riding	21	18	31	19	13.3
Road	23	12	22	34	19.4
Alley	13	12	27	13	6.8
Police check	4	25	24	6	3.2
Telephone repair	4	17	22	8	3.4
Mailman's route	4	25	19	13	7.9
TV repair	4	24	20	5	2.7
Tearing down house	7	24	26	24	13.7
Health center study	4	24	23	6	3.1
Door-to-door sales	6	20	20	10	4.6
Football	8	15	40	61	38.4
Playing in park	9	12	42	38	23.9
Bus stop	14	16	21	10	5.1
Garbage collection	0	20	18	6	2.3
Newspaper delivery	0	18	23	4	1.6
Trash collection	0	19	22	4	1.6
City street work crew	2	19	24	8	3.6
Florist delivery	6	21	24	4	2.0
H. (2)	6	11	12	8	2.3
H. (3)	8	16	15	18	7.0

*Initial indicates proper name of persom for whom setting is named.

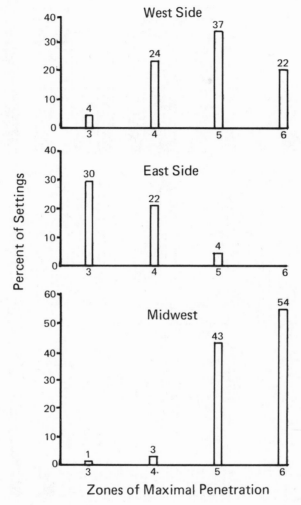

Figure 5-5
Penetration profiles of behavior settings.

is omitted from the figures but used when it makes comparisons easier.

Comparison of the three environments

Before looking at the action pattern comparison among the three environments, it is helpful to note the distinction between present and prominent mea-

sures. Barker (1968, pp. 119-120), in his listing of the action patterns of Midwest, indicates which of these are a prominent part of community life and which might be considered present but not prominent. Attributes that are present are prevalent in some degree; attribtues that are prominent are a major resource for the generation of behavior and rate 6 or more on the action pattern scale of 14.

Religion action pattern The averages for East Side

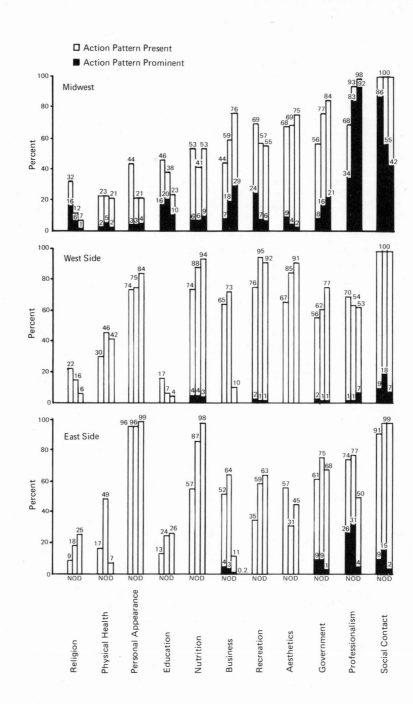

Figure 5–6
Action pattern comparisons between Midwest, West Side, and East Side. Adapted
from Bechtel, Binding, and Achelpohl, 1970, p. 14.

N = number
O = number of occurrences
D = duration

and West Side are about the same (15 and 17) and are comparable to Midwest (about 17). The only noticeable difference seems to be in terms of duration, which is longer for East Side. One would not expect the city blocks to be equal to those of Midwest since there are no churches on the city blocks. This may indicate a fairly high level of religious activity for both city blocks.

Physical health action pattern Action patterns of physical health seem to be present more than twice as much on the West Side as the East Side. The East Side and Midwest are relatively comparable. Despite a larger number of occurrences on the East Side, the lower duration and number pull the average down.

Personal appearance action pattern Perhaps this action pattern as much as any other characterizes differences among the three environments. The average for East Side is 97, for West Side 78, and for Midwest about 30. Thus, the city blocks show far greater utilization of the personal appearance action pattern across their range of behavior settings than do the people of Midwest.

The chief reason for this difference seems to be the many uniformed persons on the East and West Sides, especially the East Side. This may be an indication that the clothing scale (Barker, 1968, p. 61) needs changing. Or it may be that the use of uniforms is simply more typical of this locale and is, indeed, a measure of greater formality in dress that occurs in cities as opposed to towns.

Educational action pattern Educational action patterns for the city blocks are low compared to those of Midwest because the settings in the city blocks did not contain any schools. However, there seems to be a greater amount of educational action patterns on the East Side than on the West Side. This was caused largely by a school class visiting the East Side park.

Nutritional action pattern This action pattern shows a large difference between the two city blocks and the small town. This may be because the setting range over one particular month only will show nutrition action patterns disproportionately high compared to the one year in Midwest. However, it may also be an indication that nutrition action patterns are more

pervasive in the city block environment. For example, there is more eating in public, particularly on the West Side where more activities are outside in general and food is eaten and obtained more often outside the home. The larger prominent pattern in Midwest is due to the presence of restaurants in the town.

Business action pattern The comparatively low amount of prominent business action patterns for the city blocks compared to Midwest may be largely due to the residential character of the two blocks compared to the entire town measured in Midwest.

Recreational action patterns The high average for West Side (88) compared to only 42 for East Side is probably because there are more children on the West Side compared to more elderly on the East Side; there are also younger adults and, hence, younger families on the West Side; and, the West Side is more isolated from public transit vehicles and public services, such as street cleaning vehicles. This permits more recreational activity in the streets.

Aesthetic action pattern The very high average in West Side is due mostly to one behavior setting that involved tearing down a house during the entire period of observation. Residents highly prized this action, which gave it high aesthetic value and fits Barker's criterion of "removing the unsightly" very well (1968, p. 55).

Government action pattern The fact that all three environments are roughly comparable is due to the presence of government officials in the city blocks and government offices in the county seat of Midwest.

Professionalism action pattern The fact that Midwest is higher in professional action patterns is probably a reflection of the fact that the two city blocks are residential areas and have no businesses. Some difference may also be due to the fact that the two city blocks are in poor urban areas. Wealthier residential areas might have more professionalism because they might include more service settings, such as repairmen. It is interesting that this is the highest average for a prominent pattern that East Side has, however. West Side has some measure of professional action patterns as a prominent pattern but only half as high as East Side. This high professionalism on East Side is attributable to a greater amount of city services with paid workers such as Department of Recreation employees in the park, power and light repairmen, meter readers, and produce men selling.

Social contact action pattern All three areas compared are very high in this action pattern. It is interesting to note that as a prominent pattern, social contact is six times higher in Midwest than on either of the city blocks. This may be somewhat confirming of the "lonely" city stereotype, or it may mean that social contact occurs more in the private settings within the home.

Important aspects

Several large differences between the city and the small-town environments are suggested from these data:

1. Social contacts in the inner-city blocks seem less prominent as a feature of daily life.
2. A concern for personal appearance seems to be present in more areas of daily life in the inner city blocks than in the small town.
3. Nutritional activity seems to be more widespread in the city blocks, but some of this may be class difference.
4. There seem to be more recreational activities that pervade the white block compared to the black block. This may be due to the greater number of older people in the black block, or it may mean that recreational activities are more private in the black block and occur less in public settings.

Behavior Mechanism Profiles

Behavior mechanisms are five categories on which the behavior patterns of behavior settings are rated. Each of the five are rated on three subscales: parti-

cipation, tempo, and intensity. Average measures of N.O.D. are also frequently used.

Comparison of the three environments

Unlike the action patterns, the behavior mechanisms seemed to provide enough data for both present and prominent measures. Figure 5–7 shows behavior mechanisms.

Affective behavior Emotional behavior is higher on the West Side than on either the East Side or Midwest. This is true both in the present and prominent sense. The reason seems to be that a greater variety of different settings that are rated high in affective behavior occur on the West Side. These include both indoor and outdoor activities.

Gross motor activity Gross motor activity is relatively the same on both city blocks and considerably higher than in Midwest. Apparently behavior in the inner city is more vigorous.

Manipulative behavior Hands are used more often in the two inner-city blocks. As a prominent measure, the East Side has a higher average than the West Side.

Thinking behavior As a present feature, thinking is slightly higher in the city blocks than in Midwest, but as a prominent feature of behavior there is only half as much. This may reflect a lack of access to decision-making powers in the poor inner-city areas, or it may be another reflection of the residential character of the blocks.

Talking behavior Barker (1968, p. 122) characterized Midwest as a "talking town," but talking seems to be even more characteristic of the two city blocks. As a prominent feature of behavior, West Side has an average of 58 and East Side 32, compared to about 12 for Midwest.

Important aspects

The two city blocks seem as a general pattern to have a more vigorous and active degree of behavior mechanisms than the small town.

1. Affective behavior is more prominent on the West Side than on either East Side or in Midwest.
2. Gross motor activity is more vigorous in the city blocks than in Midwest.
3. There is twice as much thinking, as a prominent feature, of settings in Midwest.
4. The inner city seems to be even more of a talking place than the small town.

Occupancy Time

Definition

Occupancy time (OT) is the number of person-hours spent in a setting by its inhabitants. In Midwest this is the occupancy time for a year. In both the city blocks the time is calculated only on the one month of observation. Occupancy times for the two city blocks are calculated in terms of minutes. This is roughly a comparison in time units between a minute and a month for the city blocks and an hour and a year for Midwest (Occupancy times for Midwest are in terms of hours.) The differences between the city blocks and Midwest are also reflective of some of the finer discriminations the researchers made when dealing with behavior in the city blocks. Since there was only a month of observation in the city blocks, fewer of the annual settings were obtained.

Comparison of the three environments

Table 5-5 shows that East Side and West Side have roughly the same profiles with a majority of settings

N = number
O = number of occurrences
D = duration

Figure 5-7
Behavior mechanism comparisons between East Side and West Side. Adapted from Bechtel, Binding, and Achelpohl, 1970, p. 21.

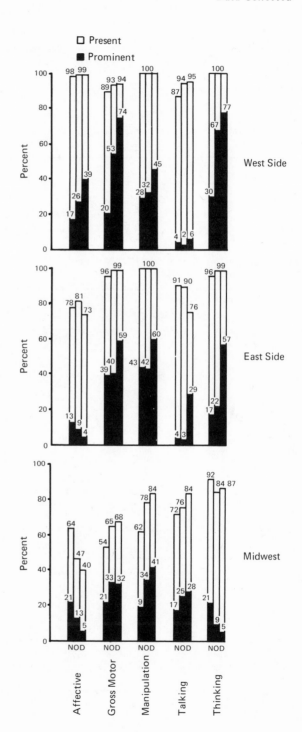

TABLE 5-5
Number and Per Cent of Behavior Settings with Occupancy Time by In-Block Residents within stated Intervals and OT by Town Residents in Midwest.

OT Interval minutes	West Side Number of Settings	Per Cent of 46
0–1	4	8.7
2–4		
5–38	8	17.4
39–97	12	26.1
98–477	9	19.6
478–1,829	4	8.7
1,830–7,625	5	10.9
7,626–33,663	4	8.7
33,664–50,000		

OT Interval minutes	East Side Number of Settings	Per Cent of 23
0–1	6	26.1
2–4		
5–38	3	13.0
39–97	7	30.4
98–477	6	26.1
478–1,829		
1,830–7,625	1	4.3
7,626–33,663		
33,664–50,000		

OT Interval hours	Midwest Number of Settings	Per Cent of 884
1	30	3.4
2–5	25	2.8
6–14	65	7.4
15–91	270	30.5
92–285	173	19.6
286–1,240	177	20.0
1,241–4,900	77	8.7
4,901–20,150	60	6.8
20,151	7	0.8

falling within the 5 minutes to 97 minutes categories. West Side, because of the greater number of settings, has a more uniform distribution into the higher ranges of intervals. Comparing all three environments, most of the settings fall within the five lowest ranges of OT intervals. The patterns are not different among the three environments, but the small amount of time for which the city blocks were measured makes comparisons more uncertain.

General Richness Index

Definition

Barker asserts (1968, p. 70) that "the richness of a behavior setting refers to the variety of behavior within its pattern of behavior." The index is computed by summing penetration ratings of the population subgroups (14 in Midwest), ratings of the 11 action patterns, and ratings of the 5 behavior mechanisms, and by weighting the sum for the OT of the setting. The formula is:

$$GRI = \frac{(\Sigma PenR + \Sigma ApR + \Sigma BmR) \quad cOT}{100}$$

Comparison of the two city blocks

Although Barker does not use the mean GRI for all settings in Midwest, this will be used to compare the two city block environments. The mean GRI for West Side is 7.88 (46 settings), and the mean GRI for for East Side is 5.19 (23 settings). These results suggest that the behavior settings of West Side are richer than those of East Side. Table 5-1 shows the GRI indexes for each of the behavior settings of East Side and West Side.

Pressure Profiles

Definition

The pressure profile (Barker, 1968, p. 124) indicates the strengths of pressure upon children and adolescents to enter and participate in behavior settings. A rating of 1 indicates entrance is required; 2-3, entrance encouraged; 4, the setting is neutral; 5-6, entrance discouraged; and 7, entrance prohibited.

Comparison of the three environments

Figure 5-8 shows an interesting contrast between West Side and East Side. West Side's profile shows most settings to be either neutral or encouraging to the entrance of either children or adolescents. East Side shows relative equality between neutrality and discouraging entrance for both children and adolescents. Midwest shows more encouragement for adolescents than for children.

Important aspects

Of the three environments, West Side seems more tolerant of adolescents and children than the other two.

Welfare Profiles

Definition

Looking at the total number of behavior settings, one can ask how many there were brought into existence for children and adolescents. A rating of 0 indicates the setting is unconcerned with welfare of children or adolescents; 1, serves the child or adoles-

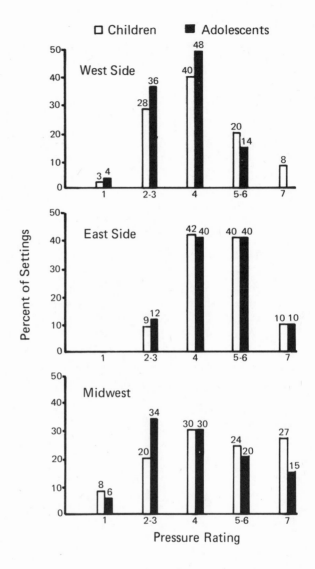

□ Children　■ Adolescents

1 = entrance required
2-3 = entrance encouraged
4 = behavior setting neutral
5-6 = entrance discouraged
7 = entrance prohibited

Figure 5-8
Pressure profiles of East Side, West Side, and Midwest.

cent; 2, serves the child or adolescent inhabitants of other settings; 3, children or adolescents serve other inhabitants.

Comparison of the three environments

Midwest has many more settings designed specifically to serve children (75 percent) or adolescents (70 percent). There are practically none in either West or East Side. This may be because there are no schools in the city blocks.

Important aspects

As the data stand, the environments of the city blocks are woefully lacking in settings that exist just for children and adolescents. In a more general sense, it must be remembered that Midwest is a self-sufficient community while the city blocks are not. In the larger community of the city, there may be a larger proportion of settings that exist for children.

Autonomy Profiles

Definition

Tbe local autonomy of a behavior setting is defined as

the degree to which four decisions regarding the operations of the setting, namely,
—appointment of performers,
—admittance of members,
—determination of fees and prices, and
—establishment of programs and schedules
occur within five geographical areas with differing proximities to the setting as follows:
—within the town,
—outside the town but within the school district,
—outside the district but within the county,
—outside the county but within the state,

—outside the state but within the nation. (Barker, 1968, p. 76)

It is obvious that when "town" is exchanged for "block" in the measures of the inner-city blocks, a great deal of comparability is lost. The town boundaries are in most ways not comparable to the block boundaries, and the relationships of town to school district and county are not comparable to the block and school district and county. Nevertheless, it is useful to compare autonomy of the three environments, keeping these limitations in mind. Ratings are from 9 to 1: 1 means that the four decisions are made on a national level; 3, state; 5, county; 7, district; and 8-9, within block.

Comparison of the three environments

West Side (figure 5-9) shows a number of settings dispersed across the various levels from 3 to 8. East Side shows many at the 5 level with two other clusters at the 4 and 7 levels. Midwest seems to have much more autonomy than either of the city blocks as one would expect in dealing with the larger unit of a town versus a city block. Moreover, Midwest is a county seat. A more proper comparison would be residential blocks of Midwest with the two city blocks (see Bechtel, 1970).

Classes of Authority Systems

Definition

Behavior settings are related to one another in a power hierarchy. The test of authority on a behavior setting, according to Barker (1968, p. 89), "is whether it determines the standing pattern of other settings via directed, intentional intervention either immediately or via intermediary settings." There are five classes of authority systems: business, churches, government, schools, and voluntary associations.

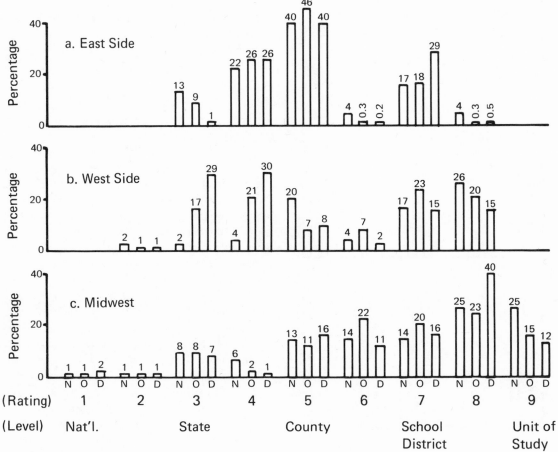

N = number
O = number of occurrences
D = duration

Figure 5-9
Autonomy profiles of East Side, West Side, and Midwest.

Comparison of the three environments

Figure 5-10 illustrates the classes of authority systems. Churches, voluntary associations, and schools are lacking from the environments of the two city blocks. The government profile of East Side is roughly comparable to that of Midwest, while West Side has roughly half the average of East Side. The same is

true for the business profile. On West Side business settings have more authority than any other category, as is true for East Side and for Midwest.

Important aspects

Apparently the authority of business pervades all three environments.

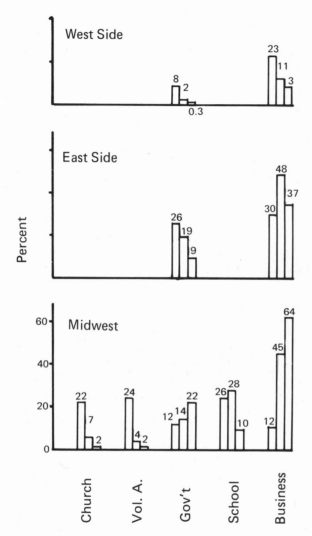

Figure 5-10
Authority system profiles of West Side, East Side, and Midwest.

Occupancy of Behavior Settings with Different Action Patterns

Definition

Another way of looking at total behavior patterns across all settings is to compile how much of a certain

action pattern takes up the total behavior in terms of occupancy time. Figure 5-11 shows the profiles of the three environments so arranged. The reader may want to compare this with the N.O.D. calculations in Figure 5-6.

Comparison of the three environments

East Side shows high presence (more than 80 percent) of action patterns in terms of aesthetics, business, nutrition, personal appearance, and social contact. West Side shows a high presence in only three categories: nutrition, recreation, and social contact. Midwest is characterized by high presence profiles in government, professional, and social contact action patterns. In Midwest, two action patterns, religion and personal appearance, are underproductive of behavior while physical health, education, nutrition, government, professionalism, and religion are underproductive of behavior on the East Side, and religion, physical health, personal appearance, business, aesthetics, education, government, and professionalism are underproductive on the East Side. In fact, the generally high level of ERIs compared to the action pattern profiles indicates there is a far greater availability of action patterns than is utilized by the population in the city blocks. Of course, the religion, education, government, and professionalism action patterns are underutilized because the buildings usually housing these activities were not present in the city blocks. (See figure 5-11.)

Important aspects

Not without some doubts do the researchers conclude from the data on OT versus action patterns that the city environment is underproductive in behavioral terms, mostly because the city blocks studied did not contain schools, businesses, or churches. Whether this accounts for all of the differences is not certain.

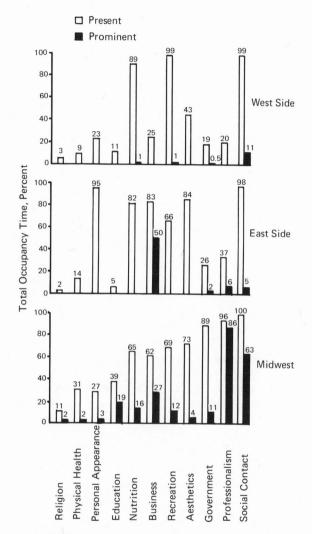

Figure 5-11
Action patterns as percent of occupancy time of West Side, East Side, and Midwest.

Behavior Mechanisms and Occupancy Time

Definition

A comparison of the total OT available for behavior mechanisms versus OT used indicates which behavior mechanisms are underutilized and which are utilized to capacity. Figure 5–12 shows OT versus behavior mechanisms.

Comparison of the three environments

According to Barker (1968, p. 133) the greatest proportion of the time of Midwest residents is allotted to behavior settings where manipulation is prominent and least to settings where affective behavior is prominent. From this method of calculating it would seem talking is most prominent. On West Side, talking is the most prominent and thinking the least prominent. On East Side, manipulation is the most prominent while thinking is the least prominent. Affective behavior is much higher on West Side than on East Side.

Important aspects

If East Side is characterized in terms of manipulation prominence, then one can speculate about blacks being on the manipulative-folk end of the folk-urban continuum (Redfield, 1960), while whites in West Side and Midwest seem to be on the verbal end. However, the fact that affective behavior is highest in the West Side would tend to contradict the whole notion of folk-urban continuum. One would expect the small-town people to be highest on the affect rating.

Genotypes: The Variety of Molar Environment

Definition

According to Barker (1965, p. 109), the variety of a community's molar environment is best measured by calculating the number of different genotypes within it. Genotypes are comprised of behavior settings whose programs are so similar as to allow for the transposing of leaders with a loss in efficiency of less than 25 per-

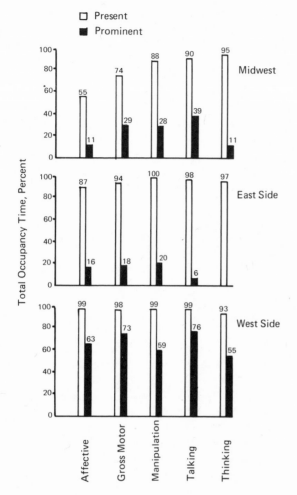

Figure 5-12
Behavior mechanisms as percent of occupancy time of Midwest, East Side, and West Side.

Comparison of the three environments

The number of genotypes for Midwest during 1963–1964 totaled 220 compared with the 12 found on East Side and 20 on West Side from October 15 to November 15, 1969. The vast difference in number of genotypes present in Midwest and the Kansas City blocks is, for the most part, due to the difference in size between the two units and the difference in the length of time of the two surveys. The most one could say on the basis of *number* of genotypes is that there is more variety to the molar environment of Midwest during a year than there is in one block of East Side or West Side in Kansas City during a month.

A look at the *kinds* of genotypes present in Midwest and absent from East Side and West Side points up the fact that the two areas differ as well in accessibility to other ecological resources. This difference is exemplified by the labels attached to each of the units. Midwest is called a town or community, implying a certain amount of self-sufficiency with regard to the fulfillment of the needs of its inhabitants. A block, on the other hand, refers to only one segment of a larger unit and need not necessarily contain the educational, administrative, religious, and business resources its residents require. As a matter of fact, if one excludes all genotypes from Midwest in which the four action patterns mentioned above are prominent, only about thirty-nine remain, most of which are prominent in recreation or social contact.

cent. The behavior settings included in one genotype should have, in general, interchangeable patterns of behavior, classes of inhabitatnts, behavior objects, milieu properties, and kinds of inputs. The genotype "basketball games," for example, contains the following behavior settings in Midwest: elementary upper school basketball game, elementary upper school basketball games out of town, and elementary upper school basketball practice.

Important aspects

The garbage collection, city water department, and power and light companies that were listed as genotypes in the city blocks are usually included in the streets and sidewalks genotype of Midwest. The police station genotype of the city blocks is also similar to the jails and sheriff genotype of Midwest. However, the listing of these genotypes from the city blocks is largely an artifact of not having a complete community for study. Garbage collection, the water department, and the power and light companies are all parts of larger settings that intrude into the life of the city blocks but are not complete as settings within the block. The police check consisted of a policeman in a car regularly making the rounds, but his rounds went far beyond the block being studied and he was part of the genotype police check, which was far removed from the block.

The surveys are probably the likeliest true difference between genotypes of the city blocks and Midwest. Surveys are very much a part of inner city life. Yet it is not inconceivable that Midwest could also be subjected to a survey. The same is true of the genotypes robberies, florist, and wrecking company. The wrecking company, however, would be less likely to occur in Midwest because the wrecking function is not yet separated from general contractor and building settings. Fence manufacturing and installing would also be likely to be included under building.

In short, except for surveys and the wrecking company, the genotypes that seem to occur in the city blocks but not in Midwest are most likely found in Midwest in some fashion. The reverse is not true, however. Many of the genotypes found in Midwest are not found in any form on the city blocks. Once again, the largest reason is that the city blocks do not constitute an entire community. It is likely that residents of the city blocks attend many of the genotypes similar to Midwest outside the block boundaries.

A review of the thirty-nine genotypes found in Midwest but not in the city blocks shows most of them to be organized social events like athletic contests, Scout meetings, hay rides, card parties, and the like. Probably if the survey of the city blocks continued over the year, many of these genotypes would have been picked up as out-of-block genotypes attended by residents.

Yet the list of these social activities is rather formidable, and a working hypothesis might be that the organized social groups and activities are fewer and less frequent in the lower-class inner city than those of the small town.

CONCLUSION

Penetration Zones

Several important areas are worth noting. Chief of these is the comparison of maximum penetration levels. A high penetration level means that a comparatively large number of persons in the setting have central roles. Certainly the higher levels in Midwest compared to those in the city blocks fit in with the researchers' observations and their expectations by the nature of the environments. West Side is a more "participating" place than East Side if only because of the greater proportion of elderly on East Side. In terms of modern parlance, it might be said from these data that Midwest is much more of a place where more people have a chance to "do their own thing" than is West Side or East Side.

Activities and Behavior Mechanisms

In terms of what people can be seen doing (talking, thinking, using their hands), there are rich contrasts among the environments. The greater attention to personal appearance (in behavioral terms) and nutritional action patterns in the city blocks marks the strongest differences between the small-town and city environments. The lower amount of social contact in the city comes as a surprise. The amount of emotional behavior on West Side, contrasted to either East Side or Midwest, is worthy of further attention. Perhaps there would have been more emotional behavior in East Side if the population were younger. It is also possible this may be a general city effect rather than being peculiar to the West Side.

Gross motor activity, manipulation, and talking are higher in the city blocks. Generally the city blocks seem to be much more active than Midwest in terms of personal styles of behavior, while Midwest is more active in its social organization.

That Midwest is more oriented to children is obvious from the data. Both city blocks have proportionately far fewer settings for children than Midwest.

In quite general terms, the results are much like one would have expected from a general knowledge of small towns and cities. Yet for specific aspects—such as talking and activity levels—there were some surprises in discovering the city blocks to be more active.

Design Aspects

The study of the two city blocks was not undertaken to uncover design problems. The data gained provide an example of how a behavior-setting survey can be carried out on a relatively small number of people over a short period. The comparisons between the city blocks and the small town demonstrate how relative statements can be made about the quality of life in each environment. The data have obvious design implications. It is clear that the exposure to settings in the city blocks is richer in the sense that there is more variety. It is equally clear the activity and participation levels of the small town are much higher than in the city blocks. If one were to accept the value that the small-town participation levels were better for residents, then a considerable change would have to be made in the incursive settings in the city blocks, permitting residents to participate in them at high power levels. This could mean physical design changes.

A good example of how participation levels in incursive settings can be changed occurred when a recent federal law required the passing of an ordinance to permit a local resident to get his own permit to do repair and rehabilitation work on his house. Previously, permits could be granted only to licensed contractors. This means that a resident can now perform his own home repairs at a 6 level of penetration.

Autonomy is also considerably increased. Such changes are not considered likely for the remaining incursive settings, such as television repair, power and ligh companies, or police. However, the home repair ordinance is expected to increase the amount of repairs on houses with significant physical design consequences.

From another perspective, one might try to change the physical design of the city blocks to force higher participation levels. For example, according to undermanning theory, the reduction of city block size should result in smaller numbers of persons per setting and thus higher participation levels. Still other physical changes might prevent a number of incursive settings by keeping many repairs and service calls outside the social contact range of residents.

REFERENCES

Barker, Roger. "Explorations in Ecological Psychology." *American Psychologist* 20 (1965):1–14.
———. *Ecological Psychology.* Stanford University Press, 1968.
Barker, R. G., and Wright, H. *Midwest and Its Children.* Row, Peterson, 1955.
Barker, R. G., and Gump, P. *Big School, Small School.* Stanford University Press, 1964.
Bechtel, Robert B. "A Behavioral Comparison of Urban and Small Town Environments." In John Archea and Charles Eastman, eds., *EDRA 2: Proceedings of the Second Annual Environmental Design Research Association Conference*, Pittsburgh, Pa., October 1970, pp. 347–353.
Redfield, Robert. *The Little Community and Peasant Society and Culture*, University of Chicago Press, 1960.
Rosenthal, Robert. *Experimenter Effects in Behavioral Research.* Appleton-Century-Crofts, 1966.
Wicker, Allen. "Size of Church Membership and Members' Support of Church Behavior Settings." *Journal of Personality and Social Psychology* 13, (1969):278–288.
Willems, Edwin. "Sense of Obligation to High School Activities as Related to School Size and Marginality of Students." *Child Development* 38 (1967):1246–1260.

6

The Observational Method: Case 2

As the complexity of problems in modern life continues to multiply, designers, planners, and public executives are being increasingly called upon to remedy the host of social ills that plague almost any settled area. "Needs of the population" and "quality of life" are phrases used with increasing frequency in architectural and planning literature. But how does one begin to grasp such complex notions? The temptation is to oversimplify, to go to a population and simply ask them what they want and then provide it. The results are often disappointing because they do not take into account the concept of changing needs (Maslow, 1954) and adaptation levels (Helson, 1964). Furthermore, even the process of asking about needs and desires has become a complex hierarchy of procedures developed by social scientists.

Barker's research has cut through much of this difficulty, but it has not substituted a simple answer. The behavior-setting survey provides a profile of an environment, which can be compared with profiles of other environments. This comparison process can diagnose the ills and prescribe a cure for a total environment and at the same time provide the central concepts and considerable detail for redesigning the environment.

The following example will show how this was done in the case of a public-housing environment in Cleveland, Ohio, called Arrowhead. The project involved nothing less than an attempt to redesign the public-housing environment using behavioral and architectural remedies in conjunction.

BACKGROUND

The Public-Housing Environment

Exactly when public housing began depends on the definition. The Public Works Administration constructed 21,000 units by 1937. The Wagner-Steagall Act of 1937, usually considered the beginning of public housing, empowered the United States Housing

Authority to make construction loans to local housing authorities and to provide subsidies that would enable rents the poor could afford. The 1949 act declared that an objective of public policy was "the realization as soon as feasible of the goal of a decent home and a suitable living environment for every American family." Unfortunately public housing has encountered a series of obstacles that continue to this day and are the root cause of most of its problems. For example, the realtors, home builders, and savings and loan leagues exerted pressures that made public housing undesirable for residents.* In a perversion of design principles, the designer who thought of leaving toilet seat covers off toilets and doors off closets was rewarded for his efforts. The result has been an image of public housing as the least desirable of all housing opportunities—the last resort of the poor. The accretion of this philosophy over the years has produced a condition of deprivation. As Freedman (1969, p. 117) said, "Here then, the esthetic and the social dimensions of the problem came together. The projects *looked* forbidding. Their size was 'beyond human scale,' the environment too big for individuals to adjust to, especially those already alienated, hostile, dependent."

HUD Background

In the early fall of 1969, the office of the director of social research of the research and technology branch of the Department of Housing and Urban Development decided to issue requests for proposals for research and demonstration projects in public housing that would incorporate social science research as the basis for design decisions. Older public housing environments had deteriorated to the point that drastic measures were needed to improve these locations to make them more livable for residents. Modernization funds were available to rehabilitate public

*U.S. Congress, Housing of Representatives, General Interim Report of the House Select Committee on Lobbying Activities, H.R. Report 3138, 81st Cong., 2d sess., 1950, p. 24.

housing, and HUD wanted to see whether social science research could provide guidelines on how to spend these funds.

The HUD Request for Proposal and its Requirements

Three housing authorities were selected and given the responsibility to solicit proposals and contract with an organization or organizations of their choice to fulfill the proposal request. The requests were virtually the same general outline for each city. Two phases were planned: phase I would involve problem identification, base line data, and recommendations and would cost about $200,000; phase II would involve implementation of the recommendations for a cost of about $750,000. Amounts varied for each of the three cities selected. The contract was to cover an eighteen-month period. These figures were arrived at by considering the optimal amounts for modernization funds and the usual time for such contracts. In each city, appropriate sites were selected that were roughly equivalent, although the Cleveland site did not contain high-rise buildings.

This chapter will deal with the full scope of the project that developed with the Cleveland Metropolitan Housing Authority, later renamed the Cuyahoga Metropolitan Housing Authority (CMHA). The other two projects were with the Allegheny County Housing Authority (Pittsburgh) and the San Francisco Housing Authority. The project grant for Cleveland was awarded to the Environmental Research and Development Foundation, for which I was director of research.

The first paragraph of the Request for Proposal (RFP) set the tone of high demand:

The purpose of this contract is to define, test, and evaluate innovative modernization techniques designed to make public housing projects more livable, more satisfying to the tenants, more economic to operate, less subject to crime, vandalism and property abuse, more conducive to helping tenants achieve self-sufficiency, self-fulfillment and upward mobility, and more acceptable to the community as a whole.

The second paragraph revealed the constraints under which the tasks were to be accomplished:

These objectives are to be accomplished within the constraint that the innovative modernization techniques proposed for Carver-Outhwaite* must be cost-effective over a reasonable period of time. The purpose of this project, it should be emphasized, is not to demonstrate how to allocate additional funds, but to determine new ways, on a pilot or experimental basis, that the usual amounts of funds available under HUD's modernization program might be more effectively allocated to achieve the objectives noted above.

In short, the goal of the project was to develop scientifically based guidelines to spend HUD modernization funds for renovating older public-housing projects. These renovations, it was learned later, had to deal only with *exterior* modifications and had to be within the sum of regular modernization budgets. The restriction to exterior modification was a problem that continued to surface both within CMHA and housing residents for the life of the project. It was one of those distinctions so easy to make in government practice and sometimes so necessary to make in accounting procedures, but so very difficult to communicate to either workers in the field or residents.

The time span of the project was defined as eighteen months, roughly ten months for phase I (planning and base line research) and eight months for phase II (implementation and evaluation). The time span was intended to reflect the usual length of modernization fund allocation and construction contracts, but as is true more often than not, both local and national conditions beyond the control of either the local housing authority or HUD intervened to expand greatly the time needed.

*The name of the public housing site for Cleveland. In Cleveland, public housing projects were called "estates" in an attempt to remove some of the labeling stigma of public housing.

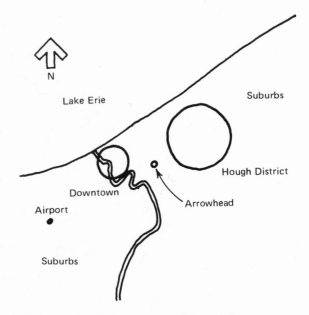

Figure 6-1
Location of Arrowhead in Cleveland, Ohio.

Physical Description

The site of Arrowhead (figure 6-1) is between the Hough District and downtown Cleveland. Project Arrowhead is a gerrymander made to look like an arrowhead. The gerrymander is cut from a larger project called Carver Park, which is itself an extension of Outhwaite homes. Carver Park has 1,051 units—771 units are three-story apartments and 260 are two-story townhouses. The Arrowhead project had 636 units and a population of 1,716 at the time the project was midway through phase I of the contract (see figure 6-2). On the site there are 112 two-floor townhouse units, 508 third-floor apartment units, and 26 first-floor flat units. There are 17.6 acres with a density of 36.1 dwelling units per acre.

Population

Carver Park was opened for occupancy in January 1943 and has been continuously occupied since. The

Figure 6-2
Map of Arrowhead.

population of Arrowhead is broken down in table 6-1.

The average length of residence for a head of household is 99.29 months, or 8 1/4 years. Fifty-one percent of the units in Arrowhead have been occupied for more than five years, which compares with a national average of fifty-four percent. Fourteen percent of the units have been occupied for fewer than 12 months, and 75 percent of the residents have lived in the study area for more than 25 months.

The average monthly rental range is from $60 (for building E-37) to $79.60 (for building J-78). The highest rent is $105 a month, the lowest is $32, and the median is $70.

The overall vacancy rate is 11 percent as of July 1, 1971; it was more than 20 percent in July 1971.

The mean income for all residents is $2,864 per annum.

TABLE 6-1
Arrowhead Area Population, January 1, 1971
Number of Residents (by Age and Sex)

Ages		Males		Females		Totals	
Infants	0–2 years	64		49		113	
Preschool	3–5 years	65		57		122	
Preteen	6–11 years	168		164		332	
Teens	12–18 years	185		157		342	
Adults	18–24 years	81		110		191	
	25–34 years	15		115		130	
	35–44 years	13	155	109	481	122	636
	45–54 years	26		88		114	
	55–64 years	20		59		79	
Aged	65 years +	65		106		171	
Total		702		1,014		1,716	

TABLE 6-2
Age and Sex Categories, as Percentages of Total Population

Ages		Males		Females		Totals	
Infants	0–2 years	3.8%		2.8%		6.6%	
Preschool	3–5 years	3.8%		3.3%		7.1%	
Preteen	6–11 years	9.8%		9.5%		19.3%	
Teens	12–18 years	10.6%		9.4%		19.9%	
Adults	18–24 years	4.7%		6.5%		11.2%	
	25–34 years	0.9%		6.7%		7.6%	
	35–44 years	0.7%	9.1%	6.5%	28.0%	7.1%	37.1%
	45–54 years	1.6%		5.1%		6.7%	
	55–64 years	1.2%		3.3%		4.5%	
Aged	65 years +	3.8%		6.2%		10.0%	
Totals		40.0%		60.0%		100.0%	

Physical Environment

There are largely two kinds of buildings in Arrowhead, the three-story brick apartments and the two-story cement block townhouses (although some townhouses were built of brick, and twenty-six units are only one-story flats. See figures 6–3 and 6–4). There is extensive vandalism throughout the project (figure 6–5). Virtually all cellars are empty with only abandoned laundry machines, or they are used as storage by maintenance. Incinerators provide a place to dispose of trash but are also a source of air pollution and the inevitable pile-up of trash dropped along all the pathways from houses to incinerators (figure 6–6). Pathways through the project are often blocked, as by the playing field fence or by playground equipment (figure 6–7).

Interiors are not discussed here because they are not the official province of the project. Suffice it to say that the plumbing stacks are inadequate to keep the toilets from clogging the plumbing for each building, windows are constantly being broken and are the prime vandalism problem, and the interior plaster is constantly falling off because of condensation, but wallboard is not used because it is "too easy to kick in."

Figure 6–4
Arrowhead two-story town houses. Courtesy of ERDF.

COLLECTION OF DATA

Observers

Residents of the study area were recruited to serve as observers. They were given training on the job to observe and record behavior as they saw it. Special emphasis was given to recording the number, sex, and age of persons, the kinds of behavior seen, and the amount of time it lasted. The observers were thirty persons who lived within the boundaries of Arrow-

Figure 6–3
Arrowhead three-story apartments.

Figure 6-5
Vandalized mailboxes. Courtesy of ERDF.

Figure 6–6
Incinerators. Courtesy of ERDF.

head. Some were housewives on welfare, others were Vietnam veterans out of work. A few were college students attending the local community college nearby. The observers were solicited through the resident council and by word of mouth throughout the housing estate. They were trained in a series of sessions at the project office and in rooms provided by Friendly Inn, the local settlement house.

The project office was a regular apartment, rented on site and converted into a suite of offices with a modest "poverty" outlook; there were no rugs, fancy appointments, or decorations. Heavy wire frames were welded to the window frames to prevent burglaries (at the insistence of the public housing management), and direction of the project took place from this office.

The observers were trained by role playing and observation in the field. Unlike the observers from the East Side-West Side project, there were none who thought they would not be paid. The concern over the spying stigma and the use of the data was alleviated when the objectives of the project were understood. There was, however, a somewhat healthy skepticism about whether anything would actually be done in the end to help residents. All of the observers needed the pay and were glad to get the job.

As a note on social perspectives, some of the observers, as was typical of previous experience, had difficulty "turning off" when the project was finished and would often drop in with news of events long after the observation period was over. A few observers took part in other phases of the project, and a handful took an increased interest in the resident council.

Once observers gained a fair reliability (more than 90 percent) with researchers in the field, they were sent to six different posts in the area and followed a

Figure 6-7a
Pedestrians going around fence to cross project.

Figure 6-7b
Fence in center of project surrounding play area.

sequence of time schedules to obtain nearly twenty-four-hour coverage for seven days a week during thirty-nine days of observation.

The Setting List

Some sixty-seven settings resulted from the observation of the thirty resident-observers (twelve full time and eighteen part time). The first step was to make a list of the settings and to test doubtful ones with the K-21 scale to measure whether settings were independent of one another. The observers merely

TABLE 6-3
Behavior Settings Catalog*

	OT
Playgrounds	30,928
Cellars	18,000
Sidewalks and paths (GM)	7,526
Security guard rounds (P, Af)	5,080
Football games (Rec, GM, M, T)	4,442
Maintenance workers' picket line (S, Af)	2,235
Bus stops	2,076
Administrative assistant and secretary's office	1,995
Stairwells	1,830
Management office (P, G, S)	1,079
Four modernization program (P)	942
Incinerators (P, G, GM)	722
Police patrol (P, G, S, Af)	654
Parking lots (P, GM)	424
Director's office (A, P, T)	408
Maintenance office (A, P, T)	380
Resident council meeting	320
Fires (S)	270
Marching (A, R, GM)	208

*Letters within parenthesis are abbreviations for action patterns and behavior mechanisms prominent in each setting. R, Religion; PH, Physical health; PA, Personal appearance; E, Education; N, Nutrition; B, Business; R, Recreation; A, Aesthetics; G, Government; P, Professional; S, Social contact; Af, Affective behavior; GM, Gross motor activity; M, Manipulation; T, Talking; Th, Thinking

confirmed the behavior in the setting list and added details. (New settings were continuously being added as the monitoring of the settings proceeded. The setting list was constantly brought up to date.) The setting list for Arrowhead appears in tables 6-3 and 6-4.

The final setting list provides a complete description of each setting. The description contains figures on occurrence (number of days in a year in which the setting takes place out of 365), duration (total hours it functions during a year), and the population (total number of *different* persons that spend any time in the setting during the year). The population was broken down into residence subgroups (in-project versus out-project), age subgroups (eleven types), sex subgroups, and class subgroups. All or nearly all were black; racial subgroups were not counted.

TABLE 6-4
Friendly Inn Behavior Settings*

	OT		OT
Main lobby (T)	3,375	Charm class (A, E, PA)	21
Montessori School (E, S)	1,584	Moving	206
Open gym (R, Af, GM, M, T)	1,338	Basketball games (R, GM, M, T)	153
Dances	816	Roads	147
United Youth (S)	780	Ohio Bell repair (P)	139
Golden Age Club (R)	660	Accidents, S, Af, T)	113
Canteen	605	*Plain Dealer* newspaper route	95
Front porch and sidewalk (R, S, Af, GM)	378	Mail delivery (P, G)	91
Arts and crafts–girls (A)	337	Milk delivery	80
4-H girls (E, R, S)	260	Newspaper (Press) routes	64
Black room	221	Black Nationalist parade	51
Adult education (E)	206	May Company delivery (B, P)	43
Adult sewing class (A)	179	Pop truck delivery (B)	34
4-H boys (E, R, S)	174	Diaper delivery	23
Drums (A, R, M)	164	Snow removal	23
Arts and crafts—adults (A)	122	Mail pick-up (P, E)	18
Sisters' Club (S)	104	Jitney taxi (B)	14
Arts and crafts—boys (A)	103	Laundry pick-up and delivery	11
National Committee to Combat Fascism (S)	98	United Parcel Post	9
Puppetry class (a)	78	Extermination	7
Newspaper drops (P)	75	Salvation Army delivery (P)	6
4-H Christmas party (R, Af)	47	Junk and veretable cart (P)	5
Creativity unlimited (A, P, R)	32	Christmas caroling (R, T, S)	5
		Robberies (R, M)	4

*Letters within parenthesis are abbreviations for action patterns and behavior mechanisms prominent in each setting.
R, Religion; PH, Physical health; PA, Personal appearance; E, Education; N, Nutrition; B, Business; R, Recreation; A, Aesthetics;
G, Government; P, Professional; S, Social contact; Af, Affective behavior; GM, Gross motor activity; M, Manipulation; T, Talking;
Th, Thinking

Occupancy time is the total number of person-hours people spent in a setting in a year. It is the most important single item of information on each setting because it indicates the relative importance of a setting to the total behavior pattern of a community. Separate occupancy times were calculated for each age category.

ANALYSIS OF BEHAVIOR-SETTING DATA

To obtain some comparative notion of the social environment present in Arrowhead, the behavior-setting measures were compared with the populations of Midwest and of East Side and West Side. While these comparison groups are not, perhaps, the most ideal, they are the only currently available studies offering comparable data, and the comparisons are useful in highlighting resources and deficits of the behavioral environment in Arrowhead.

Behavior-setting data analysis provides a succinct and comprehensive picture of life in the Arrowhead area and establishes whether the behavioral environment of the community is an asset or a liability to residents. In other words, *the behavior-setting survey provides quantitative data on whether the environment is within generally acceptable limits of physical and social scale.*

Each setting has components that are influenced by management, social activities, and design. Some settings are influenced more by one aspect of the environment than others. Thus, the decision as to whether changes should be made in management, social action, or design is considered for each setting separately. However, since all the rating scales are additive across settings, weighted by occupancy time, it is also possible to characterize the sum of settings as a total community and to make decisions about the community as a whole. For example, a low autonomy rating in one setting is not necessarily a problem. A particular setting may be especially dependent on another setting for many reasons, but, when a low autonomy rating holds for many (or all) settings in a community, a general state of over-dependence becomes clear.

The same kinds of decisions can be made for virtually all of the scales: religion, manipulation, welfare, and so forth. Some settings may be assets or liabilities by themselves. Others contribute more to a global picture. In comparing Arrowhead to the known environment of Midwest, the white small town that has high ratings as a resourceful environment, judgments can be made about Arrowhead's environment. Controls for this comparison are made by adding the low-income white (West Side) and black (East Side) housing environments.

Profile Analysis of Penetration Levels

Definition

Barker (1968, pp. 49–52) defines six zones of penetration for every behavior setting: zone 6, the single leader without which the setting would dissolve; zone 5, shared leadership; zone 4, the officer or functionary; zone 3, the bona-fide member; zone 2, the audience; and, finally, zone 1, the onlooker who adds nothing to the setting. Zones of maximal penetration levels are usually at level 5 or 6 because each setting almost

always has a leader of some kind. The more useful measure, however, in looking at residential environments is to compare the maximal penetration levels *available to residents* with the maximal zones themselves.

Data

Figure 6–8 shows the maximal penetration zones available to residents of the three environments reported in Bechtel (1970). It is obvious from these data that the two poor urban residential areas have little chance for leadership in their residential environments.

Figure 6–9 shows that the maximal penetration zones available to residents of Arrowhead are mainly at level 3 (membership), while the majority of settings operate at level 5 or 6. This indicates, as in the low-income white and Negro areas of West Side and East Side, that residents have little control over their environment. These data also confirm and add another dimension to the autonomy data.

Figure 6–10 divides the environment of Arrowhead into those settings in the area outside the settlement house and those settings inside the settlement house. It is clear that inside the settlement house established to serve them, Arrowhead residents have even less control over settings than in the remainder of their own overcontrolled environment.

The findings tend to confirm that services offered to low-income residents, as in the low-income urban private-housing environments, do something *to* the resident rather than enlist his involvement.

Profile Analysis of Action Patterns

Definition

Each of the action pattern categories explains the concern of each setting. For example, a grocery store

□ Setting Penetration Levels in Residential Area
■ Penetration Levels of Settings Available
   Just to Residents

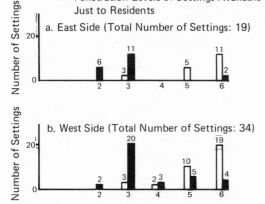

□ Maximum Penetration Zones for All Settings
■ Zones Available Just to Residents

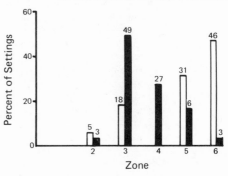

Figure 6-9
Maximal penetration zones for all settings in Arrowhead compared to penetration zones available just to residents.

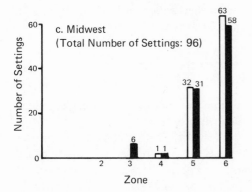

Figure 6-8
Comparison of maximal penetration levels with penetration levels available to residents in East Side, West Side, and Midwest.

out all of the behavior settings, which establishes the ecological resource index (ERI). The ERI measures the behavior as an environmental resource and estimates the general presence of that resource in an environment. See table 6-5 for a comparison of the action patterns of Midwest, East Side, West Side, and Arrowhead.

setting is concerned predominantly with business, but social contact and some eating (nutrition) also occur in this setting.

Data

Action patterns for each setting are reported from three standpoints: whether the pattern is present in a setting, whether the pattern is prominent in a setting, and whether the pattern is relatively extensive through-

□ Penetration Zones Inside Settlement House
■ Penetration Zones Outside Settlement House

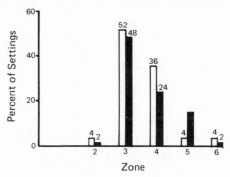

Figure 6-10
Penetration levels open just to residents.

TABLE 6-5
A Comparison of Action Pattern ERIs

Action Pattern	Midwest	West Side	East Side	Arrowhead
Religion	15–17	15–17	15–17	2.3
Physical health	22	23	23	83.1
Personal appearance	99.4	74	97	99.4
Education	37	7	21	46.7
Nutrition	55	85	80	67.2
Business	62	49.42	49.42	53.4
Recreation	62	88	52	85.1
Aesthetics	70	81	44	58.1
Government	70	65	68	70
Professionalism	87	59	67	80.3
Social contact	100	100	99	77.5

Conclusions

Deficits in Arrowhead action patterns are in the areas of religion, nutrition, aesthetics, and social contact. While it requires a value judgment to conclude that some settings of a religious nature should be added to Arrowhead, it involves less of a value judgment to say that more behavior of residents needs to be directed toward keeping the area clean and introducing more opportunities for social contact. The addition of either a snack bar or quick-stop grocery would increase the nutritional behavior.

Assets include the presence of physical health concern, the tendency to dress well, educational aspects, and a fair amount of recreational activity for adults.

Profile Analysis of Behavior Mechanisms

Definitions

Behavior mechanisms are the standing behavior patterns of the settings. They include affective behavior (expression of emotion), gross motor (muscular) behavior, manipulation (use of the hands), talking and thinking. See table 6–6 for a comparison of the behavior mechanisms in Midwest, East Side, West Side, and Arrowhead.

Conclusion

Generally the Arrowhead behavior mechanisms are at a par level with the other environments with the exception of thinking. This finding is significant for what it suggests in content for social action and management programs. Thinking is measured as taking place when decisions are made. Thus, there are fewer observable decisions made among the population of Arrowhead. There is a need to provide more opportunities for residents to decide as a part of their total behavior. Complex as this conclusion may seem, its remedy is simple: programs need to provide the residents with more decision-making opportunities.

Profile Analysis of Derived General Scores

The general richness index (GRI) refers to the variety of behavior within each setting that is available to numbers of persons at a high level of participation and over a considerable period of time. A setting has a high GRI if it has a great variety of behavior ranges that are available and used by great

TABLE 6-6
A Comparison of Behavior Mechanisms

Behavior Mechanism	Midwest	West Side	East Side	Arrowhead
Affective behavior	50	98	77	82.2
Gross Motor behavior	70	91	98	82.5
Manipulation	79	100	100	95.9
Talking	93	100	98	94.9
Thinking	80	92	86	65.9

numbers of people who can be leaders in the setting over a long time. A setting has a low GRI if it has a very limited variety of behavior ranges for very few people and few leaders for a short time period. The GRI can be averaged over all settings to give a GRI for the entire environment. Places like a general store or community drug store generally receive the highest GRI while very specialized settings like a radio station receive low GRI.

The average GRI for Arrowhead, 8.54, is relatively high and compares favorably with 7.88 for West Side and 5.19 for East Side. (Data were not available for Midwest.) This indicates that the public behavioral environment of Arrowhead is a fairly rich one and a definite resource to the residents.

Pressure is a measure of the extent to which children and adolescents are required to enter and participate in behavior settings. These are usually reported in a profile showing percent of settings at each pressure level (figure 6-11). It would appear

Figure 6-11
Pressure profile for children and adolescents in Arrowhead.

		Children		
1.5%	22.4%	32.8%	41.8%	1.5%
1 entrance required	2-3 entrance encouraged	4 neutral	5-6 entrance discouraged	7 entrance prohibited
		Adolescents		
3.0%	28.4%	32.8%	34.3%	1.5%
1	2-3	4	5-6	7

that Arrowhead children are discouraged from a greater percentage of settings than in Midwest and West Side, but a nearly comparable score is given for East Side. On the other hand, Arrowhead prohibits children from only 1.5 percent of its settings, while all three other areas exclude children from 10 percent, 10 percent, and 25 percent, respectively, of their settings. Thus, children are discouraged from a number of settings but actually prohibited from far fewer than in the other environments.

Thirty-four percent of settings in Arrowhead discourage adolescents, and another 32.4 percent are neutral. Twenty-eight percent encourage entrance compared to 35 percent in West Side, 12 percent in East Side, and 37 percent in Midwest. There seems to be a relative need for settings that encourage adolescent participation.

Welfare ratings indicate the number of settings available specifically to children or adolescents. This is an important measure of how hospitable the behavioral environment is to children in general; the measure also indicates the behavioral resources available to them. Generally, few of the settings in an environment exist just for children. Three ratings are given for each setting in figure 6-12. Arrowhead

Figure 6-12
Welfare ratings of Arrowhead behavior settings.

children	Rating:	76%	17.9%	4.5%	1.5%
		0	1	2	3
adolescents	Rating:	79%	11.9%	4.5%	4.5%
		0	1	2	3

compares very favorably with the other environments in its welfare ratings. For children, 18 percent of settings exist in Arrowhead, compared to none in West Side, none in East Side, and 20 percent in Midwest. Thus, the behavioral environment of Arrowhead, relatively speaking, is a resource to children.

A somewhat similar situation exists for adolescents, except that the situation is far less favorable generally. Arrowhead has 12 percent of its settings serving adolescents, while West Side had 2 percent, East Side had 10 percent, and Midwest 25 percent. There is probably room to create more settings for adolescents in Arrowhead.

Local autonomy ratings indicate how free the residents are to make decisions regarding the operation of the settings. In Arrowhead, autonomy is rated by decisions made:

1. Within Arrowhead area: 8-9
2. Within Arrowhead region: 7
3. Within Cuyahoga County (CMHA): 5
4. Within state of Ohio: 3
5. National level (HUD): 1.

Scores must be interpreted in terms of number of settings, occurrence of the settings, and duration of the settings. A small number of settings might have high autonomy ratings (8-9) but only occur once or twice a year (such as Christmas parties) and have low duration, (not more than a couple of hours). See figure 6-13.

In terms of duration of settings (the ones that last the longest), 68.4 percent of the decisions made on Arrowhead's settings are made at the county or CMHA level. This compares with 20 percent in Midwest, 42 percent in East Side, and 8 percent in West Side. *The evidence is unmistakable that the behavioral environment at Arrowhead is overcontrolled by the CMHA.*

DISCUSSION OF RESULTS

Arrowhead may not be typical of public-housing environments in general. Certainly not all public-

housing residents are black, but the majority (62 percent) are (HUD, OHM, 1971*). Fifty-one percent of Arrowhead residents lived there five years or more compared with about 54 percent with five years or more residence for all of public housing. Yet there is reason to believe because of the uniformity of federal regulations on public housing and the increasing pressures toward centralized management due to increasing cost (de Leeuw, 1971) that it is typical, at least in regard to the overcontrolled atmosphere. Further, the overcontrolled aspect can be seen in the thwarting of site plan and architectural design. The construction of the large wire fence in the playground without regard to pathways and the placing of sidewalks at kitchen entrances rather than at front doors permanently memorializes the heavy hand of management in all decisions. According to poverty research, the Arrowhead area seems to exemplify a dependency atmosphere. Pareek (1970) describes dependency motivation in terms all too clear to the researchers who have been in contact with Arrowhead residents: "Dependency motivation can be characterized in terms of concern for control of decisions in power motivation, and it is expressed through lack of initiative, avoidance syndromes (shifting responsibility to others, exaggerating obstacles), excessive fear of failure, seeking favors of superiors, overconformity, and aggressive rejection of authority (The so-called 'reverse reaction' to dependency)."

While the solution—to restructure the management of Arrowhead to allow local decision making and leadership—is obvious, the findings raise fundamental issues about the rendering of all types of services to poor persons, and the old saw that "helping the poor" is a demeaning practice is amply illustrated.

The characterization of Arrowhead as a dependent environment is not necessarily an indictment of CMHA, HUD, or public housing as villains that have produced a victim. The processes that have created the dependent environment began long before public

*Data obtained by telephone from the Office of Housing Management, Department of Housing and Urban Development, January, 1971.

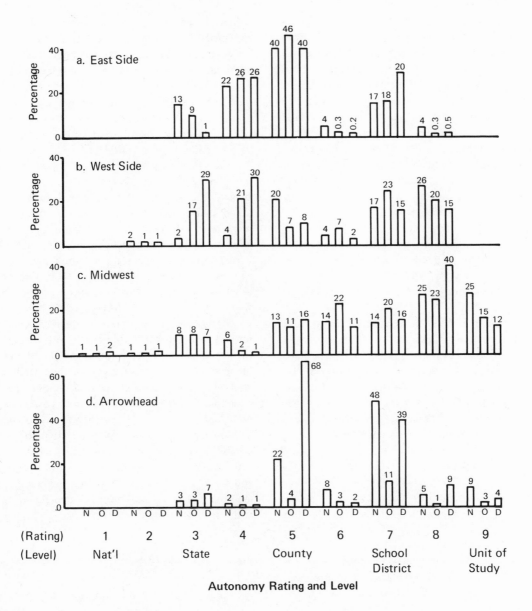

N = number
O = number of occurrences
D = duration

Figure 6-13
Comparison of autonomy ratings among Arrowhead, East Side, West Side, and Midwest.

housing and are the substance of the general condition of poverty. The basic principle is a simple one: the person who cannot make a living for himself becomes dependent upon those who provide for him. Dependency becomes a way of life in which the dependent person sets up a system of rationalizations to be able to live with himself. He becomes convinced of his own inability in order to justify his dependency; once convinced, he resists any attempt to develop his ability because this would destroy the dependency around which his life is organized. Yet the cost of dependency and its rewards of safety and comparative security is this constant demeaning of self. To balance the self-denigration, a second system of blame is set up against the provider. Whoever gives the services to the dependent person must also be inferior in some way because he is serving an inferior person. Only a second-rate person (or a saint) would perform such a task.

Arrowhead, as a composite product of thirty years of public-housing practices and policies, houses a population of dependent persons. Because the administration recognizes the dependent nature of its residents, it sets forth a number of rules for them to abide by and removes a number of decisions from their control, *only to increase the dependency.*

People in a dependent environment become preoccupied with their survival to a point where they appear to lack initiative, seem to blame others constantly for their troubles, and exaggerate the obstacles they encounter. From their standpoint, it is better not to try than to encounter so many obstacles and rebuffs. Hence, an appearance of apathy and cynicism greets any new proposals.

But there are ways in which healthy motives are invested. Teenagers, needing a place to gather, collect in the apartment building hallways to be out of public view and to have some privacy. Because teenagers are usually noisy in such gatherings, residents complain. No public toilets are available in Arrowhead, and the mistrust of teenagers is such that they are not easily admitted to apartments. The ultimate consequence is to urinate in the hallways. Finally, the urination becomes a gesture of defiance of the system designed to produce such frustration, as well as defiance of the complaining residents. The residents then become even angrier and the spiral of alienation continues upward. The teenagers then become the vanguard of the "counterdependency" to which Pareek (1970) addresses himself. They exhibit unremitting hostility toward adult authority, the obverse of the apathy in most residents.

How then, to overcome this problem—the apathy and the rebellion that are so much a part of dependency? The road is a difficult one. It must be understood that *a sign of improved conditions will be an increase of rebellion and outcries against authorities.* Once the dependent conditions are removed and residents begin to make some of their own decisions, they will become more aware of their problems and rebel against them. This is a universal phenomenon that cannot be avoided (Bechtel, 1970).*

The methods for removing dependency are described in detail within the framework of the theme of reneighborhooding Arrowhead—in the recommended management changes, in the social services activities, and in the architectural modifications. Let it be said that the most effective way to *maintain and perpetuate* a dependent environment is to construct a physical plant and social system that are beyond the capabilities of residents in terms of social and physical scale. So long as the residents must deal with physical and social dimensions beyond their own range of coping ability, they must remain dependent on the authorities who run the system.

FINAL RECOMMENDATIONS

The final recommendations were arrived at by a series of sessions between the researcher, the archi-

---

*In fact, once the residents gained their confidence in a few elections, they sued CMHA. At the time of writing, there was no way to predict such a specific outcome, but some form of rebellion was certain once the process of removing dependency began.

tect, the social action specialist, the management consultant, the project director, and the on-site coordinator. These sessions sometimes went long into the night. Several were held in motel rooms in Cleveland, others at the ERDF offices in Kansas City. Once the recommendations were verbally argued from all viewpoints, they were written in draft form and sent to all members of the team for comments and approval.

The format of the meetings was to begin with problems defined by the research and to arrive at solutions supported by research. All recommendations had been tried at least in one other location. After agreement among the team, the proposed solutions were presented to residents, chiefly by the architect. They voted on the acceptance or disapproval by a show of hands or expression of verbal consensus at the meetings. After the final acceptance by residents, the recommendations were written up and formally presented to CMHA where they were accepted in March 1972. Implementation continues through 1977.

The central theme around all recommendations is the elimination of dependency and the creation of a more self-sufficient environment.

The Project Manager

The concept of the strong housing manager (HM) implies that minimum supervision is required. Constant and detailed supervision would jeopardize successful performance by the HM. This condition, however, increases the importance of supporting the HM in the performance of his duties.

The Carver Park HM's activities do not have proper coordination or support. He is required to "shop" for guidance and support. He knows supervisory lines on an organization chart, but the chart is not productive in bringing about the substance of supervision and support.

The processing of maintenance orders is clearly out of the control of the manager. Residents have an inclination to go above his head to the central office to obtain results on complaints. This situation is further compounded by the manager's lack of control over the hiring and firing of maintenance personnel. Authority over all such project functions is not vested in the manager, and the residents know it.

ERDF recommended that an existing member of the CMHA central office staff be designated formally by the CMHA to be the coordinator supporting the Carver Park HM. This assignment would be in addition to that staff member's present duties.

Resources for Better Maintenance

The first recommendation is that a central location for the maintenance shop and stores supply must be created.

The second recommendation is that modernization funds be used to equip the maintenance facility with production control equipment, operated as part of a system to ensure authentic and constant control over all maintenance activities.

The third recommendation is that a thorough review of the centralized maintenance functions of CMHA be conducted jointly by ERDF, CMHA, and HUD. This review would be focused on examining the central CMHA maintenance functions from the standpoint of delivery capability to Carver Park.

The final recommendation is that a new system of receiving, recording, and assigning all tenant maintenance requests be designed to be operated by Carver Park personnel. One test of the effectiveness of such a system could be that the recently installed central office telephone complaint service no longer would be required to handle maintenance requests.

Improvement in Management–Resident Relations

We propose the development of a stronger Carver Park residents' council, built upon the existing council, as a mechanism to allow for greater, more meaningful resident input into the operation of Carver Park. This is the most logical vehicle for improving tenant–management relations.

New Social Services

The committee recommends that an estate management officer, other than the manager, be designated as the tenant relations officer and that at least four residents be employed as tenant relations aides.

The tenant relations officer would be one of the three management assistants. He or she would be directly accountable to the manager but would coordinate activities closely with CMHA's social services coordinator.

The resident aides would be accountable to the tenant relations officer and would receive all assignments and channel all reports, requests, and so on through his office. The main function of the resident aide is to serve as an intermediary between residents and management. The aide might also serve as the expediter when residents must depend on outside agencies and resources for the meeting of needs.

In Arrowhead, the committeee also proposes the demonstration of an elaboration of the European concept of the concierge (the doorkeeper, jack of all trades, the father image to the lonely tenant). We would call him the building superintendent. His responsibilities would include his acting as: caretaker of either one or two buildings and their grounds; custodian of the keys to the (experimental) building multipurpose room; adviser or go-between with resident aides; representative of the building's residents in the resident council; perhaps the building mailman; maintenance department's inspector of vacated units, following move outs by residents, and inspector of units prepared for reoccupancy; on-call fix-it man to handle minor complaints, such as leaking plumbing, burned-out fuses, and lock-outs on a twenty-four-hour per day basis; and expediter of work orders that

he cannot handle himself. He would live in the building, probably rent free as part of his compensation. Hopefully, he would be recruited from the ranks of the present maintenance personnel and be promoted to "Serviceman II."

Male Image

The problem is addressed in the proposed demonstration involving the hiring of resident building superintendents. But because of the high ratio of females to males, it was decided to provide greater male presence to arrive at a balance. There is a need to allow single males to live on the estate. To implement this demonstration, ERDF proposes experimentation by CMHA of an arrangement similar to that developed successfully by the Boston Housing Authority.

The arrangement described was not conceived as a direct response to the male image problem as defined in the Arrowhead project. Otherwise, however, there are many analogous circumstances, and the principles involved should be as applicable to Carver Park as they have been to several projects in the Boston program.

The key feature is to go through the steps required to designate a dwelling unit to serve a nondwelling use. This procedure is followed regularly by many housing authorities, especially in recent years, when many reasons have rationalized nondwelling use of dwelling units. Most frequently, the procedure has been used to enable the housing authority to use a dwelling for office purposes or some other direct operating function in the project. Many social and community action agencies have made use of dwellings officially through this arrangement.

There should be no reason why these arrangements could not be adapted to the particular interests to achieve demonstration opportunities for the "male image" concept. Possibly some special procedures for the clearance of the residents under this arrangement would have to be developed. These should be adapted to the particular circumstances that arise.

Smaller Social Areas

Although estate management and CMHA tend to see Carver Park as one unit, the residents use the Arrowhead area as though it were comprised of eight subunits. Evidence for this observation comes from: research surveys listing social contacts; behavior-setting data showing common "turf" areas; an architectural survey showing the interaction of behavior with building arrangements; and police and complaint data that show problems do not occur uniformly through Arrowhead.

The committee thus recommends defining seven smaller social areas that correspondingly define similar physical groups of buildings. These sociophysical areas will each receive from one to three building superintendents, a color code, and a special demonstration and auxiliary meeting and indoor recreation rooms in certain apartment building basements.

This recommendation is intended to define clearly and subtly already existing social areas. Its purpose is to aid in reneighborhooding the project and to help to build a greater sense of neighborliness among residents. By physically identifying and making clear subneighborhood social components, a total neighborhood can more easily be developed. Its intent is also to give identity to various social areas and to lessen problems of social and physical scale of Arrowhead.

Neighborhood Center

There is a lack of facilities for a comprehensive social service program and a decentralized maintenance operation. The existing settlement house is overcrowded, and operations-maintenance is scattered

in ten buildings. Research of resident needs by the community organization/social service team revealed, among other things, that additional social services for Arrowhead were essential. In a random unstructured survey, in which 491 residents were asked to enumerate any of their needs, the following five priorities were listed: improvements in maintenance, additional social services, recreational facilities and programs, architectural and site improvements (buildings, stairwells, grounds, and so forth), and exterior lighting.

In terms of social services, the needs fall into subcategories according to the following priorities: laundromat, pharmacy, clinic, shopping facilities, day-care centers, doctors and nurses, programs for senior citizens, additional meeting rooms, transportation, and "everything."

The committee recommended a neighborhood center in a multipurpose social services building and a separate building to house centralized operations-maintenance and resident council officers. (Rather than new construction, two existing structures would be converted.) It is recommended that service facilities be centralized in buildings F44, F45, and F46 (see figure 6–2).

The multipurpose social services building (F46) would contain a new laundromat and dry-cleaning facility located on the first floor of the building. The minibus system that provides transportation to hospitals, clinics, and other services would require an office-waiting area, also located on the first floor of the building. A day-care center would be provided in the basement and on the first floor by opening up nonbearing partitions to connect a series of apartments. Small quick-stop, snack-bar facilities would be provided in the basement or first floor. Additional meeting rooms, miscellaneous social services and programs, and rental spaces would be provided on the second floor. Recreation rooms would be located on the third floor. Television, games, and magazines for teenagers, adults, and the elderly and building storage could be located on the third floor.

The management-maintenance building (F44)

would contain the Carver Park management and maintenance offices, relocated and centralized on the first floor. Tenants' council offices and meeting rooms and the Arrowhead site office would also be located on the first floor. Maintenance shops and storage facilities, which are presently scattered in ten basements, would be located in the basement, second, and third floors of the building. Rear entrances to the basement for maintenance crews would be provided.

Since it is recommended that the management office be moved to F44, the space it vacates would be used for community building functions. New and enlarged programs could be housed in an enlarged Friendly Inn.

All these changes should improve the quality of social services in public housing, improve management operations, provide a centralized arena for social interaction and aesthetic focus, and intensify informal surveillance through implementation of the concept of centrality and the resulting notion of the multiplier effect.

Recreation

There has been little use of the large formal open space recreation area and heavy use of informal play areas too small for their intensive usage. Furthermore, older children frequently disrupt the recreational activities of younger children.

The committee thus recommends defining the large formal open area into three similar recreation areas and an employee parking-storage area and developing three larger and specially designed informal play areas for various age groups. Other small totlot sandbox areas would be located near certain apartment buildings. Construction of some recreation areas would necessitate building demolition, which would also serve to reduce the density of Carver Park. Recreation areas would be separated according to age groups.

Parking

The number of parking areas are inadequate, and the parking and dwelling units and building groups are not near enough.

The committee recommends more parking areas featuring closer location to dwellings where possible. Some parking areas will require building demolition (which will reduce Carver Park's density). Arrowhead area parking problems can be lessened by adding a limited number of new or enlarged off-street parking lots in critical places.

Unwin Street

The problems on Unwin Street include lack of enough parking places, vehicular traffic, and vehicular conflict with pedestrian circulation. Vehicular circulation along Unwin Street is a major problem. With visitors, employees, and service trucks parking along both sides of the street, double parking, speeders, and pedestrians, driving Unwin Street is difficult. Because there is not sufficient parking space, residents park along the street (worsening the traffic problems) and on grounds areas not designated for parking (worsening problems associated with grounds maintenance).

The committee recommends limited parking during rush hours, safety bumps to slow speeding traffic, retention of the one-way street designation, towing regulations, and a colorful crosswalk and stop sign for pedestrian safety.

Walkway System

The existing sidewalks, laid out according to obsolete design considerations, are narrow, perpendicular, and obstructed in many places by chains and fences, and they have deteriorated. They frequently do not go where pedestrians are headed. Pedestrian circulation is another design error. Sidewalks were designed according to a rigid eighteenth-century baroque concept of formality.

The committee recommends a new widened walkway system where pedestrian use is greatest. Landscaping, general lighting, information graphics, and seating areas would be designed in conjunction with the walkway system.

Special Lighting

Existing lighting, in addition to being generally inadequate, does not highlight special areas of the public-housing environment that are security hazards. [Special Lighting Demonstration—Social Area #1, building J83, H73, H72, play and parking areas only.] There should also be special security illumination of areas of buildings and grounds that produce most crime, vandalism, and accidents. Improvements in exterior lighting consist of two types of changes. General illumination features the general improvement of lighting in many demonstration areas and along the walkway system through floodlighting, for example. Special illumination, however, is more dramatic and demonstrated in only one area. Used in conjunction with general illumination, specific lighting of special features should limit crime, vandalism, and accidents and make the area more attractive aesthetically.

Graphics

Arrowhead is one large mass of undifferentiated buildings and areas with no rationale ordering of graphic identifications and no way of disseminating neighborhood information.

There should be an overall color coding system built around the concept of the previously discussed social areas. New information signs giving directions to certain areas, streets, and addresses, and *colorful* *kiosks* for neighborhood and community news are proposed. Concrete block portions of some townhouses would be given a colorful painting.

Clotheslines

There are no outdoor facilities for drying clothes. Thus, clotheslines should be provided in backyards of certain townhouses. The lines would be positioned to minimize danger to playing children and others who might be injured if they encounter the clotheslines in the course of their use of the area. Two rows of new lines would be positioned parallel to rather than perpendicular to the length of the townhouses. These lines, which would be located in backyards (technically, the front yards), would be strung at a height of six feet. This height, which most adult women can easily reach, is sufficiently high to offer little danger to children.

Special Materials

There has been physical deterioration of facilities and grounds because of inadequacy of original construction materials, inadequacy of present maintenance, heavy usage, and vandalism. More durable, *high initial cost, low-maintenance*, vandal-proof materials and hardware should be installed. Durable-glass, metal doors, roof hatches, mail slots to replace vandalized mailboxes, and unit waste compactors to replace building incinerators are also proposed.

Saturation Maintenance

Because of inadequate delivery of maintenance services the committee recommends a program of saturation maintenance targeted on the two areas of greatest maintenance need.

Superintendents' Facilities

Inexpensive work-storage facilities should be provided in all eight social areas for their respective building superintendents. Superintendents would be required to live in the social areas they serve. In the basements of eight apartment buildings would be located work stations for the superintendents.

Exterior Front Stairways

Existing interior stairwells foster a disporportionately high amount of crime, vandalism, and maintenance and are particularly disliked by many residents. Stairwell maintenance and security problems can be directly attributed to their architectural design. Located interior to the buildings, poorly lit, and usually drab, they virtually attract the abuse they receive.

As an alternative to the enclosed stairwell design, two three-story exterior stairways are proposed where stairwell problems are severe. Being more open, with better visibility, more easily lighted and maintained, the stairways will also provide a change in appearance to the apartment buildings.

Exterior Rear Stairs

Present building codes require two fire exits from apartment buildings. Access to common and proprietary areas is also required. These exits did not exist in the original buildings.

In the same social area as the previous recommendation are proposed ten half-story rear stairs at four apartment buildings.

Common and Proprietary Spaces

An axiom in medium-density, low-rise residential site planning is that groups of about four buildings should be oriented toward one another so that a space common to all is defined. The focal space would be an area for social interaction, recreation and play—a lively gathering place for residents of all ages in that building group. Concurrent with this need for a place where neighbors can get together is the need for space that residents can call their own and over which they can exert proprietary control.

Omitted in original site planning, a common space demonstration is proposed where site and architectural conditions permit. In the same area is proposed a proprietary space demonstration. Backyards and front yards, defined spatially as belonging to respective residents, would be located near perimeters of the various buildings. Demolition of an apartment building (the removal of building E37 and the addition of exterior stairs at the rear, allowing the creation of a common space) would be required to implement these recommendations. In addition, a recreation area is also proposed for part of the common space, for tots, teenagers, and adults. Extensive proprietary landscaping (trees, grass, shrubs, berming, seating) improvements are also recommended for the demonstration area. These improvements would help define the space into public, semipublic, and private areas.

Density Reduction

With thirty-nine two- and three-story buildings housing 1,716 residents packed into approximately twenty acres of land, Arrowhead building and people density is extreme in comparison with most other residential areas. The committee thus proposes converting or removing six apartment buildings and one townhouse building to reduce the population by approximately 9 percent. Residents displaced by this recommendation could be rehoused in Arrowhead and Carver Park vacancies or in other CMHA estates. Problems of social scale, the overmanned social environment previously discussed, could thus be ameliorated.

INNOVATIVE APPROACHES

For every innovation suggested by ERDF, there was some precedent or previous working example. The building superintendent had the European concierge; the tenants' council had many precedents in the poverty programs. But although each suggestion had been tried elsewhere, it would be extremely difficult to find this *combination* of suggestions anywhere else. The umbrella concept of management where all other functions, even design, are subservient to management is truly innovative.

But by far the most innovative aspect of Arrowhead is a new way of doing things. While it is not innovative in other fields (industry and commercial sales are quite used to the research-operation paradigm where new methods are discovered, tested out, and then applied), in Arrowhead for the first time a research application paradigm was used. Profile analysis uncovered a dependent, poorly designed environment. Design, management, and social action components made research-based recommendations, and then the application of these recommendations was to be evaluated by social science methods. Even if the recommendations fail as intended, enough will be learned to contribute significantly to guidelines for future modernization of public housing.

Arrowhead and the two other research-demonstration projects like it are tremendously complex. They involve the attempt to change a near-total environment, and it must be remembered that such an attempt is the most innovative step since public housing began.

APPLYING INNOVATION TECHNIQUES

It was not an exaggeration when Jay Jackson, a management consultant, said that most evaluation is done by management expecting a "pat on the back." Very few evaluations contain the built-in mechanisms to permit truly objective evaluations. And in the design field, very few evaluations are made at all.* Thus, evaluation, the most important operation in measuring performance, is usually lacking in most human endeavors. Management and design have few feedbacks to tell whether they are successful.

The lesson of Arrowhead is clear. Unless there are built-in mechanisms whereby management can have its performance evaluated by feedback from residents and more objectively by other agencies like HUD, the inevitable result is some product like the paternalism-dependency system—or worse. A one-shot demonstration like Arrowhead will not prevent that from happening.

A number of innovative social and physical techniques are constantly being developed that could be useful to HUD operations in housing. The HUD Office of Research and Technology must aggressively pursue these innovations and test them in the housing sites. This requires a permanent staff of persons equipped to deal with social and physical environmental research; in short, this means a professional team on a permanent basis. Only then can the lessons of Arrowhead be applied to other housing locations and developed.

The other (and equally important) lesson of Arrowhead is that innovative programs cannot be fragmented. An item even as small as a new doorknob cannot be tested without understanding the behavioral consequences of this seemingly insignificant item. In one project, for example, the doorknobs cost $1.50, and they often broke off. In another project they cost over $3.00; there were no such problems. Unfortunately, residents in the first project were black and those in the second were white. The white residents had all the evidence they needed that those blacks "can't take care of anything." So even doorknobs are not without social consequences, and attitudes that do not demand social evaluation of every physical change are seriously short-changing residents.

Many research techniques could have been used to

*See Ann Ferebee's editorial in *Design and Environment*, no. 8 (Winter 1971):23.

evaluate Arrowhead. Questionnaires, psychological instruments, and police and demographic data were used. But the most important innovation in research was the use of the behavior-setting survey. In a project as vast as Arrowhead, there could be no way of trying to cover all the possible changes without inundating residents with questionnaires and tests. The observation techniques of the behavior-setting survey are far less obtrusive and yet more comprehensive than any other technique. By no other technique could the global community of Arrowhead have been described and measured. Some thought the cost was high, yet the entire research effort was only 3 percent of the total Arrowhead budget.

It is the assertion of Project Arrowhead that the dependent environment is the chief problem of public and other low-income housing and that no less than a national strategy involving research and design components must be mounted to solve it.

The External Change Agent

One of the truisms of applied anthropology is that the stranger can be a powerful agent of change. Throughout the history of change in different cultures, the stranger has been able to do things forbidden or unacceptable to a native.* Therefore, the fact that ERDF staff members were from outside Cleveland and had no previous political alliances or preconceived ideas about Carver Park was a considerable advantage. There is also that element of human nature that tends to find strangers who are experts more believable than nonstrangers. Anthropologists have long taken advantage of the stranger role, and now it is time for designers and planners to do so.

*See Edward H. Spicer's *Human Problems in Technological Change*, Russell Sage Foundation, 1952, for a series of case examples.

Models

The noninstitutional organization

One of the problems likely to confront any design team of public-housing staff, or even HUD, is the rapid institutionalization of practices so that bureaucratic procedures build up to the point where adaptability to new techniques grinds to a halt. Since one of the main points of Arrowhead research is to prevent this from happening, some strategies must be developed to succeed in preventing it. Police departments try to use changes in assignment to offset it; so do the armed services and the Catholic church. But that strategy has not worked successfully. A better technique is to adopt the disposable organization in which a team is assembled to do a given job and then disbanded when the job is finished. Such a model is suggested for implementation of Arrowhead results in other public-housing projects.

The waning power model

Although there are varying constraints by law, the setting up of an organization such as a public-housing authority should be done based on the concept of waning power (that is, the authority should reach a point where nearly all of the functions of public housing are taken over by residents). This is not an easy task. But the consequences of the present model result in greater and greater dependency and greater and greater deficits. The way to move the residents out of dependency is to train them to move up the level of the organization from resident to employee to manager and so on rather than leaving them at a dead level.

The social areas concept

The concept of social areas has been discussed previously in this chapter. Indications are that housing projects should be organized into social areas of two hundred persons or fewer. This level of human, social, and physical scale permits a better development of social relations and actually works to coerce greater participation in residents in all aspects of public life. Provided it is handled correctly, it does not preclude the building of large projects. The important principle is to give each area a character of its own.

If the concept of social areas is carried out as it should be, then the social area becomes the unit for maintenance, management, and representation in government. It becomes, as it should be, a social unit on which to build large communities. Keep in mind, however, that the behavior settings should be slightly undermanned. As it is with money, it should be with people—always not quite enough.

Centralization of services

In an urban area like Arrowhead, services to the local residents should be centrally located and overlapping. This means each resident should have as nearly equal an opportunity to reach the service by foot as any other residents. Services that are overlapping also provide informal surveillance and cut down on the need for security. At the same time, this overlapping tends to spawn social settings. The model, then, is one of centrally located, overlapping services.

This principle does not hold for services that are for customers outside the locale that pull in nonresidents. Such services should be located on the edge of the project, preferably where strangers and local residents can meet on some neutral ground. This avoids conflicts over territoriality. Strangers do not come into the project as often, and they are not seen as taking services away from locals.

Personalization of services and design

This is a principle that has design and social implications. A personalized design is one that looks like it was built for people, not for the convenience of cheap construction or what some professional decides is good for the resident. Michelson (1969) mentions many examples. Essentially, this means adjusting services and design to local preferences, not applying designs from one location to another. Virtually all of public housing (with a few recent exceptions) looks institutional rather than personal. Essentially, Arrowhead was a weak example since very little of the institutional environment could be changed physically.

Socially, personalization of services means cutting out the need for long lines of people at stores, offices, and even waiting to make telephone calls. Offices should be small, not run on an assembly-line basis. It must be stressed again that the personal model of design is directly contrary to the assembly-line production model of construction, design, and services. It is more costly in the initial phase but cheaper in the long run in terms of maintenance, vandalism, and other social problems.

CONCLUSIONS

At the time of writing, it remains to be seen whether all the recommendations of Arrowhead will be carried out. Already the density reduction has taken place. The special lighting, the sidewalks and the playgrounds were implemented. But political changes since the project began make some of the social changes doubtful. Nevertheless, by the use of profile analysis, comparing the behavior setting measures of one environment with others, it was possible to diagnose and prescribe a specific environment in public housing. The reader should note two important results of the diagnosis.

1. It was *not* limited to conditions as they were. One of the criticisms of social science is that it can only describe or analyze existing conditions and not prescribe for bettering conditions. To some extent this is true, but the undermanning theory of Barker (1968) clearly prescribes a breaking down of the environment of Arrowhead into smaller units and an

increase in settings. What is important in this regard is that once the present conditions are known with some precision, the remedies are often obvious.

2. Many designers feel that social science can be of help in specific design problems such as rooms, or even smaller objects such as desks. This may be from a mistaken notion that social scientists are like human engineers and work on problems of fitting the human body to its surroundings. That kind of research has its place, but perhaps the greatest help that the social scientist can be to the designer is to supply him with a central concept by which a total environment can be characterized. Once understood, then this central concept can become the focus of both design and management changes. In Arrowhead, the central concept was dependency, and recommendations in management and design were directed toward the remedy for that situation. True enough, many social science concepts can be of use in even the microareas such as the recommendation for small offices, but the principal contribution was the global view of a dependent environment.

In other environments, Barker and Barker (1961) have characterized the position of elderly in the community as "regressed"; in urban residential areas, Bechtel (1970) characterized the environment as "passive." The possibilities of diagnosing environments by profile analysis of behavior setting data have just begun.

REFERENCES

Barker, Roger G. *Ecological Psychology*. Stanford University Press, 1968.

Barker, Roger, and Barker, Louise. "Behavior Units for the Comparative Study of Culture." In Bert Kaplan, ed., *Studying Personality Cross-Culturally*. Harper & Row, 1961, pp. 457–476.

Barker, R. G., and Wright, H. *Midwest and Its Children*. Row, Peterson, 1955.

Bechtel, Robert B. "A Behavioral Comparison of Urban and Small Town Environments." In John Archea and Charles Eastman, eds., *EDRA 2: Proceedings of the Second Annual Environmental Design Research Association Conference*, Pittsburgh, Pa., October 1970, pp. 347–353.

Bechtel, R. B.; Achelpohl, C.; and Binding, F. *East Side, West Side, and Midwest: A Behavioral Comparison of Three Environments*. Epidemiological Field Station, 1970.

De Leeuw, F. *Operating Costs in Public Housing*. Urban Institute, 1971.

Freedman, Leonard. *Public Housing*. Holt, Rinehart and Winston, 1969.

Helson, Harry. *Adaptation-Level Theory*. Harper & Row, 1964.

Maslow, Abraham. *Motivation and Personality*. Harper & Row, 1954.

Michelson, W. "Most People Don't Want What Architects Want." *Transaction* (July–August 1968):37–43.

Pareek, U. "Poverty and Motivation: Figure and Ground." In V. Allen, ed., *Psychological Factors in Poverty*. Markham, 1970, pp. 300–317.

7

The Interview Method

One of the most touted methods in ecological psychology is direct observation (Barker and Wright, 1955; Barker, 1968). Yet this method becomes unwieldy beyond the confines of a small community and when one wants data in a shorter time span than the traditional year. If, for example, one wanted to diagnose the behavioral needs for design purposes of 1,300 families, considering the high cost of trained observers for each family, there would be no choice but to sample this behavior rather than to measure all of it. Further, using a time span shorter than a year necessitates asking about rather than observing all of the behavior over a year. In short, one must resort to a random sample interview; the alternative is a prohibitively expensive research project. While such a procedure may seem at first to negate some of the advantages of the behavior-setting survey, this need not necessarily be true. It is possible to construct a questionnaire around the information needed for a behavior-setting survey and to obtain valid results.

The questionnaire was applied to seven locations in the state of Alaska in order to gather data for better design of cold regions environments. These locations were Cordova, Kotzebue, Gulkana, Murphy Dome, Campion, and Fort Wainwright. Two locations at Kotzebue were studied. The sample of 50 families was from Fort Wainwright. Research was funded by the Cold Regions Research and Engineering Laboratories, Hanover, New Hampshire, and all data are printed with their permission. Data were collected at the various sites during eight trips by the author. This research was a true architect-social scientist collaboration in that the architect, Burgess Ledbetter, also learned the behavior setting techniques and lived in Alaska with his family for eleven months.

The reader must be assured that the particular random sample survey described here was not done without observational backup. In addition to the survey, an observer lived on the housing site with a family for eleven months. Thus, the questionnaire was constructed around direct observations, and the results were validated against these direct observations. The questionnaire became a method for extending the observations to a level of generalization valid for 1,145 families.

RANDOM SAMPLING

For those not familiar with the methods of random sampling, textbooks such as Kish (1965) describe the theory and various methods used. It is important to keep in mind that the purpose of a random sample is to provide a measurement of a fraction of a population that will be representative of that population; that is, it will provide information almost as good as if the whole population were measured.

In order to accomplish representativeness, every subject in the original population must have a mathematically equal chance of being measured. This is accomplished by random selection. A popular method of random selection is to place numbers in a hat and to pick several from the hat as the random sample. When a large number of subjects is involved, however, this method is not practical, and a mathematical interval is chosen to provide an adequate sample.

The size of the sample depends upon the accuracy required from the answers. For example, in a sample size of fifty, for differences to be statistically significant at the 95 percent confidence level, they must exceed 27 percent. Thus, if 40 percent of the sample answer "yes" and 60 percent answer "no," the difference (20 percent) is not large enough to be significant. Figure 7–1, taken from Cantril (1965), shows the differences between percentages and sample size required for statistical significance. The American Psychological Association accepts 95 percent as the level of significance for a statistical test.

In the example provided here it was decided to sample 51 families out of a possible 1,145. This meant a sampling interval of 22 in order to obtain 51 families. In other words, once selecting a starting point by putting 22 numbered squares in a hat (or looking up a table of random numbers), every twenty-second person in the list of 1,145 was chosen.

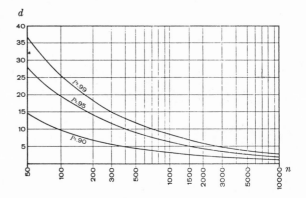

Figure 7–1
The significance of differences between categories within a single sample. Reprinted from Cantril, 1965, p. 360; copyright © 1965 by Rutgers—The State University. Reprinted by permission of Rutgers University Press.

Once having chosen, the interviewer is not allowed to select substitutes. It is a common belief that the interviewer could select the person next door if the person originally selected were not at home. This gives the person next door a second chance at selection and destroys the random sample basis.

In the example considered, 40 families, or 78.43 percent of the 51, completed the questionnaire. Considering the highly mobile population, with many soldiers on field problems and on leave, this number compares favorably with recent results of polls in large cities. In any random sampling, there will always be a certain number who cannot be interviewed.

THE INTERVIEW

An interview was constructed for families that would provide data for the standard behavior-setting survey of one year. Respondents were asked about the activities that would permit scores on the activity patterns and behavior mechanisms of Barker's scales (see the sample interview schedule in appendix B).

In order to get an accurate estimate on the amount of time spent indoors by family members, a yearly schedule was worked out for each one. The father's was usually the easiest since he had to follow regular work hours. After-work hours were specifically probed for both winter and summer months. Then, weekends were gone into with as much detail as possible. Many of the activities were scheduled for specific periods of time, and fairly accurate data could be obtained by adding in travel time to and from events.

Relatively large margins were allowed for in the activity patterns and behavior mechanisms (see appendix A for scales). The most important distinction was whether an activity was present, absent, or prominent. For example, if the members of the family did not give to any of the charitable agencies that solicited family housing, their philanthropy score was zero. Those that did give had not spent nearly enough time to account for 1 percent of total occupancy time in the house.

Aesthetics was scored by accounting for clean-up time and any additional aesthetic activity such as antiquing furniture, doing oil paintings, building cabinets, or working on similar aesthetically oriented hobbies in the home.

The most difficult item to pin down in terms of occupancy time was recreation. Hours spent watching television, working on hobbies, lounging around, and so forth were often difficult to quantify in terms of person-hours. Figures were often arrived at by family consensus.

The final procedure of filling out behavior-setting forms was to calculate total occupancy time by subtracting the total number of hours spent outside the home from the 8,760 hours in the year. Some families spent less than the full year, and their time was prorated. From the total, eight hours per night in the home were subtracted for sleeping. The figure remaining was considered the occupancy time in the house for that person. All persons in the home had their occupancy times added for a total occupancy time. Rating scales were then calculated as a percent of the total occupancy time.

Autonomy was calculated as follows: selecting

performers, 9; admitting members, 9; determining policy, 2; and financial arrangements 1, for a total of 21. The average was 5. The average score is for Barker's (1968) level 5, which is the county level. Actually, in Alaska where the data were collected no county form of government exists. The average, therefore, represents only a numerical value. The five level itself was not used in estimating autonomy levels for Alaska.

Penetration levels were calculated by considering the husband and wife as at level 5, adult offspring earning wages at level 4, children at level 3, and visitors at level 2.

Social parties, Scout meetings, and other meetings were calculated as separate settings.

THE FAMILY HOUSING ENVIRONMENT OF A MILITARY BASE IN ALASKA

Part of contract DAAG17-73-C-0104 between the Cold Regions Research and Engineering Laboratories in Hanover, New Hampshire, and the Environmental Research and Development Foundation in Kansas City, Missouri, required the development of habitability guidelines for family housing. This meant that design criteria should answer to the behavioral needs of families living in cold regions. The farthest north large military post in the United States is Fort Wainwright at Fairbanks, Alaska. About 1,300 families were living there at the time of the random sample survey in June 1974. Of these 1,300 families, only 1,145 were not in transient housing or out-processing, and they became the subjects for the survey.

Family housing on all military bases has a quality of sameness. Figures 7-2 to 7-4 show family housing at Fort Wainwright in the three types of buildings constructed there. In addition, officers at the level of major and above live in duplexes (figure 7-5). The same kinds of buildings can be seen at military bases all over the United States.

The most basic plan for family housing is organized around a court. Three buildings are clustered around

Figure 7-2
Type I: Older, larger housing units at Fort Wainwright (1,250 sq. ft.). Photograph by Wayne Tobiasson; courtesy of CRREL.

Figure 7-4
Type III: Smaller units (1,080 sq. ft.). Photograph by Burgess Ledbetter; courtesy of CRREL.

this court, and there are eight families in each building (figure 7-6). A variation of this is the single building, holding eight families, standing alone. Some bases provide both kinds of housing.

Traditionally, military officers have had larger and better quarters than enlisted men. Often, however, this difference is blurred when locations have shortages of various types of housing. A second distinction is often made at field grade, or the rank of major and

above. At Fort Wainwright, field grade officers can live in duplex houses, while lower-ranked officers live either in the single buildings standing alone or in the three-building courts. The site plan of housing strives to separate officers from enlisted men and bachelor soldiers from families, while at the same time making central services equally available to all parties. A contradiction to the latter motive is the now-outmoded defense posture that held until very recent times. When conventional bombs were the most feared wea-

Figure 7-3
Type II: Large units built in the 1950s (1,250 sq. ft.). Photograph by Burgess Ledbetter; courtesy of CRREL.

Figure 7-5
Officers' duplexes at Fort Wainwright.

pon, the directive was to disperse critical buildings so that the least number could be harmed by a single bomb. The result is that most military bases have residences and amenities related at great distances to each other. With modern weapons, the directive has been relaxed somewhat.

These, then, are the three features most common to military family housing: segregation by rank and marital status, uniformity of construction, and relatively large distances to amenities.

The structures themselves are only slightly modi-

Figure 7-7b
Arctic entrance exterior at officers' quarters, Fort Wainwright.

Figure 7-6
Family housing buildings organized around a parking court.

Figure 7-7c
Arctic entrance interior in a house at Hanover, N.H. Note hooks for hanging clothing and doors to outside and house interior.

fied for cold regions; they have thicker insulation (six inches as opposed to four), vapor barriers, higher roof loads because of snow, and thermal windowpanes. In most cases foundations over permafrost are avoided in family housing. In several cases arctic entrances are used for the front entrances to housing, and in all cases, where cars are to last the winter, electrical outlets must be provided to keep engines and batteries warm overnight.

Figure 7-7a
Arctic entrance exterior at Kotzebue.

DERIVING HABITABILITY GUIDELINES

The process of deriving habitability guidelines from behavior-setting data is shown in figure 7-8. The process is considered in ten steps.

Step 1: data collection Data was collected by various methods. Key to the observations is having someone or several people live on the site for several months. In addition to the main observer, two observers were hired who were living on the site at the time, and two more additional observers moved onto the site for periods varying from several days to five months.

Records of various organizations were combed for data on person-hours, visitors, special events, absences, and other data collected in the course of doing business. Interviews were held with many personnel to learn about their jobs and duties and how the organizations functioned. Photographs were taken of all sites studied.

Most of these data (except photographs) were compiled on the behavior-setting information sheet in appendix A.

Step 2: results The behavior-setting survey data were arranged into seven categories, including action pattern profiles, behavior mechanism profiles, autonomy scores, welfare and pressure scores, population data, general richness indexes, and ERI data.

Step 3: analysis of results The results of the first three categories in step 2 were made into bar graphs. These bar graphs constitute the profiles that are compared to similar or different environments in order to define differences and similarities. A more sophisticated analysis of this kind would use discriminant function analysis, a multivariate analysis technique. Because this type of analysis is so costly, it was not used for this study. Profile comparisons were not tested statistically. Therefore, the analysis consists of listing differences and similarities of the profiles. Although the last four categories—welfare and pressure scores, population data, general richness indexes, and ERI data—were not made into bar graphs, they are considered part of the profile comparison data.

Step 4: results Profile comparisons proceed from the most global to the most specific. First, Fort Wainwright as an army post was compared to Federal Aviation Association (FAA) sites, Aircraft Control and Warning stations, and other civilian environments previously studied by behavior-setting survey. This results in a characterization of Fort Wainwright as a total environment. The best characterization seemed to be a temporary environment. Organizations and divisions within Fort Wainwright—family housing, transient housing, barracks, and selected work environments—were compared. Then, within each of these units, more detailed comparisons were made until the level of behavior setting was reached. The question was asked, Does the behavior fit the environment? A fit is determined by observations, reports of informants, answers to questionnaires, or all of these. For example, do the residents want fences in their yards? Do the residents who have fences like them? Do the fences keep out children and dogs as some claim? The answers to these questions then lead to the decision whether to recommend fences as a habitability guideline.

Step 5: inference of guidelines Once the results of the analyses are clear, the process of inferring guidelines is fairly simple. Using the example of fences above, if most people want fences and the fences are observed to fulfill the functions intended, then fences would be a recommendation. However, the requirement is to keep dogs and children out of neighboring yards and away from each other. Fences may be recommended for this particular situation, but another post with no dogs and very few children may not have the same need and hence would not have such a requirement.

Step 6: trial guidelines The guidelines finally arrived at were a result of five or six preliminary guidelines that were tried out with various authorities and users and tested against research data.

Step 7: preliminary drawings A preliminary drawing preceded the final drawing and would often raise questions that could be answered only by going back to the original data and doing further analysis.

Step 8: reiteration It then became necessary to go

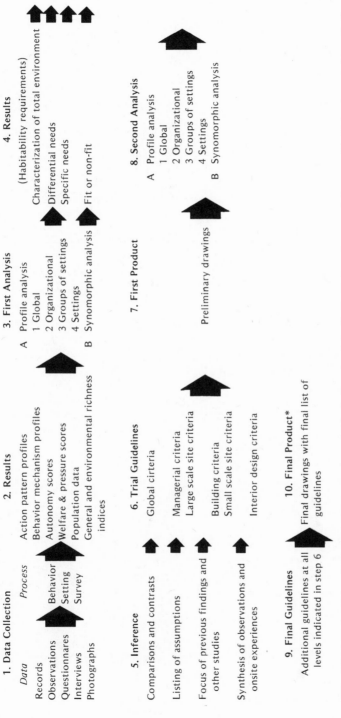

1. Data Collection

Data   *Process*
Records   Behavior
Observations   Setting
Questionnares   Survey
Interviews
Photographs

2. Results

Action pattern profiles
Behavior mechanism profiles
Autonomy scores
Welfare & pressure scores
Population data
General and environmental richness indices

3. First Analysis

A Profile analysis
   1 Global
   2 Organizational
   3 Groups of settings
   4 Settings
B Synomorphic analysis

4. Results

(Habitability requirements)
Characterization of total environment
Differential needs
Specific needs
Fit or non-fit

5. Inference

Comparisons and contrasts

Listing of assumptions

Focus of previous findings and other studies

Synthesis of observations and onsite experiences

6. Trial Guidelines

Global cirteria

Managerial criteria
Large scale site criteria

Building criteria
Small scale site criteria

Interior design criteria

7. First Product

Preliminary drawings

8. Second Analysis

A Profile analysis
   1 Global
   2 Organizational
   3 Groups of settings
   4 Settings
B Synomorphic analysis

9. Final Guidelines

Additional guidelines at all levels indicated in step 6

10. Final Product*

Final drawings with final list of guidelines

*The "final product" is a final product for purposes of this study only. Actually the design recommendations need to be implemented by actual construction after which this process will be performed again to evaluate the efficacy of the guidelines.

Figure 7–8
Process of Deriving Habitability Guidelines

back to the data, the notes, and the photographs and answer questions, which would then permit a new list of requirements.

Step 9 Final guidelines were derived from legal requirements.

Step 10 Final drawings could be made.

THE RESULTS

Data from the questionnaire were tabulated on behavior-setting code sheets (see table 7-1) as in an ordinary behavior-setting survey. These data will be dealt with separately. In addition, a number of questions were asked about specific design features of the houses and general aspects of the environment.

Behavior-Setting Data

In addition to the sample survey at Fort Wainwright, complete behavior-setting surveys were made of forty-two housing units at four different FAA locations. These locations were Murphy Dome, Kotzebue, Gulkana, and Cordova, all in Alaska. The FAA maintains these sites to service airports (flight service stations) and assist in air navigation through operation of radar stations, radio direction finders, and other navigational devices. These sites differ from military housing not only in being civilian but also in being much smaller and of different construction. Most of the FAA houses are single-family dwellings (figure 7-9), and a few are apartments (figure 7-10). Comparing FAA housing with the military provides some important clues as to how a military housing environment differs from a civilian one.

Figure 7-11 lists the action patterns comparing FAA family housing with family housing at Fort Wainwright.

Action patterns

There are seven action patterns on which the FAA families show a lower percentage of total occupancy

Figure 7-9
FAA single-family dwellings.

time than the family housing at Fort Wainwright. These include religion, education, business, government, and professionalism as present percentages and recreation and social contact as prominent percentages.

The army emphasizes religion a great deal with staff chaplains and church buildings to care for the residents. The FAA leaves religious pursuits entirely at the discretion of residents. Therefore, the lesser percentage of religion action pattern for the FAA is not only in accord with observed behavior but possibly due to FAA personnel going off the FAA compound for pursuit of religious activities.

Figure 7-10
FAA apartments.

TABLE 7-1
Behavior Setting Code Sheet Used in Cold Regions Study

Name _____

Genotype #   1-4: _____   Authority System   9-10: _____   No. of Occurrences: 12-14: _____

Behavior Setting No.   5-8: _____   Class of Authority System 11: _____

| Occupancy Time of Base Subgroups | | | | Max. Pene. of Subgroups | | Action Pattern |
Group	Col. No. No. P.		Col. No. O.T.	Group	Col. No.	Rate
On Base						
Inf	ML	15-18:	42-46:	Inf	26:	Aes: 5:
	C	19-22:	47-51:			Bus: 6:
Presch	ML	23-26:	52-56:	Presch	27:	Prof: 7:
	C	27-30:	57-61:			Educ: 8:
Y S	ML	31-34:	62-66:	Y S	28:	Govt: 9:
	C	35-38:	67-71:			Nutr: 10:
O S	ML	39-42:	72-76:	O S	29:	PersAp: 11:
			End of Card (2)			Phil: 12:
			Behavior Setting	Adol	30:	PhysH: 13:
			No. 1-4:			Rec: 14:
O S	C	43-46:	5-9:	Adult	31:	Rel: 15:
						Soc: 16:
Adol	ML	47-50:	10-14:	Aged	32:	
	C	51-54:	15-19:			Mechanism Rate
Adult	ML	55-58:	20-25:	Males	33:	AffB: 17:
	C	59-61:	26-30:	Females	34:	GroMot: 18:
						Manip: 19:
Aged		63-66:	31-35:			Talk: 20:
				Negroes	35:	Think: 21:
				Whites	36:	
Males	ML	67-70:	36-41:			Gen Rich: 22-23:
	C	71-74:	42-46:			
				Social C. Pen. L.		
Building No. 75-78:				I	37:	Pressure Rating
				II	38:	Child 24:
End of Card (1)				III	39:	Adol: 25:
Behavior Setting				IV	40:	
No. 1-4:						
				Grand Max. 41-42:		Welfare Rating
						Child: 26:
Females	ML	5-8:	47-51:			Adol: 27:
	C	9-12:	52-56:			

TABLE 7-1 (Continued)

Negroes	13–16:	57–61:	
Whites	17–20:	62–67:	
On Base	ML	21–24:	68–73:
Total	C	25–28:	74–78:

End of Card (3)
Behavior Setting No. 1–4:

Off Base	ML	29–32:	5–9:
Total	C	33–36:	10–14:
Grand Total		37–41:	15–20:

Total Duration 21–25

Performers (number)

On Base	ML	43–45:
Total	C	46–48:
Off Base	ML	49–50:
Total	C	51–53:

Grand Total 54–57:

Perf/Pop. 58–59:

White Perf. 60–63:
Negro Perf. 64–66:

End of Card (4)
Behavior Setting No. 1–4:

Autonomy Rating
Wtd: 28:

Social C. O.T.	
I	29–33:
II	34–38:
III	39–43:
IV	44–48:

E, O or I   49:

Jan.	50:
Febr.	51:
March	52:
April	53:
May	54:
June	55:
July	56:
Aug.	57:
Sept.	58:
Oct.	59:
Nov.	60:
Dec.	61:

(End of Card 5)

The education action pattern is present in a greater percentage of the occupancy time of family housing at Fort Wainwright because the soldiers tend to take more correspondence courses at home, while most of the educational upgrading at FAA takes place on the job.

There is less business action pattern in the FAA family settings because FAA personnel seem to order less through mail catalogs and do more ordering and have commercial parties (such as Tupperware parties) in their recreational buildings (figure 7-12). In addition, army people sell more goods from their homes as part-time jobs.

Recreation is a prominent feature of the family occupancy time of Fort Wainwright compared to the family occupancy time of FAA. There are at least two reasons for this. One is that recreational spaces are provided outside the home and close by the FAA personnel, and parties, luncheons, birthday celebrations, and other activities take place there. While recreational space is provided at Fort Wainwright, it is farther from housing and much less utilized. Another reason why the out-of-home recreational facilities of the FAA are more utilized than those at Fort Wainwright has to do with the size of the post. Data independently collected for air force sites show that participation in recreational pursuits decreases as the size of the post increases. Table 7-2 shows how every activity except auto hobby shop has a higher participation level for smaller populations. The reason why the auto hobby shop participation level is not higher at the remote bases is that at some locations

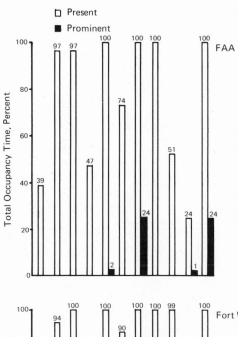

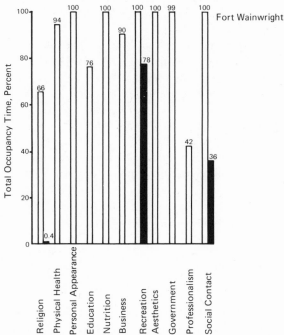

Figure 7-11
Action patterns of FAA and Fort Wainwright family housing
by percent of occupancy times.

Figure 7-12
FAA recreation building, Cordova, Alaska.

autos are not available. These data tend to confirm
Barker's (1960, 1968) undermanning theory.*

It would seem then that the two factors of distance
and size of installation operate, possibly with other
variables, to bring more recreation to the family environment at Fort Wainwright.

Social contact is higher as a prominent feature of
life in Fort Wainwright housing compared to FAA.
This contrasts to talking behavior mechanism, which
has a higher prominence for FAA. Usually talking
and social contact are correlated. The difference is
due to more contacts being made outside the home
for FAA.

Professionalism is higher in the Fort Wainwright
settings because there are more paid persons inspect-
ing the premises and more cases of the soldiers bringing work home. In addition, several of the army wives
sell merchandise from the home.

*A criticism of the air force data might be that the remote
stations are more isolated than the large bases and that this
might account for the differences. Some of this factor may
account for the differences but many of the "remote" bases
are near civilian towns and villages, and by contrast many of
the single men at large bases are very isolated by lack of
transportation.

TABLE 7-2
Participation Levels

Activity	Remote Sites (N = 15) (Av. Pop. 253)	Eielson AFB (Pop. 3,208)	Elmendorf AFB (Pop. 9,138)
Gymnasium	76.6%	47.5%	54.2%
Library	72.3%	39.0%	38.1%
Bowling	70.0%	60.2%	43.9%
Recreation center	58.1%	22.7%	20.4%
Photography and electronics hobby	23.8%	7.6%	9.0%
Wood hobby	20.0%	12.7%	12.6%
Auto hobby	18.1%	35.6%	31.3%
Golf course	15.8%	3.4%	11.6%

Source: From Attachment 2, Study No. AAC 74-006, *Analysis of AAC Recreation Opinion Survey*, 4 February 1974 (categories "1-3 times a month" and "once a week or more" combined).

Behavior mechanisms

Behavior mechanisms do not differ appreciably between the two types of housing with the exception of talking, which is more prominent in the FAA housing. The difference is probably due to a higher ratio of children in the FAA units. There are 111 children for 42 units in FAA contrasted to 69 children for the 40 units of the Fort Wainwright sample. The presence of children raises the rating for talking behavior mechanism.

Other measures

The GRI shows that FAA family housing has a higher mean score (29.8) than Fort Wainwright family housing (25.9). Since the FAA action pattern scores were the lower of the two and the behavior mechanisms similar, the difference can be attributed to the greater number of children at FAA. The GRI score is influenced by action pattern and behavior mechanism scores and by different age levels.

Penetration levels, as an average, were scored the same for FAA as family housing at Fort Wainwright. There were a few single individuals living in apartments at the FAA locations, however, tending to make the FAA level slightly higher since these persons were rated at level 6.

Local autonomy for the FAA was at level 6 because FAA personnel had slightly more to say about their housing than personnel at Fort Wainwright.

In conclusion, the military environment in comparison with the FAA environments seems to emphasize more recreation in the home. Three other action patterns are significant: education, business, and professionalism. These all have consequences for designing a different type of house for the military.

Problems Uncovered by Observation of Synomorphs*

Parking

Originally, most housing at Fort Wainwright was constructed with an arctic entrance at the front door,

*Synomorphs is a term used to designate an environment-behavior relationship below the behavioral level of a behavior setting. Sitting in a chair is an example of a synomorph; so is watching television.

assuming most traffic would enter there. The stairway giving access to bedrooms on the second floor was also placed next to the front door, giving immediate access to the upstairs without having to cross the living room. However, since all parking of vehicles is in the rear, the traffic pattern for the house originates through the back door, and the front door is seldom used. This means that a person wanting to come in from the outside to go to the bathroom must go through the kitchen and cross the center of the living room to get upstairs. In addition, coats, which were supposed to be hung in the spacious arctic entrance, are now hung in the back entrance, already crowded with garbage (figure 7-13).

A further consequence of frequent use of the back door was that, unlike the door of an arctic entrance, it collects moisture at the edge and will often freeze open.

And, since the backyard is visually accessible from the kitchen, and most of the traffic originates in the parking lots, the front yard then becomes unused and is often turned over to the dogs (figure 7-14).

Living spaces

It was found that living spaces were not utilized to their fullest capacity. The basements were eagerly utilized for additional living space by families that could afford the time to finish off and wire the basement themselves. Yet because of the unavailability of studio beds, few were able to have multiple use of the bedrooms, and most living activity was crowded into the living room.

Synomorph Problems

The basement was the most frequently mentioned item in the housing questionnaire. Most residents wanted the basement finished off to add to their living space. They also expressed a need for more electrical outlets and more dry storage space. The boiler in the middle apartment basement of each building

Figure 7-13
A back door becomes crowded with coats, boots, and garbage. Photograph by Burgess Ledbetter.

was also a source of complaint. Most of these apartments are noticeably hotter. The boiler cuts into the usable space in the basement, and noise and vibration are another source of complaints.

Outdoor storage was considered a problem by some (10 percent) because regulations do not permit storage of snowmobiles, motorcycles, or similar equipment indoors. The general security of any items left outdoors is poor.

Some respondents (25 percent) indicated satisfaction with the living room. However, some problems were noted because of the traffic pattern, and the

Figure 7-14
Front yards were unused and given over to dogs. Photograph by Burgess Ledbetter; courtesy of CRREL.

use of the desk and phone in the living room caused some difficulty. Some residents moved the desk to the basement.

The dining room was not mentioned by residents, but the counter separating the kitchen and dining room drew praise from the residents who had them (figure 7-15).

The kitchen drew comments from 35 percent of the residents, who said they needed more electrical outlets and more shelf space. Some residents, to satisfy the need for shelf space, had built shelving into the broom closet in the kitchen.

A second bathroom was needed by 37.5 percent of the residents. This was directly tied to the size of the family since childless couples did not mention it.

Acoustics in bedrooms was the only complaint about this part of the house. Since the wall facing the next apartment was so permeable to sound, residents avoided placing their beds against this wall, severely restricting the furniture arrangements.

Validity of Results

Twenty-seven senior occupants* were also interviewed, and the results of these interviews are gener-

*Senior occupants were residents who had higher rank and longer service records than the other residents in the building.

ally comparable with the random sample. Table 7-3 lists a comparison of the two groups with each other on selected variables. In addition, it compares the results on the questionnaires with the answers of the habitability project observer who lived in family housing for eleven months. As can be seen from the results, the observer's experiences in working, cleaning, cooking, and dressing were comparable to the random sample and the senior occupants. His rating of Fort Wainwright was much lower, however.

CONCLUSIONS AND RECOMMENDATIONS

Three strategies were adopted to apply the conclusions to family housing. First is a minimal remodeling strategy. Assuming funds are scarce, there is a plan for expending at minimal cost in order to improve the family housing environment and make it more suitable to human needs. The second strategy is one of maximum remodeling. Short of tearing the buildings down and building new, this strategy proposes how they can be rehabilitated for long-term future use. The third strategy deals with design of new construction.

Figure 7-15
Formica counter separating the kitchen from the dining area drew praise from residents. Photograph by Burgess Ledbetter; courtesy of CRREL.

TABLE 7–3
Differences Between Senior Occupants, Random Sample, and Observer,
Fort Wainwright Housing Survey, June, 1974

Question	Senior N = 27	Random N = 40	Observer N = 1
Rank	2.85	2.70	2.00
Occurrences (days)	340.37	308.8	298.00
Length of stay (months)	20.81	17.33	11.00
Child visitors (hours)	496.24	598.06	126.00
Adult visitors (hours)	425.93	695.90	320.00
Husband hours	4553.89	4580.48	4548.00
Wife hours	7064.96	6380.50	6195.00
Cleaning hours (per week)	13.15	13.17	14.00
Government regulations (per week)	2.67	2.49	1.00
Cooking (per week)	20.44	19.58	28.00
Dressing (winter)	32.78	40.66	30.00
Dressing (summer)	12.29	20.58	15.00
Rating of Fort Wainwright	4.06	3.87	6.00

Minimal Remodeling

1. First priority is finishing off the basement in family housing. This includes waterproofing some foundations from the inside, insulating the walls, putting up new surfaces, and installing electrical outlets in the wall, an acoustical ceiling, and a resilient floor surface. Finishing off the basement will increase the living space for families and permit either play space for children kept indoors during the long winters, a possible fourth bedroom, or a study area, or parts of all of these.

2. Second priority is to provide paint for the wall surfaces of the apartment. Many residents complained of the colors or the condition of the wall surfaces, and 32.5 percent expressed a desire to have them painted. The residents should be able to choose the paint and do the work themselves.

3. Third priority is increasing the number of electrical outlets in the kitchen.

4. Next priority is the setting up of fences in the yards. A majority of residents supported this, several very strongly.

5. An outside storage shed for various kinds of equipment would alleviate much of the pressure for storing inside the house.

6. A paved or brick patio should be laid in either the front yard or backyard. In single row houses, the patio would be in the backyard while in the housing courts the patio would be in the front yard.

Major Remodeling (Figure 7–16)

1. Adding more space to the back of the house is first priority. This would incorporate a second bathroom, a storage closet, and a combination arctic entrance-mudroom.

2. The living room should be extended over the front porch, and the porch should be extended with an overhead cover out into the yard.

3. The traffic pattern should be rearranged so that traffic goes through the new rear entrance to the side of the living room under the old stairs.

The new wing in the back and the new front extension, while reducing yard space, would increase the indoor living space considerably and add to privacy in the yards, both critical issues with residents.

4. Parking lot size should be increased by bringing curbs closer to the rear entrance.

5. A roof structure or carport should cover the cars to assist in keeping snow off the car.

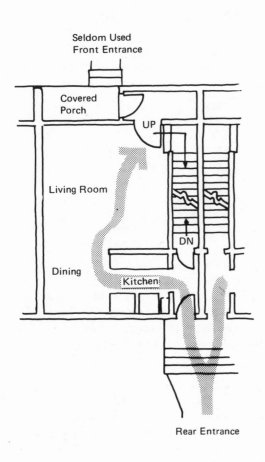

Present Configuration

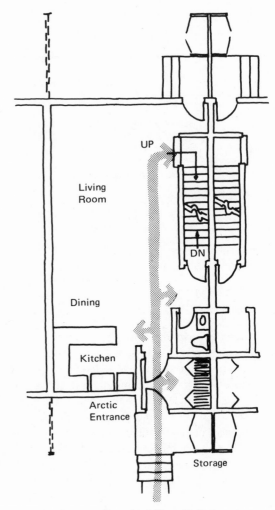

Proposed Remodeling

Figure 7-16
Major remodeling of family housing.

6. All new houses should include a finished basement with the same features as provided under minimal remodeling.

7. A second bathroom should be added, preferably in the new wing but possibly in the basement. This

could be a half-bath rather than a full bathroom.

8. Children's furniture needs to be available for selection by residents. The current GSA furniture is only for adults and is inadequate. This should include the option of studio beds for children's rooms so that

the bedroom space could also serve as a play room. Smaller dressers for children would satisfy storage requirements and increase space in bedrooms.

New Construction (Figures 7-17 and 7-18)

1. The family houses should preferably be duplexes (or triplexes) on the cul-de-sac site plan.
2. Three-floor houses as opposed to ranch type are more economical in cold regions because of the decreased amount of foundations and roofs.
3. New housing should provide a garage to protect cars from the ravages of winter.
4. Fenced-in yards should be provided uniformly.
5. Outside patios should be installed. Nearly all residents are currently having to barbecue on the steps.

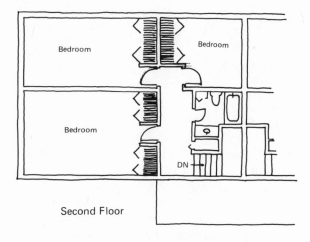

Second Floor

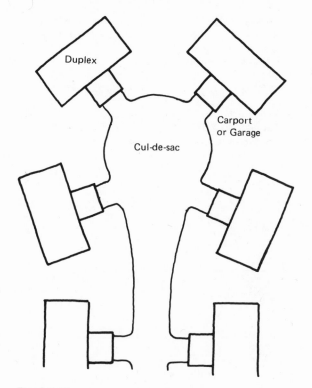

Figure 7-17
Duplexes on cul-de-sac street arrangement.

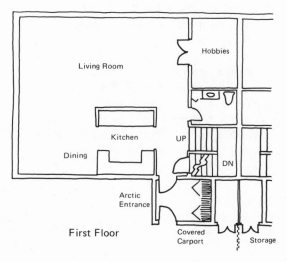

First Floor

Figure 7-18
New construction design suggested for family housing.

6. Previous problems would be eliminated by having one and a half bathrooms (and possibly one in the basement), a mudroom, outside storage, a better defined dining area, and a sewing or hobby space adjoining the rear living area.
7. A humidifier should be provided in the living room and bedrooms.

8. Floors in the living room and bedrooms should have wall-to-wall carpeting, largely for acoustical purposes.

9. Children's furniture and studio beds should be available.

FINAL COMMENTS

The interview method is a radical departure from previous ecological studies not only on the basis of being an interview procedure but also on the fact that this was the first ecological psychology study of behavior inside the house. Families in houses were never considered in any of the previous studies mentioned. What, then, has been learned from this first ecological study of families?

First, the behavior of families in the home is greatly affected by the behavioral resources available in the community as a whole. FAA families in one location (Kotzebue) go outside the home for a great many of their recreational, religious, and other activities while more isolated families do not.

Second, as the size of the surrounding community increases, the tendency seems to be to seek more entertainments in the home. Whether this is true of nonisolated communities outside of Alaska remains to be seen.

Third, the inadequacy of house design is evident from just a few of the observations and questionnaire items. Obviously the designs did not take behavior into account but seemed to function on a traditional concept of what is needed in a house.

Fourth, many alterations can be made to modify house design that are not prohibitively expensive but that go far toward increasing comfort and habitability.

And, finally, the behavior-setting dimensions seem stable enough so that even relatively small samples such as this one can yield conclusive information about designing a better environment.

REFERENCES

Barker, Roger. "Ecology and Motivation." In Marshall Jones, ed., *Nebraska Symposium on Motivation.* University of Nebraska Press, 1960, pp. 1–49.

——. *Ecological Psychology.* Stanford University Press, 1968.

Barker, Roger, and Wright, Herbert. *Midwest and Its Children.* Row, Peterson, 1955.

Cantril, Hadley. *The Pattern of Human Concerns.* Rutgers University Press, 1965.

Kish, L. *Survey Sampling.* Wiley and Sons, 1965.

8

The Analysis of Behavior-Setting Data

General Purpose

The analysis of behavior-setting data provides a tool for the solution of many environment-behavior problems. But while much of the analysis depends on the direction needed to solve certain problems, the researcher must never lose sight of the fact that the behavior-setting survey is designed to uncover problems not considered in the early formulation of a study. Therefore, it is useful to adopt a standard procedure of analysis and then examine all the data results systematically to ensure that no aspect has been overlooked. While it is true that this often results in data not useful in terms of immediate criteria, in the long run the researcher is accumulating comparative data for future studies. Even the most unremarkable action pattern scores can be of value when used in comparison with other environments.

The action pattern profile of the barracks at Fort Wainwright, Alaska, for example, presents a uniform picture of 100 percent present scores for each action pattern (figure 8-1). Looking at the profile by itself, one might conclude that it tells practically nothing about the quality of life in the barracks. Yet, when compared to family housing at the same location (figure 8-2) or to community life in Midwest (figure 8-3), it becomes clear that barracks life has one of the most lackluster profiles of an environment ever collected. The usefulness of behavior-setting data accumulates as more environments are investigated.

Occupancy Time

Occupancy time is the most basic kind of information collected about a setting. If possible, all the persons present in a setting over the period of a year are multiplied times the number of hours each one was present in the setting. However, in many cases

137

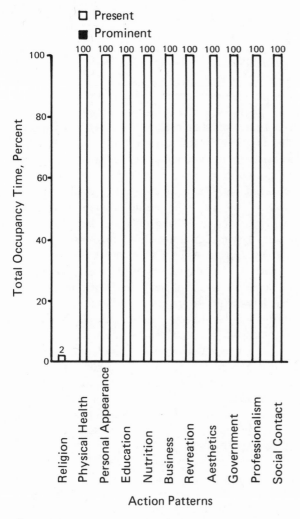

Figure 8-1
Action patterns for men's barracks at Fort Wainwright.

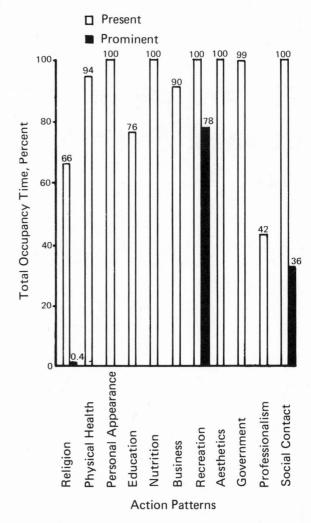

Figure 8-2
Action patterns for family housing at Fort Wainwright.

exact figures are not available, and the average attendance is often multiplied times the number of hours.

Some researchers may be inclined to believe that total occupancy time for an environment will equal all the waking hours for all the people in the environment. Theoretically, however, it should equal *more* because occupancy times overlap. For example, in tabulating the occupancy time of a delivery man, he is counted both as a visitor to each setting where he

makes a delivery and for all deliveries as part of his own setting. Thus, the total of all occupancy times in all settings should come out to more than the waking periods of all persons in the environment.

In practice, it is not known whether occupancy time will come out to equal waking hours because all of Barker's previous studies considered only public settings and did not cover the behavior in homes. Also, even though Bechtel and Ledbetter (1976) did

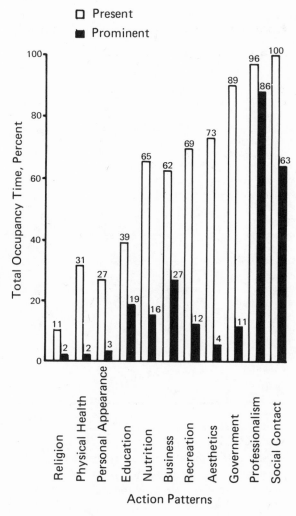

Figure 8-3
Action patterns for Midwest.

study homes, all of the occupancy times of the entire community were not calculated. Occupancy time is the base figure on which all other scales can be rated in terms of a percentage.

Number, Occurrence, and Duration

Number, occurrence, and duration are three calculations made from behavior-setting data in order

to calculate the ecological resource index, which is an average of these three figures.

Number is the number of behavior settings in a particular environment. Action patterns, behavior mechanisms, and even penetration levels and autonomy can be measured in terms of the percentage of behavior settings in which a certain score occurs. For example, aesthetics could be scored 5 in 10 percent of all the settings, or 12 percent of all settings could have an autonomy score of 9.

Occurrence is the number of days in the year in which a setting occurs regardless of how long the setting lasts during the day. The maximum number is 366 in a leap year and 365 in an ordinary year. To calculate the percentage of occurrence for any scale, the number of settings in which the score occurs is added for a subtotal amount of occurrence in those settings. Then this subtotal is divided by the grand total of occurrences to obtain a percentage.

Duration is the total number of hours a setting lasts during a year. In an ordinary year this could not be more than 8,760 hours if the setting functioned all 365 days without stopping. Percentage of duration is calculated the same way as occurrence, by adding the duration amounts for every setting with a given score on the scale in question and dividing this sum by the total duration.

When the number, occurrence, and duration are calculated for each of the scales desired, then the average percentage of all three becomes the ERI. According to Barker (1968), the ERI is a fair estimate of the availability of a particular behavior to the inhabitants of an environment. As such, the availability is a resource for people to take advantage of as they choose. The ERI is usually calculated for each setting, with the total of all settings in an environment equal to 100 percent.

At this point it should be noted that number, occurrence, and duration are different bases of calculations from total occupancy time (OT). For example, calculations based on number, occurrence, and duration can be very different from calculations based on OT. Figures 5-6 (page 80) and 5-11 (page 89) show profiles for action patterns for the same environments (East Side, West Side, and Midwest) using number, occurrence, duration (figure 5-6), and occupancy time (figure 5-11).

The advantage of using OT as a basis is that it is a better measure of the total behavioral environment when families are being measured. Number may be misleading if there are a large number of settings with few people and short duration. Occurrence may be misleading for a large number of settings meeting only a short time each day, and duration may be misleading when there are large numbers of people in the settings. Thus, OT provides the best basis for judging how pervasive a certain action or behavior is throughout the family environment.

Of course, for certain reasons, one also wants to know number, occurrence, and duration. For example, a certain behavior may be present in all settings but account for little OT.

Action Patterns and Behavior Mechanisms

Action pattern and behavior mechanism rating scales are, according to Barker (1968), not especially reliable and in some cases have not been obtained. However, this is not a limitation in the usual analysis of these data since they are usually scored as either present (any score of 1 or above) or prominent (any score of 6 or above). An example of how this scoring increases reliability is illustrated in table 8-1, which shows the raw scores obtained by two researchers, Bechtel and Ledbetter, after rating the supervisor's office behavior setting at the FAA station in Murphy Dome, Alaska. The reliability of these scores can be calculated in several ways. First, looking strictly at only the scores on which the two observers agree exactly, the agreement is only 40 percent. Another more generous way to calculate reliability is to consider in agreement all those scores that are only plus or minus one point away from each other. In that case, agreement is up to 80 percent. The Spearman correlation coefficient is 0.61. However, by Barker's usual method of scoring either present or prominent, agreement would be 100 percent since all scores are

TABLE 8-1

Reliability on Supervisor's Office, Action Pattern Ratings Murphy Dome, FAA

| | Observers | | |
	Bechtel	Ledbetter	Differences
Aesthetics	4	4	
Business	4	3	−1
Professionalism	4	2	−2
Education	4	2	−2
Government	4	3	−1
Nutrition	4	4	
Personal appearance	4	3	−1
Philanthropy	4	4	
Physical health	4	4	
Recreation	4	3	−1
Religion	4	4	
Social contact	4	3	−1
Affect	4	4	
Gross motor	3	2	−1
Manipulation	3	1	−2
Talking	3	2	−1
Thinking	3	2	−1
Pressure	2	2	
Welfare	2	2	
Autonomy	4	2	−2
Total	72	56	

present and none are prominent. For this reason, the researchers feel there is reason to believe that the reliability is high enough to meet scientific standards. There is no known example in the literature of where these scores have been used in any way other than present or prominent.

One example does not provide final evidence, however, and more data need to be collected.

General Richness Index

There arises a problem in calculating the general richness index (GRI) with each environment, and that comes in constructing the occupancy time matrix for the symbol represented in the formula as cOT. This symbol stands for the code number of the OT of the particular setting being measured. This code number is provided for the environment of Midwest by Barker (1968) in his appendix I. For each new environment studied, a new matrix and code list must be calculated. However, for quick comparisons, Barker's appendix could be used provided the OT range does not exceed that of his table too drastically.

Penetration Levels

Penetration levels are calculated with fair reliability even in raw scores but often the data are used by separating performers, who score from 4 to 6, from nonperformers, who score from 1 to 3. A handy way to tell whether a setting or an environment has a high or low ratio of leadership is to calculate the performer-population ratio, which tells what percent of the population of a setting are leaders. These data are useful for assessing a rough estimate of undermanning. For example, in the three aircraft control and warning stations studied (average population 252) by Bechtel and Ledbetter (1975), it was found that the performer-population ratio of the stations was 0.65, or that 65 percent of the population of the average setting were leaders. By contrast, at the larger post of Fort Wainwright (population 7,500), the performer-population ratio was 0.45, thus tending to confirm that larger organizations provide fewer leadership opportunities. Some caution must be injected, however, because the same limitations in calculating are inherent without taking occupancy time into account. Essentially this is a calculation based only on number of settings.

LIMITATIONS OF BEHAVIOR–SETTING DATA

Designation of Cytosettings and Synomorphs

In terms of data needed for the design professions, perhaps the most serious limitation of the behavior-setting survey is the lack of formal analysis below the level of the behavior setting. Though Barker mentions cytosettings and synomorphs, there is no formal way to collect data comparable to that which is done for the whole setting. For this reason, it is essential for the researcher to observe each setting carefully, take photographs, and question inhabitants so that the use of every object and physical aspect of the setting is understood. It is useful to list cytosettings and synomorphs though these may be too numerous in some cases.

The cytosettings are the major divisions of the setting program. In a church service, they are the choir processional, the hymns, the reading of scripture, the sermon, announcements, collection, and the recessional. Each cytosetting has a different function yet is part of the whole setting in that the same people take part using the same location.

Synomorphs are even finer divisions. They are single behavioral events like sitting in the pews, using the kneeling boards, walking in the aisles, and other single events that involve one behavior and its necessary physical object.

Every setting can be analyzed in terms of the cytosettings and the synomorphs, Other methods of research such as human engineering or time-motion studies have been working with cytosettings and synomorphs for some time, yet these have not yet been done with the organizing perspective that the whole setting gives.

At the present stage, then, the researcher is left on his own as to how to go about studying below the setting level. The author suggests organizing observations by the use of the K-21 scale for a beginning. This permits arranging the objects and behaviors in any setting into their order of importance in determining the identity of the setting and locating its boundary problems.

The Inadequacy of Action Patterns and Behavior Mechanisms

Any researcher in the field of behavior settings sooner or later comes to realize that certain types of behavior are missed by being classified into the eleven action patterns and five behavior mechanisms. The behavior mechanisms are especially faulty. Affective behavior does not differentiate laughing from crying. Gross motor behavior does not differentiate walking from carrying. Manipulative behavior does not differentiate typing from working radar screens. And talking does not differentiate announcing over the radio from conversing with one's friends. Yet, to differentiate these categories further confronts one with the overwhelming dilemma of cataloging all of observable human behavior or even, as Phillip Thiel (1970) is attempting, of cataloging all human experiences in an environment. Clearly, greater differentiation is needed, but the task of attempting new categories cannot be taken lightly.

Autonomy

Autonomy is perhaps the easiest of the rating scales to change because its concept remains very much the same, only extended to lower levels. Autonomy is inadequate in current use because it refers to an entire community rather than a setting. Thus, if the decisions in any setting are made in the community of which that setting is a part, then the setting is rated 9, the highest level. Yet this is inadequate because the setting itself may not be autonomous but have all its decisions made outside the setting. Therefore, as currently used, the autonomy rating does not measure levels of autonomy within a community as well as it could.

It is proposed that the scale be extended to twelve levels as follows:

12 with the setting entirely
10 within the same genotype
9 within the immediate community
7 within the school district
5 within the county
3 within the state
1 within the nation.

Level 5, within the county, proved inadequate for the Alaskan study (Bechtel and Ledbetter, 1976) because Alaska does not have counties. No recordings were made for that level but, of course, some averages could equal 5. It becomes apparent with time that the behavior-setting methodology must be adapted with use in order to ensure its becoming more universal and at the same time more specific for the needs of the designer.

REFERENCES

Barker, Roger. *Ecological Psychology.* Stanford University Press, 1968.

Bechtel, Robert B., and Ledbetter, C. Burgess. "The Temporary Environment." Final report of the Cold Regions Habitability Research Contract No. DAAG17-73-C-0104, U.S. Army Cold Regions Research and Engineering Laboratory, Hanover, New Hampshire, October, 1976.

Thiel, Phillip. "Notes on the Description, Scaling, Notation, and Scoring of Some Perceptual and Cognitive Attributes of Physical Environment." In H. Proshansky, W. Ittelson, and L. Rivlin, *Environmental Psychology.* Holt, Rinehart and Winston, 1970, pp. 593–618.

9

Behavioral Focal Points: A Schema for Community Design

One of the concepts Barker and Wright mentioned in their 1955 study of a small town of 750 was "core setting." The core setting was not fully defined and was later dropped in the 1968 book (Barker, 1968).

Barker and Wright mapped the behavior settings of Midwest by using the core setting as the central point around which to arrange all other settings in the community. But the core setting has much more than a mapping function. In the live community of Midwest, it is the setting accessible to the largest number of the fourteen population subgroups. In other words, it is the one place in the community most accessible to young and old, male and female, all social classes and races.

In an observational sense, the core setting is really the behavioral focal point of the community. It is the spot from which one can observe the greatest variety and number of community inhabitants, and it is also the place where most of the community gossip can be heard. It is the place where an inhabitant can go to learn what is new. People are attracted to the focal point because "that's where the action is." One can be in touch with a greater number of events here than in any setting.

It is not possible to understand the full significance of a focal point, however, until one compares the focal point of Midwest with those of other communities. Figure 9-1 shows the Barker and Wright (1955) map with Clifford's Drug Store as the focal point of Midwest. Figure 9-2 shows the focal point and behavior settings of the community in Project Arrowhead. The steps of Friendly Inn are the focal point. Each base map has the focal point surrounded by the remainder of the behavior settings in the community. The size of the circle for each setting is determined by the GRI of the setting. The distance from the focal point is determined by the dependence of that setting on the focal point, and the settings are clustered together according to their common membership in a genotype.

It can be seen from figure 9-2 that although the porch of Friendly Inn serves the definition of the focal point as being the place most accessible to

Figure 9-1
Base map of behavior settings of Midwest. Reprinted from Barker and Wright, 1955, p. 143; by permission of Roger Barker and Herbert Wright.

Each setting is represented by a circle whose diameter is proportional to the general richness index of the setting. The distance of each setting—Clifford's Drug Store at the center of the diagram—is proportional to its independence (K-value) from that setting. The position of each setting is proximate to other settings belonging to the same variety.

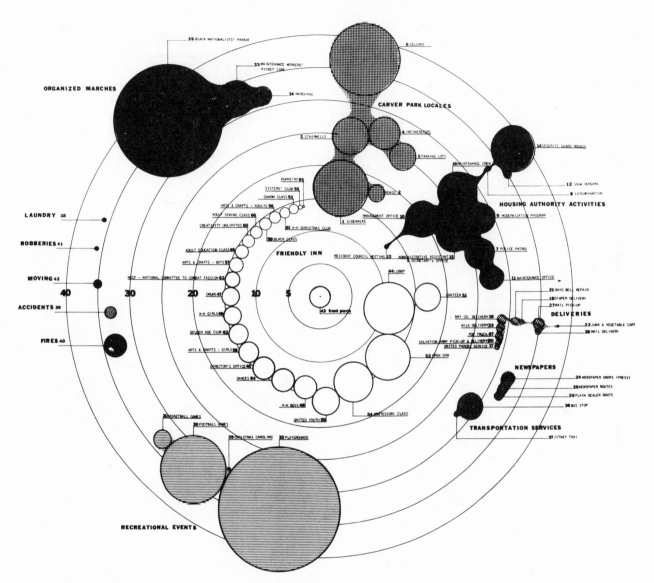

Figure 9–2
Base map of behavior settings of Arrowhead. Courtesy of ERDF.

the greatest variety of ages, sexes, and races, it turns out to be among the lowest in richness. Many other settings, both near and far on the dependency measure, are much richer. The consequence is not to reconstruct the map around the richest setting arbitrarily but to recognize that the focal point that lacks richness diagnoses a community that has not utilized its focal point to the fullest extent possible.

Arrowhead, according to other data and community opinions, is a fragmented community. This conclusion is further reinforced by the fact that the varieties of settings are not closely related. Recreational events are not related to the marches (the two richest settings) and are completely independent of the focal point. The other settings also arrange themselves into a fragmented community picture.

By inference from these two examples, one can derive maps to illustrate the ideal integrated and the ideal fragmented community as in figure 9–3. Ideally the focal point is the richest setting with the next richest circle of settings adjacent and dependent, and their satellite settings adjacent to them, each succeeding circle to the outside of the diagram being less rich and less dependent on the focal point.

Returning to the Barker and Wright diagram in figure 9–1, it can be seen that the focal point in Midwest is also not the richest behavior setting in the community but it is among the richest. Thus, even in the Midwest community there is room to progress toward the ideal in use of the focal point.

Of course, this ideal community is unimodal, and it is possible to conceive of communities that are bimodal or trimodal with one focal point. However, at some point one arrives at the situation pictured on the lower part of figure 9–3, which is the fragmented community with a small or entirely lacking central focal point and which approaches the condition more or less represented by the community of Arrowhead.

The mapping of community behavior-setting data by the three criteria of richness, dependence, and variety can be a useful diagnostic tool. The designer can decide from the beginning which type of community he wants to create.

Some of the uses of focal points as design concepts are illustrated from the Cold Regions Habitability Study. Figure 9–4 shows the dispersed site of a typical aircraft control and warning station (AC&W) in Alaska. These buildings, constructed in the 1950s, were connected by a series of long, narrow corridors called "tunnels" even though they were above ground and had windows. Such a site prevents focal points from developing.

One commander, sensing that there was no natural

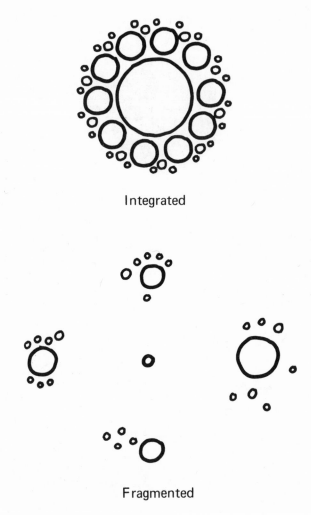

Integrated

Fragmented

Figure 9–3
Ideal types of communities.

central gathering place in which informal contact could be made (and, hence, informal business done), made a point of going to the various gathering places on the site such as the NCO club, the enlisted men's dining room, and other areas to chat with the men and casually suggest certain kinds of work be done. Another commander, not recognizing the limitations of the site, did not seek out these isolated

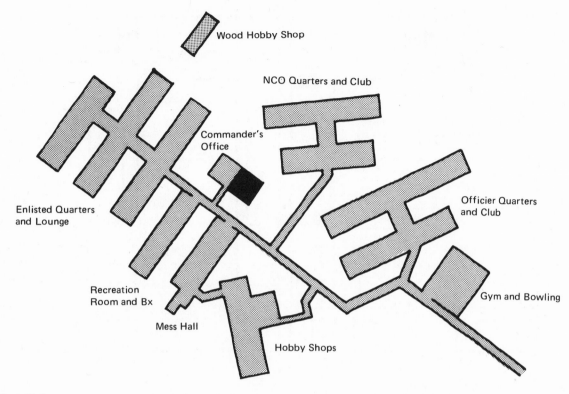

Figure 9-4
Tunnel system of dispersed station. Adapted from Ledbetter, 1974, p. 4; courtesy
of CRREL.

gathering places and became isolated. The informal
contact, and hence the informal business, was lost,
and it required an increasing use of formal channels
and paperwork to get even less work accomplished.
Shortly, a morale problem developed. Yet the second
commander was behaving only according to standard
procedures.

The presence of a focal point for this site would
not guarantee that informal business would be conducted or that morale would improve, but it would
provide the increased opportunity of informal contact
and a greater chance for an informal system to
develop.

A good illustration of a focal point occurs in the
design "accident" at Cape Lisburne, the most north-

erly of the AC&W stations in Alaska. Figure 9-5
shows a light well designed at the center of a composite building on the base. Figure 9-6a shows an
overall view of the base with the composite building
on the right side of the figure. The light well and the
behavior of the mean as a response to its design were
studied intensively for a few days by a team of three
observers. The results of this study follow.

When the building was originally designed, the
architect intended to have a totem pole in the center
and a bench along the wall with bright lights illumi-
nating the space from the second floor ceiling. It was
conceived as a relatively static space. Somehow, the
totem pole and bench never got in place, and the lights,
partly because of energy conservation and partly

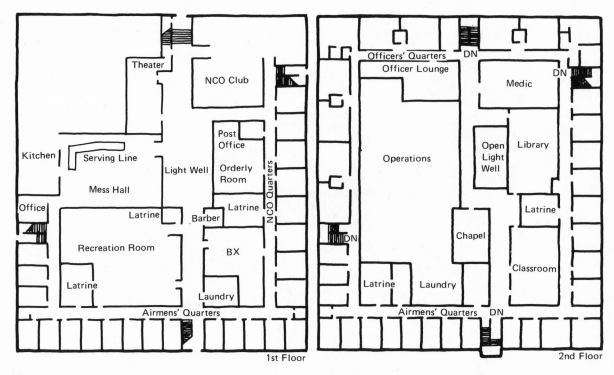

Figure 9-5
Cape Lisburne AC&W station floor plans. Reprinted from Bechtel and Ledbetter, 1975, p. 54; courtesy of CRREL.

because they would be so difficult to replace when they burned out, were turned off by maintenance personnel. Instead of following the original design purposes, the men took over the space as their own, buying large vinyl-covered lounge chairs to place around the center. A fireplace was added to the wall, and a bearskin rug hung over it. In short, it became a lounge room with three sides open to traffic around the light well.

But much more began to occur than just lounging and watching the crowd. Because the recreation room (see figure 9-5 for location) was already crowded, a "fooshball" game was moved into the southwest corner of the space. A scale for weighing was placed next to the dining room entrance, and a mailbox was al-

ready present just inside the south entrance of the light well.

In conjunction with these unplanned changes, the original design purpose also had a powerful influence on behavior in the light well. The light well was designed as the main axis of all pedestrian traffic. In this regard, the light well, as a behavioral focal point, had much in common with the focal point of Barker's small town, which was located at the juncture of the main north-south traffic arteries.

There is an important difference between the light well as a behavioral focal point and Barker's drugstore, however. All the traffic in the light well is pedestrian, and it goes *through* the physical area of the light well rather than past it on an outside street. Thus, all of

Figure 9-6a
Cape Lisburne Station.

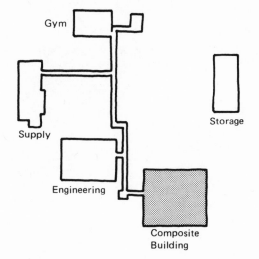

Figure 9-6b
Plan of Cape Lisburne.

the pedestrians have a chance to interact with each other and the occupants of the light well. But there would have been no occupants in the light well had it not been for the placement of chairs there. Thus, the men created their own focal point. Figure 9-7 shows the light well area with men seated in the chair area at right. Others stand in the lunch line at

Figure 9-7
Light-well area. Photograph by Burgess Ledbetter; courtesy of CRREL.

center and play at left. The way the behavioral focal point of the chairs functions in the whole community is shown by the diagram in figure 9-8.

Notice that figure 9-8 shows a heavy cluster of settings around the focal point in contrast to Midwest (figure 9-1) and Arrowhead (figure 9-2), which have focal points relatively isolated. It would seem that Cape Lisburne approached the ideal integrated community as depicted in figure 9-3 more nearly than either Midwest or Arrowhead. The focal point has many settings closely associated with it, and some of these are fairly rich. And, those richer settings in food services are physically near to the focal point even though not dependent on it.

The focal point diagrams can be compared with the physical layouts of the communities mentioned. Figure 9-9 shows an aerial view of Midwest, and figure 9-10 shows a plan of Arrowhead. Notice that both physically and in the diagrams, the focal points tend to be centrally located. This means only that focal points should be equally accessible to all persons in the community, and the best way to accomplish this is by a central location that takes a minimal amount of travel and effort to reach it. The first principle, then, of designing focal points is to locate them centrally.

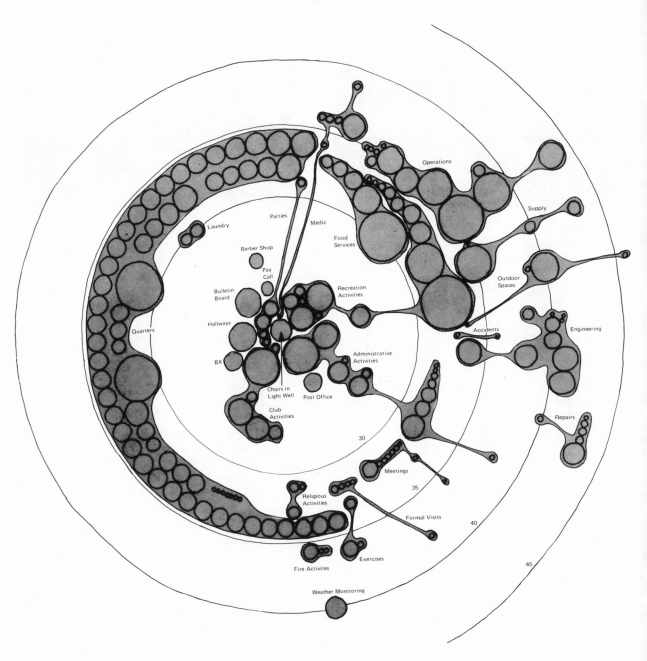

Figure 9-8
Base map of behavior settings of Cape Lisburne AC&W station.

Figure 9-9
Aerial view of Midwest. Arrow points to behavioral focal point, Clifford's Drug Store. Courtesy of Roger Barker.

The second principle is to make the focal point a crossroads of traffic by locating necessary and well-attended functions near it. This traffic should come in closest possible contact with the focal point. The physical layouts of each community show that traffic from essential activities flows by the focal points. In Midwest, the focal point is next to the county courthouse on the main street of the town and with banks, grocery, and hardware stores nearby. In Arrowhead,

the focal point is on the only street through the project. People going to the housing office or Friendly Inn must pass by, and all walkways go past it. At Cape Lisburne, no one goes to meals, the BX, hobby shop, commander's office, or movies or sees the bulletin board without going past the focal point.

The third principle is to make the focal point as rich as possible without requiring a social commitment. This means the focal point should have no

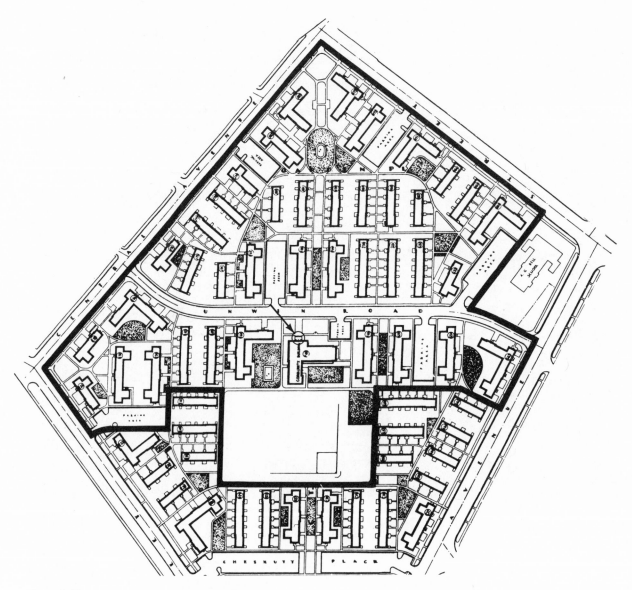

Figure 9–10
Physical plan of Arrowhead. Arrow points to behavioral focal point, the steps of the Friendly Inn. Courtesy of ERDF.

important ongoing activity of its own. People come without a social commitment to see or do anything in a formal sense. They can come just to gossip or to sit and do nothing. They can look in to see if there is anyone they know present and, if not, leave. The focal point can have facilities for serving food or coffee, but sometimes even this is a distraction.

The fourth principle is to make the focal point with as few visual boundaries as possible. One of the most important motives of a focal point is to make it easy for people to see and be seen by others. This is not accomplished by solid walls. The focal point should be open on at least three sides. One of the reasons why the drugstore at Midwest is not more successful is that it is enclosed within walls and thus requires some kind of social commitment to enter.

A fifth principle of focal points is that there must be places where a number of people can be seated. One of the reasons why Arrowhead's focal point is so poor is that it does not have facilities for anyone to sit down. People will sit on the steps but they are uncomfortable and sitting there obstructs others from coming and going. By having a deliberate seating arrangement, people can be exposed to the traffic flow without obstructing it.

Once these principles have been incorporated into the focal point design, then the remainder of the community can be designed much like the bubble diagram, with other facilities and transportation radiating out from it.

REFERENCES

Barker, R. *Ecological Psychology.* Stanford University Press, 1968.

Barker, R., and Wright H. *Midwest and Its Children.* Row, Peterson, 1955.

Bechtel, Robert B., and Ledbetter, C. Burgess. "The Temporary Environment." Final report of the Cold Regions Habitability Research Contract No. DAAG17-73-C-0104, U.S. Army Cold Regions Research and Engineering Laboratory, Hanover, New Hampshire, October, 1976.

Ledbetter, C. Burgess. "Undermanning and Architectural Accessibility." U.S. Army Cold Regions Research and Engineering Laboratory, Hanover, New Hampshire, Special Report 213, October 1974.

10

A Theory
of Human Scale

At several places in this book, undermanning theory has been mentioned. This chapter will attempt to summarize the research related to this theory and to show its general application to design. Undermanning would perhaps be better termed a theory of human scale because its central proposition is that human organizations need to be of a certain scale in order to derive positive benefits from the environment. Once that scale is exceeded, not only do the benefits correspondingly decrease, but pressures begin to build from the environment that are detrimental to the function of any organization. The design for a building that will enclose any organization needs to take advantage of these beneficial environmental forces and to attempt to control the detrimental effects.

UNDERMANNING THEORY

It was in the 1960 Nebraska symposium on motivation that Roger Barker first proposed his theory of undermanning (Barker, 1960). As a result of comparisons between a small town in England and a similar but smaller town in Kansas, he noticed profound differences in behavior that could be related to the size of behavior settings.

The Surroundings

In the 1960 paper, Barker describes three main consequences and eleven secondary consequences of people who are placed in small settings:

(1) There is a greater claim that a smaller setting makes on each person.
   a. He has to work harder.
   b. He has to do greater and more important work.

(2) In a smaller setting, because there are fewer numbers, there are more and wider forces acting on each person to produce:

a. A wider variety of activities
b. Less sensitivity to and less need to evaluate differences between people
c. A lower level of maximum performance.

(3) Because the wider range of forces act together, their joint influence will produce:
a. Greater importance for each person in the setting
b. More responsibility for each person in the setting
c. Greater self-identity for each person in the setting
d. Lower standards and fewer tests for admission to the setting
e. Greater insecurity
f. More frequent occurrences of success or failure.

First, since a smaller setting must do the same work as a larger setting, each person in the smaller setting has to work harder, and the important work is shared among fewer people. Therefore, each person in the smaller setting takes on a larger and more important work load.

Second, since the behavior program of each setting requires that certain work be done, the obligations, the pressure to perform, and all of the psychological forces in a setting are increased for each individual as the number of individuals gets fewer. This results in each person's getting a wider variety of activities. The number of activities remains the same for a setting, but as people get fewer, each person has to take up more activities. And, with a bigger activity load, each person will have less time to worry about his differences with others. He simply becomes less sensitive because he is busier. Also, as a consequence of this busyness, the maximum level of performance will suffer. The quality of work of a busy craftsman is not as high as the quality of work of an unhurried craftsman. There is less time to take care.

Third, because these forces to perform are stronger and have a wider base for each person in the setting, the individual acquires new importance. Small settings value each member more because each member is more necessary to the continuance of the setting. A small club is more hurt by one member's dropping out than a large club. But more importance and more things to do also mean more responsibility. Each person has a larger stake in the setting and is counted on more by the others. Consequently, these elements of importance and responsibility make the individual feel he has greater worth and self-identity. He has more value as a person, and others in the setting will communicate this to him. They will show they miss him if he does not show up for work.

These pressures on people in the small setting make them more eager to accept new members. A new member will help take the load off them. Accordingly, members of a small setting will be less strict about membership requirements. The large setting members will try to keep others out. They are already overloaded.

Perhaps a negative consequence of the small setting is a greater insecurity. With smaller numbers, it seems as though the work never gets done. Everyone must constantly make an effort, and this is likely to create insecurity. Curiously, this negative aspect of undermanning is neglected in most of the literature but it seems to show up in the extreme undermanning condition Srivastava describes (Srivastava, 1974).

Often in smaller settings people will be forced to do work they are not qualified for, and this may be a source of discomfort and insecurity.

Finally, with everyone working at near peak and with everyone doing more kinds of activities, successes and failures will be more frequent for each person. The result is probably more immediate feedback for each person, and conceivably this could act to increase performance level. This factor may tend to decrease insecurity because with a greater amount of feedback, a person is more aware of how he stands and performs in an organization.

Research on undermanning has generally attempted to prove or disprove each of the above eleven points. Generally, with the exception of the insecurity factor, and perhaps the level of performance, each point has been upheld by some evidence.

The Size

One of the most important aspects of undermanning is that small undermanned settings seem to be a consequence of small organizations and that large overmanned settings are spawned in large organizations. Large towns have relatively fewer but larger settings for their population while small towns have relatively more but smaller settings. Thus, there seems to be some law of the structure of organizations, communities, cities, or any other human enterprise that produces overmanning as a result of bigness and growth and undermanning as a part of the nature of smallness. It is important to keep in mind, however, that it is the influence of the smaller setting that is the critical influence on behavior.

The First Set of Data

There was considerable evidence to support all of Barker's allegations. Considering the forces toward participation, there was evidence to show that as both setting size and size of organization increased, so did an index of lack of participation: absences. In ninety-one factories, absences increased linearly as did the size of the factory (Acton Society Trust, 1953). And in the British coal pits, attendance rates declined with the size of the operation (Acton Society Trust, 1953). At eleven air bases, absence increased with the size of the base (Baumgartel and Sobel, 1959). In the textile industry, absence increased with the size of the room (Hewitt and Parfit, 1953).

But it was from the comparison of the larger English town with the smaller Kansas town that Barker mustered most of his evidence. Although the Kansas town had only half as many people as the English town, it had 1.2 times as many behavior settings. Further, even when one looked at the number of important tasks, there were 1.7 times as many in

the Kansas town as in the English town. On the average, the citizens of the Kansas town acted in leadership roles three times as often as those in the English town. Considering the acceptance of less qualified members into settings, adolescents in the Kansas town had 3.5 times more responsibility than adolescents in the English town.

Thus, it seemed as though Roger Barker had built a case for saying that the population structure of the environment had far-reaching consequences for human behavior.

THE SCHOOL STUDIES

It was in the volume *Big School, Small School* (Barker and Gump, 1964) that undermanning theory received its most comprehensive presentation. Willems (1964a) reviewed the literature up to 1964 that supported undermanning theory. Roger and Louise Barker (1964) showed that number of behavior settings increased much less than population. Gump (1971) claims that while population of schools increased by a factor of 65, number of settings increased only by a factor of 8. Roger Barker and Eleanor Hall (1964) showed that participation in interschool and extracurricular activities was greater for smaller schools. Gump and Friesen (1964) found that large- and small-school students participate in the same *number* of settings but that small-school students participate in a wider variety of extracurricular activities. A larger portion of small-school students hold positions of importance and responsibility, and they hold central positions in a wider variety of school activities than do large-school students.

Gump and Friesen (1964) also catalog more competence satisfactions developing in small-school students than large-school students. Small-school students had more direct responsibility and central authority while large-school students had more vicarious satisfactions. This is because of the more central positions that small-school students tend to hold in activities. Some students in large schools hold these same positions and have the same competence satisfactions, but because relatively less of the population in a large school holds such positions, there is more vicarious satisfaction throughout the total population. Gump (1971) assesses the small-school experience as being one of gaining more general competence.

Willems (1964b) relates how the small school and its smaller settings result in greater forces toward participation in settings. Small-school students felt more responsibility and obligation toward the settings than did large-school students as a result of these forces.

Campbell (1964) studied the effects of school consolidation and demonstrated that students from a small school moving to a larger one would feel a decrease in pressures to participate.

Barker (1964) and Barker and LeCompte (1964) show that participation in a broad range of school and community events is also clearly related to the size of the community. Smaller communities seem to foster greater participation levels.

One of the important concepts Barker and his colleagues dealt with is what they call the "school size illusion" (Barker and Barker, 1964). On the surface, everyone is impressed with the seeming advantages of a larger school. It has many facilities and an impressive array of equipment. But when one objectively compares student performance, the small school requires more of its students in a wider range of extracurricular activities. Barker and Gump (1964) came very close to saying (but do not) that small schools produce more competent people per square foot than do large schools.

Table 10–1 summarizes some of the most critical comparisons between large and small schools.

The clearest message of *Big School, Small School* is "that the negative relationship between institutional size and individual participation is deeply based and difficult, if not impossible to avoid" (Barker and Gump, 1964, p. 201). The implications of this remark cannot be underestimated. It means that as organizations grow larger, individual participation deteriorates. But what is the optimal size of an organization? And can the effects of size be controlled or compensated for by splitting organizations up into small settings? The answers are not yet forthcoming but later research sheds some light—and raises further problems.

THE CITY-TOWN PROJECT

Herbert Wright (1969) set out to explore whether children between six and eleven years raised in a small town tended to have different cognitive experiences from those raised in a large town. He used two techniques to measure what children knew about the community they grew up in. One technique was to ask the child to construct the community out of wooden blocks, naming each structure. Another technique was to ride or walk around the community asking the child to name people and jobs in the fifty houses nearest to him. The results were a further

TABLE 10–1
Comparative Data for Big School and Small School

Variables	Ratio Between Big and Small Schools		
	Big		Small
Number of persons present in extracurricular behavior settings	3	:	1
Number of behavior settings performed by students	1	:	2½
Number of reasons given for participation in behavior settings	1	:	2½
Number of obligation responses given for participation in behavior settings	1	:	6
Number of satisfactions expressed by students	5	:	6

demonstration of undermanning principles. The children from the small community were able to name more elements in the block game than children from the larger town (201 versus 132, total for matched pairs of children). And the small-town children were able to describe twenty jobs of adults living in the neighborhood versus 7.5 for the large-town children. Also, in elements beyond the neighborhood, the small-town children identified 160 versus 112 for the large-town children. Table 10-2 summarizes Wright's critical data.

The inescapable conclusion is that children in the small town know more about these aspects of the environment than do large-town children. Wright proposes two reasons for this. First, small-town children are exposed to fewer elements and thus have more repetition for each element. Repetition being necessary for learning, it is only natural they would learn more. Second, since small-town children participate more deeply in activities (supported by other data), they remember them more.

THE WORK OF ALLAN WICKER AND HIS ASSOCIATES

Following on Barker's undermanning theory directly, Allan Wicker (1968) demonstrated that it

was the experience of being in a performing role in the school setting that was the chief determiner of all the positive undermanning experiences discovered by previous research. In other words, some students in large schools also have these positive experiences because of their leadership positions. This confirms Gump and Friesen's (1964) findings.

Wicker's (1969, 1971) studies of churches support the school studies as being generalizable to churches as well. Members of small churches participated in more kinds of activities, had more leadership positions, spent more time in the activities, attended church more often, and contributed more money.

Looking at assimilation into membership in churches, Wicker and Mehler (1971) found that new members of a small church had greater assimilation. Wicker, McGrath and Armstrong (1972) expanded these findings to wider national and state levels. However, the relationship between member participation and church membership size was linearly, not negatively, accelerated, and *capacity* (in terms of the number of participants who could be accommodated) was as effective as size of church membership in predicting attendance.

The factor of capacity appears here for the first time in the undermanning literature, and its importance cannot be underestimated. Capacity was defined by Wicker et al. (1972) as seating capacity, combined with number of meetings. This definition

TABLE 10-2
Comparative Data for Large and Small Communities

Variables	Large Community	Small Community
Populations	About 33,000	500–1,400
Number of places children get to	53	35
Number of elements presented by children about their town	132	201
Number of elements beyond neighborhoods known by children	112	160
Percentage of children on street without parents (autonomy)	58	87
Percentage of children with low setting penetration, zones 1 and 2 (noninvolvement, lack of initiative and leadership)	31	21.5
Number of neighborhood adult jobs known	7½	20
Setting reentrance rate	2.9	3.6
Mean hours per setting	2.4	3.1

accounted for 69 percent of the attendance measure in one study and 77 percent in another.

The designer is more constrained to feel capacity is a static factor determined by room dimensions. Actually, physical capacity of any room can be increased by increasing the number of times it is used. This is only possible up to a point, however, for there are time limits, such as hours in a day.

Another important aspect of manning is the number of persons attempting to occupy the setting. Even though a setting may have a large capacity, if no one attempts to enter it, it will remain undermanned. Thus, two critical qualifications have been added to the organization size-setting size relationship, as in figure 10-1. Most of the relationships in figure 10-1 are supported by Wicker's data, but it is uncertain as yet what a small organization with small capacity but large population supply would do. Presumably, it would grow and exceed its physical capacity.

Wicker et al. (1972) might not agree with the formulation shown in figure 10-1 because they define the relationships as follows:

undermanning: applicants $<$ maintenance minimum $\leqslant$ capacity

adequate manning: maintenance minimum $\leqslant$ applicants $\leqslant$ capacity

overmanning: maintenance minimum $\leqslant$ capacity $<$ applicants

The maintenance minimum is defined as the number of performers and nonperformers required to keep the setting in operation. Obviously undermanning and overmanning are unstable conditions by this view, and adequate manning is stable (Wicker et al. say quasistable). It is the latter statement that may not be supported in nature. There are several relevant questions: Do organizations and/or settings reach an adequate manning stage and cease growing? Or do they go through all three stages depending on applicants (population supply) and capacity? Or do both of the above apply? Church memberships have been known to exceed and then create new capacities, and they have also been known to decline. There does not seem to be evidence that organizations or settings stop at the adequate manning level unless they have reached the limit of population supply. Perhaps the dynamics of these relationships depend on still other forces yet to be assessed like attraction to the setting or organization by outsiders, or usefulness of the setting to the organization, or support for the setting within the organization. The dynamics of the setting-organization relationships are not yet clear. Further research needs to be done to determine whether certain settings in an organization are more critical than others and how the relationships of settings change with size.

Wicker's work in the laboratory was discussed by Petty (1975). His current work goes beyond the definition of undermanning as originally stated by Barker (1960) and ranges into problems of overmanning and

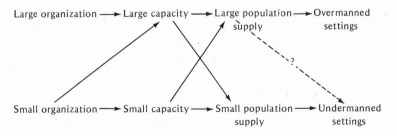

Figure 10-1
Size of organization as related to setting size.

how the concepts of manning may be used to provide a better definition of crowding (Wicker, 1973).

COST AND UNDERMANNING

There is an important area of undermanning not yet touched on by the research of Barker and his colleagues. That is the area of financial cost and undermanning. Most of the research has been couched in terms of how undermanning or overmanning relates to the psychological state of the persons in the setting. The job enrichment literature does deal with financial advantages, but job enrichment arose entirely independently of undermanning theory and seems to deal generally more with the assembly line than the organization as a whole.

The only available figures are concerned with city size. Lamm (1973) presents figures to show that in cities of less then 50,000, education in the United States is provided at $12 per capita, but for cities of 300,000, the figure is double, for cities of half a million double again, and for cities of a million or more, the cost is $85 per capita.

Crime rates seem to follow a similar pattern. In cities less than 10,000, there are 12.8 robberies per 100,000; there are 117.6 robberies per 100,000 for cities over 250,000, and the cost of police protection doubles.

Lamm quotes other figures showing the cost of population increase. A hundredfold increase in population translates into a 1,200 increase in roadways. Public health is twelve times more expensive per capita in cities of over a million than in those of less then 50,000. Welfare costs the citizen of a city of over a million *eighty-eight times* more than in a city of less than 50,000. What are the possible reasons for these cost increases? According to undermanning theory, if people in smaller settings work harder, then people in larger settings and larger organizations do not work so hard. Furthermore, overmanned settings have a much higher personnel cost than undermanned. These two factors alone might account for the differential.

THE PROBLEM OF TASK

In his paper on laboratory studies, Petty (1975) discusses the tasks given to laboratory subjects in order to test their performances within optimally manned and undermanned conditions. He suggests that cognitive as well as motor tasks need to be tested in the future. But this raises the much larger issue of how the task in the setting defines the degree of manning. For example, it is clear that an eight-man baseball team is undermanned. But is a four-man baseball team twice as undermanned as an eight man or, because of relative deficit, three times as undermanned? In short, how does the number of people lacking to do a given task define the degree of undermanning? Undermanning by any of the definitions given above does not permit a measure of how severe or to what degree undermanning occurs in any setting.

Perhaps a more cogent way to pursue the measure of degree is to look at the performance roles within each setting. After all, Wicker (1968) demonstrated that positive experiences usually associated with undermanning accrue from being in a certain leadership role in a setting, not from being without sufficient numbers to get the job done. The importance of being without sufficient numbers is that it forces people into more central roles, and it is the experience of these central roles that is the causal factor in all the positive benefits. The logical consequence to all this is to give every person the most central role possible. This conclusion forces us to the position so popularly spoken of as having "too many chiefs." Or does it? Do the findings of undermanning really point out what so much of industry is already finding (O'Toole et al., 1973)—that we need far fewer supervisors and should give far greater autonomy to workers on the line? The success of such endeavors at the Pet Food plant in Topeka (Walton, 1972) and the Volvo assembly line in Sweden seem to be independent confirmations of this way of thinking.

Yet can anyone really accept this line of reasoning? Should we do away with baseball managers and let the teams manage themselves, or do away with teachers and let pupils manage themselves? No one who is an observer of the current state of our society can deny trends in this direction. What is sorely needed is research that will tell us how far we can go in supplying central roles to members of settings and organizations.

UNDERMANNING AND DESIGN

There is an obvious connection between a theory that talks about numbers and design consequences of those numbers. The person who asks how we can translate undermanning into specific design concepts should refer to Lozar (1975) and Ledbetter (1974). Yet these illustrations are not adequate as a final answer because the development of the theory goes beyond these particular applications. The general principle of undermanning would support reducing the scale on any large project. For example, in a large housing project, the houses should be arranged in clusters to develop smaller units. In a large office building, the tendency to mass numbers of people in a large room should be avoided. Any design that fosters small settings should help derive the benefits of undermanning from the environment.

One of the areas needing solution is the element of physical capacity. We have already seen (Wicker et al., 1972) where the capacity of a church was a determinant of attendance. This suggests that undermanning could be directly related to room size (Barker's illustration of room size and absence in the textile plant) or other physical determinants of capacity, but the relationships are not yet sufficiently developed. A designer could not directly program a textile plant for fewer absences without doing more research on each particular plant. Undermanning, however, will sensitize him to the need for small rooms.

For the architect or designer who can think in terms of behavior settings as rooms and organizations as buildings and of communities as hierarchies of settings, undermanning theory and behavior settings can offer a far richer set of concepts for design than other methods—if for no other reason than it gathers together data on the total environment and relates how that total environment can be organized for design purposes.

Perhaps what undermanning theory is really saying to the designer is that human scale relates closely to what designers refer to as physical scale. The two are defined by size. When a building or community gets too large, the designer says it is "out of scale." Similarly, undermanning theory may be telling us that there are limits to social structure and that when human organizations reach a certain size, they are out of scale. Scale then becomes the physical capacity of a setting, and it is both architecturally and behaviorally defined.

Milgram (1970) supports this notion with the concept of overloading. Persons in crowded environments become overloaded with sensory inputs and must discriminate out of awareness the feelings and needs of those around them, as well as the physical surroundings.

The undermanned environment, for all its present incompleteness in understanding, is an ideal environment that strives to achieve the maximum positive experiences for the greatest number of people, and it does so by deliberately structuring the number of people in each setting to be less than most people require. Nature has already done this in small towns, small schools, small churches, and small organizations in general. It is a cure for the problem of bigness, and this has some immediate consequences for design.

CONCLUSIONS

Reassessment of Original Theoretical Points

Of the eleven original points Barker (1960) set up as consequences of an undermanned setting, seven seem to have been firmly demonstrated by research, two modified, and two have been generally missed by research. Of the original points researched, the more important studies are listed below:

1. Gump and Friesen (1964) report satisfaction in

hard work as one of the thirty-nine measures of satisfaction mentioned by more than 20 percent of the subjects. But it was not central to their findings, and this point was changed (Barker, 1965) to "being challenged." No study has come up with unequivocal evidence that people in small settings actually work harder, but most studies infer this conclusion from their findings. Srivastava (1975) comes close to showing this, but in severely undermanned settings. Petty (1971) showed subjects saw themselves as working harder. Thus, this point of the theory still has a strong assumptive quality but has no final objective evidence so far. Wicker (1973) adds "spending longer hours" to this point.

2. Gump and Friesen (1964) report inhabitants of smaller settings engaging in more difficult and more important tasks. This finding is confirmed by Wicker (1968, 1969), Wicker et al. (1972), Petty (1971), and Willems (1965) and seems to be one of the most solidly confirmed of the points.

3. A wider variety of activities for small-setting occupants is a general finding (Gump and Friesen, 1964; Wicker, 1969). This seems to be another solidly confirmed finding, but as Petty (1971) says, the research done is on organization size, not setting size.

4. Less sensitivity to and less need to evaluate differences among people is another point that is more inferred from results than demonstrated, but Petty (1971) did show some tendency for undermanned performers to see more task-oriented rather than personality-oriented qualities in members of the setting. By no means were results considered more than indirect. Actually, this point should probably be merged with point 9 since less sensitivity to differences among people should permit greater receptivity to new members.

5. Undermanning will produce a lower level of maximum performance. If one looks at the literature, only the Srivastava (1975) study shows a clear lowering of maximal performance in smaller settings, but these were severely undermanned. Many of the studies (i.e, churches) did not contain settings or organizations that measured an objective performance level. The school studies (Barker and Gump, 1964) did not report on academic performance. Baird (1969) showed that in a national sample of 21,000 high-school students, small-school students reported higher accomplishments in four out of six areas: leadership, music, drama, speech and writing. If these data reflect academic achievement, the results would contradict expectations from undermanning. In fact, the job enrichment data (Walton, 1972) indicate an increase in maximal performance level as a result in undermannning. This is also confirmed by the air force manpower studies (Callander, 1970).

6. Greater importance of each person in the setting is a finding confirmed by the school (Gump and Friesen, 1964; Willems, 1965; Wicker, 1968) and church studies (Wicker, 1969; Wicker et al., 1972).

7. Greater responsibility is also a finding of most studies (Gump and Friesen, 1964; Willems, 1964; Wicker, 1968; and, Petty, 1971). This is one of the points most firmly demonstrated.

8. Greater self-identity is a consequence and closely related to what Gump and Friesen (1964) call the competence satisfaction. Perhaps the main thrust of the *Big School, Small School* findings centers on this issue but is also closely related to points 6 and 7.

9. Lower standards and fewer tests for admission was not generally supported by Petty (1971) or by Hanson and Wicker (1973). However, some questions remain since Wicker and Mehler (1971) clearly showed members were better accepted in smaller churches. There seems to be a distinction between stated requirements and actual acceptance in the group. There may not be a difference in stated requirements, but the smaller group accepts new members more readily.

10. No finding seems to support directly the notion of greater insecurity. Barker's (1960) reasoning is faultless, but clear, objective findings on this subject are lacking. The job enrichment data (O'Toole et al., 1973) would seem to contradict it, and this point may actually be contradicted itself by point 8.

11. More frequent occurrences of success or failure do not occur in the laboratory studies set up by Petty

(1971) and Hanson and Wicker (1973) but experiences of success or failure do not seem to influence acceptance of new members. This is a point where more research needs to be done.

In considering results of undermanning research so far, one must keep in mind that the bulk of the research has been done on organizations rather than settings. Most of the above results (except Wicker and his colleagues) accrue to the effects of smaller organizations. Wicker's laboratory studies tend to deal more with the setting itself. This may create an artificial situation since most settings occur in the context of some organization or community, but it makes the setting relationships clearer in terms of members' behavior.

The finding that large organizations tend to form larger and relatively fewer settings and that smaller organizations tend to form relatively more but smaller settings seems very conclusive. From Barker's original data (1960) through the *Big School, Small School* studies to Wicker's church studies, the relationship seems clear.

Considering the above findings, it is now time to revise Barker's original list, at least for heuristic purposes. Before that is done, however, it must be understood that a clear definition of the undermanning condition is still lacking. Barker's (1960) original definitions were largely comparative. The small Kansas town was undermanned compared to the English town. Small schools were undermanned compared to large schools. Wicker's studies attempted to operationalize undermanning with the concept of maintenance minimum, which was the minimal number of performers required to bring in enough nonmembers to keep the setting operating. Yet this leaves the area between some point below maintenance minimum up to just below the point of adequate manning as the area for undermanning study. As yet, this requires a new definition of undermanning for each situation studied.

The same definitional problem exists in organizational size. The organization-setting size relationship has not been researched except on a comparative

basis. Therefore, any statements about undermanning theory must begin with these two caveats. Perhaps two new terms should be introduced to clarify the goals of future research. (1) We need to define the area of undermanning where the maximum amount of the benefits of undermanning can occur. This is the optimal size of a setting. (2) We need to define the same area for the size of an organization if it is shown that organization size absolutely determines setting size, and this should be an optimal organization size or the golden organization-to-setting size ratio (*golden ratio* for short). This recognizes that above and below these setting and organization sizes, the positive benefits of undermanning will be reduced. Therefore, providing these optimal conditions are met, the following results should occur:

1. Wider variety of activities.
2. Increased level of maximum performance.
3. Greater importance and increased sense of self-identity through increased competence.
4. Higher participation level accompanied by more responsibility and greater felt needs to participate.
5. Greater tendency to accept new members into the group.

Further qualifications in terms of capacity and population pressures have already been discussed.

Connections with Other Theories

In the field of anthropology, there are similarities between undermanning and Redfield's (1963) folk-urban continuum. Redfield sees traditional or folk cultures as being prevalent in the villages of all cultures in the world. Redfield's face-to-face social structure is possible in small settings and small cultures. But in cities, a new kind of structure is necessary because no one can know the names and faces of so many people. Therefore, roles rather than persons become the units of function with which people deal. The folk continuum has many of the characteristics of small-community undermanned settings while the urban continuum could easily be the overmanned bureaucracies of the cities.

In sociology there is a similarity between undermanning and Parkinson's (1962) law of expansion of organizations. Certainly, the behavior of large organizations and overmanned settings has a great similarity to the expansionist behavior Parkinson described.

In psychiatry the Sullivanian school would predict that the childhood development of any individual would have a healthier environment in which to flourish in undermanned settings. The child's chances to participate would be so much greater. The Erickson school would say the adolescent's chances to find identity are greater in the undermanned environment.

In ethology, territoriality in the undermanned world is not a problem because there is enough territory for everyone, but when overmanning occurs, there tend to be battles for territory and perhaps even a herding instinct coming forth in response to overpopulation.

Calhoun's (1964) behavioral sink can be explained in terms of the breakdown of setting boundaries due to overmanning.

The similarities of undermanning theory to the new job enrichment movement have already been pointed out. And Ledbetter's (1974) paper shows that the air force has already been using the principles of undermanning in their staffing assignments. Undermanning theory, then, cuts across many disciplines and many areas of practical application. It takes on the appearance of being a universal law of the structure and function of human society. As such, its principle has so many possible applications that the thought of them is staggering to the most grandiose imagination. In fact, independent applications of undermanning principles can be seen in many areas of industry today.

FUTURE RESEARCH

Wicker's (1973) studies, attempting to better define crowding by testing out overmanning conse-

quences, may have the significance of opening up a whole new branch of manning research that could become more important than all the undermanning research done so far.

The extreme undermanning condition described in Srivastava (1975) points out how undermannning can go too far and destroy functioning. This, too, is an area needing more research and one that can have serious impact in such undermanned institutions as the mental hospital.

Petty's (1975) request to expand the tasks given to laboratory subjects to the cognitive realm would expand the generalizability of present laboratory work.

The Lozar (1975) and Ledbetter (1974) studies show the promise that undermanning theory gives to the design professions. Perhaps with diligence and continuing effort designers will begin to see that the tools of undermanning theory and research can make them better designers by providing the means to better understand the requirements of the behavior they enclose with their spaces and how the structure of space can change the structure of behavior.

REFERENCES

Acton Society Trust. *Size and Morale.* 1953.

Baird, L. "Big School, Small School: A Critical Examination of the Hypothesis." *Journal of Educational Psychology.* 60 (1969):253–260.

Barker, Roger. "Ecology and Motivation." In Marshall Jones, ed., *Nebraska Symposium on Motivation.* University of Nebraska Press, 1960, pp. 1–49.

———. "Community Size and Activities of Students." In R. Barker and P. Gump, eds., *Big School, Small School.* Stanford University Press, 1964, pp. 154–171.

———. "Explorations in Ecological Psychology." *American Psychologist* 20 (1965):1–14.

———. *Ecological Psychology.* Stanford University Press, 1968.

Barker, Roger, and Barker, Louise, "Structural Characteristics." In R. Barker and P. Gump, eds., *Big School, Small School.* Stanford University Press, 1964, pp. 41–63.

Barker, Roger, and Gump, Paul. *Big School, Small School.* Stanford University Press, 1964.

Barker, Roger, and Hall, Eleanor, "Participation in Interschool Events and Extracurricular Activities." In R. Barker and P. Gump, eds., *Big School, Small School.* Stanford University Press, 1964, pp. 64–74.

Barker, Roger, and LeCompte, W., "Adolescents in the Towns of Midwest County." In R. Barker and P. Gump, eds., *Big School, Small School.* Stanford University Press, 1964, pp. 172-192.

Baumgartel, H., and Sobel, R. "Background and Organizational Factors in Absenteeism." *Personal Psychology* 12 (1959):431-443.

Calhoun, J. "Population Density and Social Pathology." *Scientific American* 206 (1962):139-148.

Callander, B. "Remote Riddle Gets Close Look." *Air Force Times,* June 17, 1970.

Campbell, W. J. "Some Effects of High School Consolidation." In R. Barker and P. Gump, eds., *Big School, Small School.* Stanford University Press, 1964, pp. 139-153.

Gump, P. "Linkages Between the Ecological Environment and the Behavior and Experience of Persons." Paper presented at the Conference on Ecology of Human Living Environments, University of Wisconsin, Green Bay, 1971.

Gump, P., and Friesen, W. "Participation in Nonclass Settings." In R. Barker and P. Gump, eds., *Big School, Small School.* Stanford University Press, 1964, pp. 175-193.

Hanson, L., and Wicker, A., "Effects of Overmanning on Group Experience and Task Performance." Paper presented at the Western Psychological Association Convention, Anaheim, Calif., 1973.

Hewitt, O., and Parfit, J. "A Note on Working Morale and Size of Group." *Occupational Psychology* 27 (1953): 38-42.

Lamm, R. *Equilibrium Magazine* 1 (1973):4-8.

Ledbetter, C. Burgess. "Undermanning and Architectural Accessibility." U.S. Army Cold Regions Research and Engineering Laboratory, Hanover, New Hampshire, Special Report 213, October 1974.

Lozar, Charles. "Application of Behavior Setting Analysis and Undermanning Theory to Supermarket Design." In D. H. Carson, ed., *Man-Environment Interactions, Part II.* Dowden, Hutchinson & Ross, 1975, pp. 271-279.

Milgram, S. "The Experience of Living in Cities." *Science* 167 (1970):1461-1468.

O'Toole, J.; Hansot, E.; Herman, W.; Herrick, N.; Liebow, E.; Lusignan, B.; Richman, H.; Sheppard, H.; Sephansky, B.; and Wright, J. *Work in America.* MIT Press, 1973.

Parkinson, C. *Parkinson's Law and Other Studies in Administration.* Houghton Mifflin, 1962.

Petty, R. "The Assimilation of a New Group Member: A Laboratory Study of Behavior Setting Theory." Master's thesis, University of Illinois, 1971.

———. "Experimental Investigation of Undermanning Theory." In D. H. Carson, ed., *Man-Environment Interactions, Part II.* Dowden, Hutchinson & Ross, 1975, pp. 259-269.

Redfield, R. *The Little Community and Peasant Society and Culture.* University of Chicago Press, 1960.

Strivastava, Rajendra K. "Undermanning Theory in the Context of Mental Health Care Environments." In D. H. Carson, ed., *Man-Environment Interactions, Part II.* Dowden, Hutchinson & Ross, 1975, pp. 245-258.

Walton, R. E. "Workplace Alienation and the Need for Major Innovation," unpublished manuscript, May 1972.

Wicker, A. "Undermanning, Performances, and Students' Subjective Experiences in Behavior Settings of Large and Small High Schools." *Journal of Personality and Social Psychology* 10 (1968):255-261.

———. "Size of Church Membership and Members' Support of Church Behavior Settings." *Journal of Personality and Social Psychology* 13 (1969):278-288.

———. "Undermanning Theory and Research: Implications for the Study of Psychological and Behavioral Effects of Excess Populations." *Research in Social Psychology* 4 (1973):185-206.

Wicker, A. and Mehler, A. "Assimilation of New Members in a Large and a Small Church." *Journal of Applied Psychology* 55 (1971):151-156.

Wicker, A.; McGrath, J.; and Armstrong, G. "Organization Size and Behavior Setting Capacity as Determinants of Member Participation." *Behavioral Science* 17 (1972): 499-513.

Willems, E. "Review of Research." In R. Barker and P. Gump, eds., *Big School, Small School.* Stanford University Press, 1964a, pp. 29-37.

———. "Forces Toward Participation in Behavior Settings." In R. Barker and P. Gump, eds., *Big School, Small School.* Stanford University Press, 1964b, pp. 115-135.

———. "Participation in Behavior Settings in Relation to Three Variables: Size of Behavior Settings, Marginality of Persons, and Sensitivity to Audiences." Ph.D. dissertation, University of Kansas, 1965.

Wright, Herbert. *Children's Behavior in Communities Differing in Size.* University of Kansas, 1969.

Appendix A

BEHAVIOR SETTING INFORMATION SHEET   GENOTYPE NO. . . . .
Setting Name . . . .
Data collected by . . . . ;   date . . . . ;   . . . .
     ,, ... ;   ,, ... ;   . . . .
     ,, ... ;   ,, ... ;   . . . .
Class . . . .
Location . . . .
Time (duration/occurrence) . . . .
. . . .
. . . . Total hours duration . . . .
Unit . . . .
Locus . . . .
GENERAL DESCRIPTION
     Soma:

Journalistic Description:

POPULATION

	PEN L	SC 1		SC 2		SC 3		SC 4	
		MALE	FEMALE	MALE	FEMALE	MALE	FEMALE	MALE	FEMALE
ON POST MILITARY									
ON POST CIVILIAN									
OFF POST MILITARY									
OFF POST CIVILIAN									

Aesthetics ....

PARTICIPATION: Does any behavior in this setting make things beautiful or remove the unsightly?

No.   Yes- Percent of OT: 1-2, 21-40, 41-60, 61-80, 81-100.

SUPPLY: Are beautifying materials supplied to other settings?

No.   Yes- Percent of OT: 1-20, 21-40, 41-60, 61-80, 81-100.

EVALUATION: Is there approval or criticism of beautiful things here?

No.   Yes- Percent of OT: 1-50, 51-100.

TEACHING and LEARNING: Is beautification of the environment specifically and formally taught and learned in this setting?

No.   Yes- Percent of OT: 1-50, 51-100.

Business ....

PARTICIPATION: Does business activity occur in this setting?

No.   Yes- Percent of OT: 1-20, 21-40, 41-60, 61-80, 81-100.

SUPPLY: Does this setting supply business materials for another setting?

No.   Yes- Percent of OT: 1-20, 21-40, 41-60, 61-80, 81-100.

EVALUATION: Is business judged and appraised here?

No.   Yes- Percent of OT: 1-50, 51-100.

TEACHING and LEARNING: Are business practices taught and learned in this setting?

No.   Yes- Percent of OT: 1-50, 51-100.

Professionalism ....

PARTICIPATION: Do any of the performers in this setting receive financial recompense?

No.   Yes- Percent of OT of all performers: 1-20, 21-40, 41-60, 61-80, 81-100.

SUPPLY: Does this setting supply materials for paid work in another setting?

No.   Yes- Percent of OT of all performers: 1-20, 21-40, 41-60, 61-80, 81-100.

EVALUATION: Are paid performers judged in this setting?

No.   Yes- Percent of OT: 1-50, 51-100.

TEACHING and LEARNING: Is there specific job training here?

No.   Yes-   Percent of OT: 1-50,   51-100.

Education . . . .

PARTICIPATION: Does teaching and learning in individual or group lessons take place here?

No.   Yes-   Percent of OT: 1-20,   21-40,   41-60,   61-80,   81-100.

SUPPLY: Does this setting supply materials for teaching or learning in other settings?

No.   Yes-   Percent of OT: 1-20,   21-40,   41-60,   61-80,   81-100.

EVALUATION: Is education overtly appraised in this setting?

No.   Yes-   Percent of OT: 1-50,   51-100.

TEACHING and LEARNING: Is there learning about educational process or method in this setting?

No.   Yes-   Percent of OT: 1-50,   51-100.

Government . . . .

PARTICIPATION: Is the behaviour in this setting controlled by the government in any way?

No.   Yes-   Percent of OT: 1-20,   21-40,   41-60,   61-80,   81-100.

SUPPLY: Does this setting supply materials for governmental activities in other settings?

No.   Yes-   Percent of OT: 1-20,   21-40,   41-60,   61-80,   81-100.

EVALUATION: Are governmental activities openly judged here?

No.   Yes-   Percent of OT: 1-50,   51-100.

TEACHING and LEARNING: Is there teaching and learning about government, history, law etc. in this setting?

No.   Yes-   Percent of OT: 1-50,   51-100.

Nutrition . . . .

PARTICIPATION: Does eating, drinking, preparing, or serving food occur here?

No.   Yes-   Percent of OT: 1-20,   21-40,   41-60,   61-80,   81-100.

SUPPLY: Do people get food or eating utensils to use in another setting?

No.   Yes-   Percent of OT: 1-20,   21-40,   41-60,   61-80,   81-100.

EVALUATION: Do people judge or express appreciation or criticism of food here?

No.   Yes- Percent of OT: 1–50,   51–100.

TEACHING and LEARNING: Do people learn and teach ways of preparing and serving food here?

No.   Yes- Percent of OT: 1–50,   51–100.

Personal Appearance . . . .

PARTICIPATION: Do people prepare for this setting by getting especially groomed or attired?
Do people get groomed or attired here?

No.   Yes- Percent of OT: 1–20,   21–40,   41–60,   61–80,   81–100.

SUPPLY: Do people obtain items of adornment or dress in this setting?

No.   Yes- Percent of OT: 1–20,   21–40,   41–60,   61–80,   81–100.

EVALUATION: Are clothing and grooming appraised here?

No.   Yes- Percent of OT: 1–50,   51–100.

TEACHING and LEARNING: Does teaching and learning grooming or dressmaking occur in
this setting?

No.   Yes- Percent of OT: 1–50,   51–100.

Philanthropy . . . .

PARTICIPATION: Are voluntary contributions of time, materials or money made to worthy
causes in this setting?

No.   Yes- Percent of OT: 1–20,   21–40,   41–60,   61–80,   81–100.

SUPPLY: Does this setting provide material or money for philanthropic purposes in other settings?

No.   Yes- Percent of OT: 1–20,   21–40,   41–60,   61–80,   81–100.

EVALUATION: Is philanthropic activity openly recognized and appraised?

No.   Yes- Percent of OT: 1–50,   51–100.

TEACHING and LEARNING: Do people teach and learn about the need and methods of philanthropy?

No.   Yes- Percent of OT: 1–50,   51–100.

Physical Health . . . .

PARTICIPATION: Is physical health promoted in this setting?

No.   Yes- Percent of OT: 1–20, 21–40, 41–60, 61–80, 81–100.

SUPPLY: Does this setting supply medical or sports equipment for use in other settings?

No.   Yes- Percent of OT: 1–20, 21–40, 41–60, 61–80, 81–100.

EVALUATION: Is physical health appraised in this setting?

No.   Yes- Percent of OT: 1–50, 51–100.

TEACHING and LEARNING: Does formal teaching and learning about health problems occur here?

No.   Yes- Percent of OT: 1–50, 51–100.

Recreation . . . .

PARTICIPATION: Does this setting provide pleasurable activities for its inhabitants?

No.   Yes- Percent of OT: 1–20, 21–40, 41–60, 61–80, 81–100.

SUPPLY: Does this setting supply materials for recreation in other settings?

No.   Yes- Percent of OT: 1–20, 21–40, 41–60, 61–80, 81–100.

EVALUATION: Is appreciation or criticism of recreation openly expressed?

No.   Yes- Percent of OT: 1–50, 51–100.

TEACHING and LEARNING: Are people instructed in recreational activities?

No.   Yes- Percent of OT: 1–50, 51–100.

Religion . . . .

PARTICIPATION: Are there religious observances in this setting?

No.   Yes- Percent of OT: 1–20, 21–40, 41–60, 61–80, 81–100.

SUPPLY: Are materials for worship in another setting provided in this setting?

No.   Yes- Percent of OT: 1–20, 21–40, 41–60, 61–80, 81–100.

EVALUATION: Is religion approved or criticised in this setting?

No.   Yes- Percent of OT: 1–50, 51–100.

TEACHING and LEARNING: Are people instructed in religious forms and values in this setting?

No.　　　Yes- Percent of OT: 1–50, 51–100.

Social Contact . . . .

PARTICIPATION: Does interpersonal behaviour occur here?

No.　　　Yes- Percent of OT: 1–20, 21–40, 41–60, 61–80, 81--100.

SUPPLY: Does this setting supply the means of social behaviour in other settings?

No.　　　Yes- Percent of OT: 1–20, 21–40, 41–60, 61–80, 81–100.

EVALUATION: Is there specific approval or disapproval of social behaviour in this setting?

No.　　　Yes- Percent of OT: 1–50, 51–100.

TEACHING AND LEARNING: Are social forms and skills taught in this setting?

No.　　　Yes- Percent of OT: 1–50, 51–100.

Affective Behaviour (Emotion) . . . .

PARTICIPATION: Does overt emotional expression occur in this setting?

No.　　　Yes- Percent of OT: 0–9, 10–33, 34–66, 67–90, 91–100.

TEMPO:　　What is the **fastest rate** at which affective behaviour normally varies in this setting?
　　　　　　0–very constant emotional expression, little variation occurs
　　　　　　1–about average fluctuations, within middle range of other settings
　　　　　　2–variable emotionality, somewhat above middle range of other settings
　　　　　　3–frequent, wide swings in affective behaviour

INTENSITY: How intense is the **greatest regular** emotional expression in this setting?
　　　　　　0–apathetic, low intensity of affective behaviour
　　　　　　1–affectivity within middle range of other settings
　　　　　　2–emotional expression high, above middle range of other settings
　　　　　　3–intensely emotional behaviour occurs

Gross Motor Activity . . . .

PARTICIPATION: Does large muscle activity occur here?

No.　　　Yes- Percent of OT: 0–9, 10–33, 34–66, 67–90, 91–100.

TEMPO:　　What is the **top speed** at which gross motor activity normally occurs?
　　　　　　0–slow movements, below the middle range of other settings
　　　　　　1–about average, within the middle range of other settings

2–fast actions, above the middle range of other settings
3–as fast as is physically possible

INTENSITY: What is the **maximal amount** of energy used when the large muscles are active in this setting?
0–weak movements, energy below the middle range of other settings
1–medium energy expenditure, within the middle range of other settings
2–strong movements, energy expenditure above the middle range of other settings
3–greatest possible force used

Manipulation ....

PARTICIPATION: Are the hands used in the behaviour pattern of the setting?

No.   Yes- Percent of OT: 0-9,   10-33,   34-66,   67-90,   91-100.

TEMPO: What is normally the **top speed** of manipulation in this setting?
0–slow movements, below the middle range of other settings
1–about ordinary, within the middle of other settings
2–fast actions, above the middle range of other settings
3–as fast as possible

INTENSITY: What is the **greatest force** normally used by the hands in this setting?
0–weak, below, middle range of other settings
1–about average, within middle range of other settings
2–strong, above middle range of other settings
3–force is at maximum level possible

Talking ....

PARTICIPATION: Do people talk or sing in this setting?

No.   Yes- Percent of OT: 0-9,   10-33,   34-66,   67-90,   91-100.

TEMPO: What is the **maximal speed** of talking or singing?
0–slow utterances, below the middle range of other settings
1–average, within the middle range of other settings
2–fast verbalization, above the middle range of other settings
3–as fast as possible

INTENSITY: What is the **greatest loudness** of talking or singing in this setting?
0–very low and soft speaking or singing
1–average, within the middle range of other settings
2–loud verbalization, above the middle range of other settings
3–maximal loudness possible

Thinking . . . .

PARTICIPATION: Does problem-solving and decision-making occur here?

No.   Yes- Percent of OT: 0-9, 10-33, 34-66, 67--90, 91-100.

TEMPO: What is the **top speed** with which decisions are usually made and problems solved?
    0-slow thinking, below the middle range of speedy decisions in other settings
    1--average, with the middle range of other settings
    2-fast thinking, above the middle range of other settings
    3-very fast, lightening-quick decisions

INTENSITY: What is the **maximal level** of problem-solving occuring in this setting?
    0-low intellectual level, below the middle range of other settings
    1-above average, within the middle range of other settings
    2-sharp thinking occurs, above the middle range of other settings
    3-really difficult decisions are made and problems solved

Pressure . . . .

Children's Occupancy of this setting:
    1-required
    2-urged
    3-invited
    4-neither encouraged nor discouraged
    5-tolerated
    6-resisted
    7-prohibited

Adolescent's Occupancy of this setting is:
    1-required
    2-urged
    3-invited
    4-neither encouraged nor discouraged
    5-tolerated
    6-resisted
    7-prohibited

. . . . . . Occupancy of this setting
    1-required
    2-urged
    3-invited
    4-neither encouraged nor . . . .
    5-tolerated
    6-resisted
    7-prohibited

Welfare: Child . . . .

0-This setting is neutral to the welfare of children; it is neither more nor less devoted to them than to other groups
1-This setting exists primarily for the welfare of its child members; if there were no child members the setting would cease.
2-This setting has no child inhabitants (members or performers), but it fosters other settings that are primarily for the welfare of children.
3-In this setting child performers serve an adult, adolescent or mixed-age membership. If there were no child performers the setting would close or be severely handicapped.

Welfare: Adolescent . . . .

0–This setting is neutral to the welfare of adolescents; it is neither more nor less devoted to them than to other age groups.

1–This setting exists primarily for the welfare of its adolescent members; if there were no adolescent members this setting would cease.

2–This setting has no adolescent inhabitants (members or performers) but it fosters other settings that are primarily for the welfare of adolescents.

3–In this setting adolescent performers serve an adult, child, or mixed-age membership. If there were no adolescent performers the setting would cease or be severely handicapped.

Autonomy . . . .

What are the sites of power for carrying out the following functions of this setting, and what is the relative power of each site?

   (a) Selecting the Performer:

             SITE   RELATIVE POWER

       9–within the Immediate Block

       7–within the Rural District Community

       5–within the County (City)

       3–within the State

       1–within the Nation

   (b) Admitting Members (Customers):

       Where are the membership requirements set?

             SITE   RELATIVE POWER

       9–within the Immediate Block

       7–within the Community

       5–within the County (City)

       3–within the State

       1–within the Nation

   (c) Determining Policy:

       Where are plans and programmes made?

             SITE   RELATIVE POWER

       9–within the Immediate Block

       7–within the Community

       5–within the County (City)

       3–within the State

       1–within the Nation

   (d) Establishing Financial Arrangements:

       Where are fees and prices set?

             SITE   RELATIVE POWER

       9–within the Immediate Block

       7–within the Community

       5–within the County (City)

       3–within the State

       1–within the Nation

Appendix B

FORT WAINWRIGHT HOUSING QUESTIONNAIRE
Cold Regions Habitability Project

1. Child visitors per week?   Winter _____
                                          Summer _____
    How long do they stay? _____

2. On post adult visitors per week?   Winter _____
                                          Summer _____
    How long do they say, each visit? _____

3. Off post adult visitors per week?   Winter _____
                                          Summer _____
    How long do they stay, each visit? _____

4. Hours spent inside the quarters per day?

	Week Day		Saturday		Sunday	
	Winter	Summer	Winter	Summer	Winter	Summer
Mother	____	____	____	____	____	____
Father	____	____	____	____	____	____
Children #1	____	____	____	____	____	____
#2	____	____	____	____	____	____
#3	____	____	____	____	____	____
#4	____	____	____	____	____	____

    Do you consider these average for your neighbors?
    Yes _____ No _____ Above average _____ Below _____

5. Hours per week at home spent cleaning? _____

6. Hours per week at home purchasing items, e.g., Sears, Avon, Tupperware? _____

7. Hours per week at home spent doing homework, correspondence courses, etc.? _____

8. Hours per week at home following government regulations? _____

9. Hours per week at home cooking, serving, and eating meals? _____ *177*

10. Hours per week contributed to charitable organizations? _____

11. Hours per week dressing and/or preparing to go out?   Winter _____
                                                               Summer _____

12. Hours per week spent sick, tending to the ill, exercising for health? _____

13. Hours per week spent on recreation? _____

14. Hours per week spent in religious activities, e.g., church, prayers, etc.? _____

15. Do you say prayers at every meal?   Yes _____ No _____
    Do children say prayers at bedtime? Yes _____ No _____

16. If you have no children, do children visit here?   Yes_____ No _____
    How often? _____ (wk.) How long do they stay? _____

17. What would you say is the way you adjust to the climate here?

    _____ Try to shut it out
    _____ Try to go along with it
    Summer   _____ Pull down shades to make it dark
    _____ Try to stick to a time schedule, despite the hours of sunlight

    _____ Try to shut it out by staying indoors and not looking out of windows
    Winter   _____ Try to go along with it
    _____ Try to stick to a time schedule, despite the hours of darkness

18. If a friend in the service in the 'lower 48' was considering volunteering for duty at Fort Wainwright (or Alaska), what you would advise them is:

    A. Desirable about Fort Wainwright

    B. Undesirable about Fort Wainwright

19. How would you rate the post for providing for the needs of families; on a scale of 1 (excellent) to 7 (very bad):

    1|————————|————————|————————|————————|————————|————————|7
           2   3   4   5   6
    Excellent   Very Bad

20. What services could be provided that would improve the post for families?
    _____
    _____
    _____
    _____

21. If family housing were to grant you approximately $1,000 to be spent on your quarters for any items, what would you request?

_____

_____

_____

22. On the plan, indicate where you:

    A. Sit in the yard talking with neighbors
    B. Cook out
    C. Your children play in the summer
    D. Your children play in the winter

    Comment on the adequacy of the above space to satisfy your needs:

23. On the plan, indicate where on post you would prefer to live.
    Why?

24. Is there any part of your house that you think needs to be improved?

25. Is there any part of your house that is especially good?

Index

Achelpohl, C., 23, 24, 32, 61, 64, 67, 118

Action patterns and subscales, 59–60, 77, 121
  evaluation and appreciation, 59–60
  participation, 59
  reliability of, 140
  supply, 59
  teaching and learning, 60

Action patterns and summary of comparisons, 79–82, 103–104, 126–129, 137–138, 139
  (*see also* Aesthetics, Business, Education, Government, Nutrition, Orientation, Personal appearance, Philanthropy, Physical health, Professionalism, Recreation, Religion, Social contact)
  Arrowhead, Eastside, Midwest, and Westside, 103–104
  barracks and family housing of Fort Wainwright, 137–138
  Eastside, Midwest, and Westside, 79–82
  FAA family housing with Fort Wainwright family housing, 126–129
  as per cent of occupancy time, 89
    Eastside, Westside, and Midwest, 88–89
    Midwest, 139

Activity patterns, 121 (*see also* Action patterns)

Acton Society Trust, 156, 164

AC&W. *See* Air Force Control and Warning Station

Adams, J., 15

Adelberg, T., 8, 14

Adolescents (*see also* Teens)
  as having no place to gather in Arrowhead, 108
  pressure rating
    in Arrowhead sidewalks, 65
    compared for Arrowhead, Eastside, Westside, and Midwest, 105
    in Eastside, Westside, and Midwest, 85
  welfare rating comparison
    Arrowhead, Eastside, Westside, and Midwest, 105
    Eastside, Westside, and Midwest, 85–86

Adults, age limits, 97

Advocacy design, 4, 5
  (*see also* Design client-centered)

Advocacy planning, 4, 5

Aesthetics action pattern
  Alaska, how scored in, 121
  definition, 60
  summary of comparisons
    Arrowhead, Eastside, Westside, and Midwest, 104
    barracks with family housing at Fort Wainwright, 138
    Eastside, Westside, and Midwest, 80–81
    FAA family housing with Fort Wainwright, 124
Affective behavior mechanism
  definition, 63
  subscales, participation, tempo, and intensity, 62–63
  summary of comparisons
    Arrowhead, Eastside, Westside, and Midwest 104–105
    Eastside, Westside, and Midwest, 82–83
Aged, 97
Age groups (breakdown), 97
Air Force
  data comparing participation in activities of small and large bases, 128–129
  location of study sites in Alaska, 119
  undermanning, 162
Air Force Control and Warning Station (AC&W), 124, 141
  compared to larger bases, 128–130
  definition of, 146
Akers, R., 23
Alaska, 119, 121, 126, 137, 146, 147
  recommendations for family housing, 133–135
  study sites in, 119, 126
Alexander, C., 2, 7, 13, 31
Alinsky, S., 4, 13
Allen, V., 118
Alone, different meanings of, 18
Altman, I., 9, 13, 15
American Psychological Association standard for statistical significance, 120
Angel, S., 13
Archea, J., 32, 67, 91, 118
Architectural scale, 161
  human scale vs, 161

Arctic entrances, 123
  examples of, 123
  problems with, 130
  recommendations for, 133
Ardrey, R., 7, 13
Armstrong, G., 158, 164
Arousal (*see also* Satisfaction sites)
  increasing and decreasing, 8
  sites, definition, 8
Arrowhead, 4, 49, 58, 65, 93–118, 143, 151, 153
  action patterns comparisons, 102
  analysis of data on, 101
  background, 93–95
  behavior setting list, 100
  collection of data, 98
  dependency in, 106
  ERDF office in, 99
  ERI comparisons, 103
  Friendly Inn behavior setting list, 101
  graphics recommended for, 113
  GRI comparisons, 105
  incomes of residents, 97
  local autonomy of, 106
  location of, 95
  number of units, 95
  observers for, 99
  penetration levels available to residents, 102
  physical description of, 98
  population statistics, 96–97
  pressure comparisons, 105
  profile of behavior mechanisms, 104
  social areas in, 111, 116–117
Arrowhead recommendations
  better maintenance, 109
  building superintendent as concierge, 110
  clotheslines, 113
  common and proprietary spaces, 114
  density reduction, 114
  exterior front stairways, 114
  exterior rear stairs, 114
  graphics, 113
  improved management-resident relations, 109–110
  kiosks, 113

male image, 110
neighborhood center, 111–112
new social services, 110
parking, 112
project manager, 109
recreation, 112
saturation maintenance, 113
smaller social areas, 111
special lighting, 113
special materials, 113
superintendants' facilities, 114
Unwin street, 112
walkway system, 112–113
Authority systems
classes of, 86
definition, 86
Eastside, Westside, and Midwest in, 87–88
Autonomy
Alaska, as calculated in, 121
Arrowhead, as calculated in, 106
definition, 86
summary of comparisons
Arrowhead, Eastside, Westside, and Midwest,
106–108
Eastside, Westside, and Midwest, 86–87
FAA locations in Alaska, 130
new scale suggested, 142

Baird, L., 162, 164
Bandura, A., 8, 13
Barker, L., 118, 156, 164
Barker, R., 9, 10, 13, 21, 22, 23, 30, 31, 32, 33, 40,
48, 58, 60, 61, 62, 64, 66, 67, 68, 70, 77, 79,
81, 82, 84, 85, 86, 89, 92, 93, 102, 117, 118,
119, 120, 121, 129, 136, 143, 153, 154, 156,
157, 159, 161, 162, 163, 164, 165
Basement, uses of, in Alaska, 131
Bauer, R., 2, 13
Baumgartel, H., 14, 156, 165
Beals, A., 4, 15
Bechtel, R., 2, 4, 5, 10, 12, 13, 23, 24, 32, 58, 60,
61, 64, 65, 67, 69, 86, 91, 108, 118, 137,
142, 153

Behavior
design inhibiting, 12
effects of environment on, 24
in museums, 12
non-observable aspects, 31
Behavioral categories, Arrowhead, 50–51, 53–55
Behavioral focal point
for Arrowhead, 151
for Cape Lisburne, 147
construction, principles of, 150–153
definition, 143
ideal characteristics, 150–153
at junction of corridors, 148
for Midwest, 143, 151
principles for designing, 150–153
uses of, 147
Behavioral sink, definition, 7
Behavior episodes, definition, 22
Behavior mechanisms (*see also* Gross motor behavior,
Manipulative behavior, Talking, Thinking)
definitions, 62–64
problems with, 140
profiles, 82
reliability of, 140
subscales, 62–63
participation, 62
tempo, 62–63
intensity, 63
summary of comparisons with
Arrowhead, Eastside, Westside, and Midwest,
104–105
Eastside, Westside, and Midwest, 82
Fort Wainwright, FAA, 128, 129
with percent of OT, 89
Behavior setting (*see also* Boundary)
boundary, 33
problems, 33–48
capacity, 158–159
data, limitations of, 141
definition, 22–23
descriptive aspects of, 55, 58
dimensions, 24
interdependence (K-21) scale, 25–29

overlapped, 34
quantitative aspects, 58–59
size, 10, 154
summary of theory and problems, 9
Behavior setting survey
description of, 24
observation method, 68–118
case 1, 68–92
case 2, 92–118
questionnaire method, 119–136
rating scales for, 49–67
Behavior specimen records
definition, 21–22
examples of, 23
Bettleheim, B., 4, 13
Binding, F., 9, 10, 24, 32, 61, 64, 65, 67
Birdsell, J., 24, 32
Blackman, A., 1, 13
Bolling, R., 4, 14
Boundary
creating, 37
definitions, 33–48
problems, 33–48
examples of how to solve, 33–48
Bricks-and-mortar syndrome, 17
Brolin, B., 1, 10, 13
Burgwyn, H., 14
Business action pattern
definition, 60–61
subscales to, 59–60
summary of comparisons
Arrowhead, Eastside, Midwest, 104
Eastside, Westside, Midwest, 81
FAA and Fort Wainwright, 129

Calhoun, J., 7, 13, 164, 165
Callander, B., 162, 165
Campbell, D., 12, 13
Campbell, R., 36
Campbell, W., 157, 165
Campion, 119
Canes and crutches, use of, 51
Cantril, H., 120, 136

Canty, D., 1, 14
Cape Lisburne, 147, 149, 151
Carman, J., 12, 14
Carson, D., 1, 15, 165
Centralization of services, 117
Chain fences, use of, 51
Chandigarh, 3
Chapin, F., 7, 14, 30, 32
Churches, 162
trips to, 55
Citizen participation, 4, 13
City-Town Project, 157
Client-centered design, 3, 5, 13
Clifton, J., 4, 14
Clotheslines, 113
Clothing scale, 61
CMHA, 94
Coffin, C., 13
Colarelli, N., 37, 48
Collins, J., 6, 12, 14
Cold regions, 146 (see also Alaska)
Cold Regions Research and Engineering Laboratories.
See CRREL
Common and proprietary spaces, 114
Comstock, G. A., 6, 23
Concierge, 115
Control syndrome, 17
Conway D., 10, 12, 14
Coolfont model, 11
Corbusier, 3
Cordova, 119
Core setting, 143
Cost
Arrowhead, research of, 116
calculating total, 19
initial vs total, 19
social science, consulting of, 19
undermanning, 160
cOT
calculation, 141
definition, 140
Craik, K., 1, 14
Crowding, 7

CRREL, 119, 121
Cytosetting, 141

Dashiell, J. F., 18, 20
Davidoff, P., 4, 13
Day hall, Kirkbride, 35
Deasy, C., 4, 13
Dembo, T., 22, 31
Dempsey, D., 3, 7, 13
Density reduction, 114
Dependency, 13
    atmosphere, 106
    definition, 5
    evolution of, 108
    motivation, 106
    reverse reaction to, 106
Dependent environment, 106
Design
    aspects
        Alaska, 133–135
        Arrowhead, 108–114
        Eastside, Westside, 92
    central concept for, 118
    client-centered, 3, 5, 13
    evaluation of, 11
    model, 12
    new pathway of, 10
    perversion of, 94
    practice, methods of, 3–13
        Neodemocratic, 3–5, 13
        Neotechnological, 5–10
        traditional (paternalistic), 2–3, 13
    undermanning, 10, 161
    use of social science in, obstacles to, 16–20
Designer and researcher teams, 5, 10, 11
Deviation countering circuits
    definition, 30
    dimensions, 7
    K-21 scale of, 25, 26–29
Direct observation, disadvantages of, 119
Dispersed site, 146
Disposable organization, 116

Distances to amenities as a characteristic of military
        bases, 123
Dogs, 54, 131
Door problems, in Alaska, 131
Dry cleaner, trips to, 51
Dubos, R., 2, 14
Duijker, H., 6, 14
Duplexes, 122
Duration, definition, 58–59, 77–139

Eastman, C., 32, 67, 91, 117
Eastside, 69, 71, 74
    behavior settings, 77
    comparison with Westside and Midwest, 79
    comparisons with Arrowhead, 103–107
    description of, 69, 71
    location, 69
    population of, 71
    selecting observers for, 69
Eclecticism, 11
Ecological perspective, 22
Ecological psychology, 16, 22
Ecological validity, 22
Ecological resource index. *See* ERI
Economic philistinism, 2
Education action pattern
    comparisons
        Eastside, Westside, and Midwest, 81–92
        Eastside, Westside, Midwest, and Arrowhead, 104
        FAA family housing with Fort Wainwright, 129
    definition, 61
    subscales for, 59–60
English language, inadequacy of, 18
Entwisle, D., 6, 14
Environmental psychology research, incremental
        model of, 11
Environmental Research and Development Founda-
        tion. *See* ERDF
Epidemeological field station, 69
ERDF, 94, 99
ERI, 88, 103, 139
    comparison of Eastside, Westside, Midwest, and
        Arrowhead, 104

definition, 77–79
Erickson, E., 164
Esser, A., 7, 14
Estates, in public housing, 95n
Etzioni, A., 2, 14
Exterior stairways, Arrowhead, 114
External change agent, 116

FAA, 124
   description of housing, 126
   families going outside community for recreation,
      136
   family housing compared to Fort Wainwright, 126–
      130
   location studied in Alaska, 126
Factionalism, definition, 4
Factions, in public housing, 4
Fairbanks, Alaska, 121
Family housing
   on military bases, 121–123
   military plan for, 121–122
Federal Aviation Administration. *See* FAA
Ferebee, A., 1, 14, 115
Fighting, on sidewalks, 53
Focal points. *See* Behavioral focal point
Fort Wainwright, 119, 122, 137
   compared with FAA family housing, 126–130
   description of, 121
   housing on, 121–123
Freedman, J., 7, 14
Freedman, L., 94, 118
French, D., 4, 14
Frequency, definition, 58
Freud, S., 9. 14
Friendly Inn, 101
   behavior setting list, 101
   penetration levels available to residents, 102–103
Friesen, W., 64, 156, 158, 162, 165
Frijda, N., 6, 14
Frustration, regression, 22

Galbraith, F., 20
General Richness Index. *See* GRI

Genotype
   comparisons of Eastside, Westside, and Midwest, 91
   definition, 58
   example, 58
Global scales, 64–67 (*see also* Penetration levels, GRI,
      Pressure scale, Welfare scale, Autonomy)
Golden ratio for undermanning, 163
Good, L., 6, 14
Goodenough, W., 1, 14
Gough, H., 6, 14
Government action pattern
   comparisons
      Eastside, Westside, and Midwest, 80–81
      Eastside, Westside, Midwest, Arrowhead, ERI,
         104
      FAA and Fort Wainwright family housing, 129
   definition, 61
   subscales, 59–60
GRI
   calculating, 140
   comparisons
      Eastside, Westside, and Midwest, 84
      Eastside, Westside, Midwest, and Arrowhead,
         104–105
      FAA family housing and Fort Wainwright, 130
   definition, 65, 84
   formula, 65, 84
   ranges, 65
Griffin, M., 17, 20
Gross motor behavior
   comparisons
      Eastside, Westside, and Midwest, 82
      Eastside, Westside, Midwest, and Arrowhead,
         104–105
   definition, 63
   subscales, 62–63
Gulkana, 119, 126
Gump, P., 9, 10, 13, 14, 64, 77, 156, 157, 158,
      162, 165

Habitability
   criteria for, 121, 124
   cold regions project, 121, 146

deriving guidelines for, 124–126
guidelines, 121
Hagevick, C., 1, 7, 14
Hall, E. R., 156, 164
Hall, E. T., 1, 6, 14
Hanson, L., 162, 163, 165
Hansot, E., 165
Harrington, M., 2
Hatch, C., 4, 14
Heise, D., 6, 14
Helson, H., 93, 118
Here-comes-that-jargon-again syndrome, 18
Herman, W., 165
Herrick, N., 165
Hewitt, O., 156, 165
Holland, J., 8, 14
Hillix, W., 31, 32
Hooper Avenue School Study, 4
Housing, military
basic plan for, 121–122
family, recommendations for, 133–135
rank and, 122
segregation by rank and status, 123
uniformity of construction, 123
Housing and Community Development Act of 1974,
1n
HUD, 94
biennial awards for design excellence, 1
request for proposal for Arrowhead, 94
Human scale, 161
vs. architectural scale, 161

ICED conference, 14
Ideal community, 146
fragmented, 146
integrated, 146
Infants, age definition of, 97
Informal business, as necessary for the functioning
of organizations, 147
Inkeles, A., 6, 14
Innovation
approaches, 115
models, 116–118

Insecurity, and undermanning, 162
Interviewing, 68, 120
Ishikawa, S., 13
Ittelson, W., 1, 15, 142

Jackson, J., 6, 14
Jensen, A., 6, 14
Jones, M., 136

K, seven dimensions of, 25
Kansas City
city market, 34
Star city room, The, 34
zoo, 3
Kees, W., 10, 11, 15
Kelly, H., 9, 15
Kiosks, 113
Kirkbride, T., 35
Kish, L., 120, 136
Klein, N., 14
Kotzebue, 119–126
Kramer, R., 4, 14
K-21 scale, 25–29
examples of, 39, 40, 40–47
interdependence scales
behavioral objects, 27
behavior mechanisms, 29
leadership, 26
molar action units, 27
population overlap, 26
spatial, 26
temporal contiguity, 28–29
reliability, 39
sample K values, 25
total range of possible scores, 29
used to change office design, 40–47
uses of, examples, 39–40

Lamm, R., 160, 165
Lang, J., 11, 12, 14
Lasswell, T., 4
Laundry, trips to, 51
Leckwart, J., 20

LeCompte, A., 34, 36, 48, 157, 165
Ledbetter, C., 40, 119, 142, 153, 161, 164
  discussion of applying K-21 scale to office design,
    40–47
Leeuw, F. de, 106
Levinson, D., 6, 14
Lewin, K., 7, 21, 22, 31
Liebow, E., 165
Lighting, special, 113
Light well, 146
Limited access across boundaries of behavior settings,
  34
  nursing station example, 34–36
Littering, 55
Little, K., 9, 14
Living room, 131
Local autonomy. See Autonomy
Lockouts, 54
Logan, T., 14, 32
Lozar, C., 161, 164, 165
Lusignan, B., 165
Lynch, K., 2, 14

McClelland, D., 6, 14
McGrath, J., 158, 165
McHarg, I., 2, 14
McNamara, M., 15
Major remodeling strategy, 133–134
Manipulation behavior mechanism
  comparisons of
    Eastside, Westside, and Midwest, 82–83
    Eastside, Westside, Midwest, and Arrowhead,
      104–105
  definition, 63
  as percent of occupancy time of Eastside, Westside,
    and Midwest, 90
Mann, L., 1, 7, 14
Marsden, H., 7, 14
Marx, M., 31, 32
Maslow, A., 93, 118
Mayan temples, 11
Medievalism, the new, 11
Mehler, A., 158, 162, 165

Michelson, W., 1, 14, 117, 118
Midwest, 21, 69
  comparisons with
    Eastside and Westside, 79–92
    Eastside, Westside, and Arrowhead, 103–108
Milgram, S., 161, 165
Minimal remodeling strategy, 133
Miranda decision, 2
Mitchell, W., 15, 67
Modal personality, 6
Molar environment, 89
Moos, R., 6, 15, 30, 32
Monument syndrome, 16
Moynihan, P., 4, 15
Murphy Dome, 119, 126
Murray, J., 23

Nader, R., 2
National character studies, 6
Neighborhood center, at Arrowhead, 111–112
Neutra, R., 3, 7
New construction strategy, 135
New social services, Arrowhead, 110
Noninstitutional organization, 116
Number of behavior settings, 77, 139
  compared to OT, 139–140
Nurses' station, 35
Nutrition action pattern
  comparisons of
    Eastside, Westside, and Midwest, 80–81
    Eastside, Westside, Midwest, and Arrowhead, 104
  definition, 61
  percent of OT used for comparison of Eastside,
    Westside, and Midwest, 89

Observers
  Arrowhead, 98–99
  comparison with questionnaire data, 132
  description of, 70, 98–99
  Eastside, Westside, 69
  living in Alaska, 119
  recording data from, 69
  records, examples of, 50

reliability, 70, 99
selecting, 69, 98–99
training, 69, 99
Occupancy time
contrasted with NOD, 139–140
definitions, 49, 59, 83, 139
Occurrence, definitions, 59, 139
Operant conditioning, 8
Operant learning, 7
Operator, researcher as, 31
Optimal manning, 158
Orientation action pattern, 59n
Osmond, H., 37, 48
Ostrander, E., 17, 20
O'Toole, J., 160, 165
Outdoor storage, 131
Overmanning, 159

Paar, A., 7, 15
Panel on social indicators, 2
Paper and pencil tests, 6
Pareek, U., 5, 15, 106, 108, 118
Parfit, J., 165
Parking, 131
Parkinson, C., 164, 165
Participation subscale
action patterns, 59
behavior mechanisms, 62
Paternalism, 5
definition, 3
Paternalistic attitude, of designers, 3
Pattern analysis, *also* pattern sequences, 7, 30
Pawley, M., 1, 15
Pay scale, 62
Penetration levels
available just to residents, Arrowhead and Friendly
Inn, 102–103
calculation of leaders, 141
comparisons
of Eastside, Westside, and Midwest, 74–79
of FAA family housing and Fort Wainwright, 130
definition, 64, 102
Performance/population ratio, 141

Perloff, H., 14
Personal appearance action pattern
comparisons
of Eastside, Westside, and Midwest, 80–81
of Eastside, Westside, Midwest, and Arrowhead,
104
of FAA family housing and Fort Wainwright,
126–129
definition, 61
Personality and personality-culture research, 5, 9
Personalization
of design, 117
of services, 117
Petty, R., 10, 15, 159, 160, 162, 164, 165
Philanthropy action pattern, 59n
Physical health action pattern
comparisons
of Eastside, Westside, and Midwest, 80–81
of Eastside, Westside, Midwest, and Arrowhead,
104
of FAA family housing and Fort Wainwright,
126–129
Population, 59
age definitions, 97
of Arrowhead, 97
of Eastside, 77
overlap formula for K-21 scale, 26
of Westside, 77
Preschool, age definition, 97
Pressure scale
comparisons
of Eastside, Westside, and Midwest, 85
of Eastside, Westside, Midwest, and Arrowhead,
105
definition, 65
Preteen, age definition, 97
Prevocational skills area boundary problems, example
of, 34
Professionalism action pattern
comparisons
of Eastside, Westside, and Midwest, 80–81
of Eastside, Westside, Midwest, and Arrowhead,
104

of FAA family housing and Fort Wainwright,
126–129
definition, 62
Profiles. *See* Action patterns, Behavior mechanisms,
Pressure scale, Welfare scale, and Penetration
levels
Progressive architecture, 15
Project manager, Arrowhead, 109
Proshansky, H., 1, 15, 142
Pruitt Igoe, 3n, 17
Publish-or-perish motive, 5

Querencia, definition, 36, 47
Questionnaire
interview, 68
method, 119–136
mail, 68
used in Alaska, 119, Appendix B
used in Arrowhead, 4
validity of, 132

Radial hospital design, 20
Random sampling procedure, 120
Rapoport, A., 7, 15
Raush, H., 10, 15
Recreation action pattern
comparisons
of Eastside, Westside, and Midwest, 80–81
of Eastside, Westside, and Midwest contrasted to
OT, 84
of Eastside, Westside, Midwest, and Arrowhead,
104
of FAA family housing and Fort Wainwright,
126–129
definition, 62
Redfield, R., 89, 92, 163, 165
Relaxing sites, 8
Religion action pattern
comparisons
of Eastside, Westside, and Midwest, 79–81
of Eastside, Westside, and Midwest contrasted
to OT, 84
of Eastside, Westside, Midwest, and Arrowhead,
104

of FAA family housing and Fort Wainwright,
126–129
definition, 62
Request for proposal. *See* RFP
Research application model, 115
Reliability
of action patterns and behavior mechanisms, 140
of K-21 scale, 39
of observers, 70, 99
Research hurdles for designers to overcome, 5
RFP, from HUD for Arrowhead, 94–95
Richman, H., 165
Rivin, L., 1, 15, 142
Rodman, H., 6, 15
Rogers, C., 3, 15
Rorschach Test, 6
Rosenthal, R., 68, 92
Rubinstein, E., 23
Ruesch, J., 11, 15

Sample K-21 values, 25
Sanoff, H., 2, 6, 11
Satisfaction sites and theory, 8
Saturation maintenance, 113
Scales
action patterns, 60–62
subscales, 59–60
autonomy, 66–67
behavior mechanisms, 63–64
subscales, 62–63
K-21, 25–29
penetration levels, 64
pressure, 65
richness (GRI), 65
welfare, 66
Schoggen, M., 21, 32
Schoggen, P., 21, 32, 40, 48
Schools, 156–157, 162
Seaton, R., 6, 12, 15
Semantic differential, 6
Sephansky, B., 165
Shelly, M., 8, 15
Sheppard, H., 165
Sherif, M., 14

Shopping centers, 8
Sidewalks and paths, Arrowhead, 50–55
  falls on, 51
Siegel, B., 4, 15
Siegel, S., 37, 48
Silverstein, M., 13
Size, problems of
  churches, 158
  cities, 160
  schools, 156–157
  towns, 157–158
Skinner, B., 8, 14, 15
Sleeper clause of the Economic Opportunity Act of
    1964, 4n
Smith, M., 49, 67
Smithsonian conference on appraising museums'
    effectiveness, 13
Sobel, R., 165
Social areas, 111, 116–117
Social contact action pattern
  comparisons
    of Eastside, Westside, and Midwest, 80–81
    of Eastside, Westside, and Midwest contrasted to
      OT, 84
    of Eastside, Westside, Midwest, and Arrowhead,
      104
    of FAA family housing and Fort Wainwright,
      126–129
Social diagnosis, by behavior setting survey, 117
Social modeling, 8
Social services, Arrowhead, 110
Sociofugal space, 37
Sociopetal space, 37
Soma of behavior settings, definition, 58
Sommer, R., 1, 6, 15, 30, 32
Spatial interdependence test, 26
Special materials demonstration, Arrowhead, 113
Spicer, E., 2, 15, 116
Spiegel, H., 4, 15
Srivastava, R., 155, 162, 164, 165
Stanley, J., 12, 13
Stranger, power of, as external change agent, 116
Streets, city vs. small town, 50
Studer, R., 7, 15

Sturdavant, M., 20
Sundstrom, E., 7, 15
Superintendent facilities, Arrowhead, 114
Syndrome
  control, 7
  definition, 16
  here-comes-that-jargon-again, 18
  monument, 16
  we-already-know-that, 17
Synomorph
  definition, 130
  limitations of, 141
  observation of, 131
  problems discovered by study of, 130–131

Talking behavior mechanism
  comparisons
    of Eastside, Westside, Midwest, 82–83
    of Eastside, Westside, Midwest contrasted to OT,
      89–90
    of Eastside, Westside, Midwest, and Arrowhead,
      104–105
  definition, 63
TAT test for achievement motivation, 6
Teaching and learning subscale for action patterns,
    60
Teens, age definition of, 97
Tehran Bazaar, 34
Territoriality, 7
Theory, uses of, 10
Thibault, J., 9, 15
Thiel, 142
Thinking behavior mechanism
  comparisons
    of Eastside, Westside, and Midwest, 82–83
    of Eastside, Westside, and Midwest contrasted to
      OT, 89–90
    of Eastside, Westside, Midwest, and Arrowhead,
      104–105
  definition, 63
Total building cost, 19
Traffic problems, Arrowhead, 53
Transducer, researcher as, 31
Trites, D., 19, 20

Undermanned environment, description of the, 161
Undermanning
  acceptance of new members and, 162
  Air Force data in support of, 129
  in centralization of services, 117
  churches and, 158
  connections with other theories, 163–164
  cost and, 160
  definition problems, 163
  design and, 161
  experiences of success and failure and, 163
  extreme, 155
  golden ratio for, 163
  hard work and, 162
  insecurity and, 162
  list of Barker's eleven consequences of, 154
  list of new seven consequences of, 163
  optimal, 158
  overmanning and, 159
  participation in recreation and, 129
  problem of task in definition of, 160
  reassessment of, 161
  review of, 154
  school accomplishment and, 162
  schools and, 156
  setting capacity and, 154
  short summary of, 10
  standards for new members and, 162
Unit, definition, 58

Van der Ryn, S., 9, 15
Vetoing circuits, definition, 30

Wagner Steagal Act, 93
Wallace, A., 6, 15
Walters, R., 8, 13
Walton, R., 160, 162, 165
We-already-know-that syndrome, 17
Welfare scale
  comparisons
    of Eastside, Westside, and Midwest, 85–86
    of Eastside, Westside, Midwest, and Arrowhead,
     105–106
  definition, 65–66
Westside
  aesthetics, compared with Eastside and Midwest, 60
  behavior setting list, 78
  compared with Eastside and Midwest, 74–92
  compared with Eastside, Midwest, and Arrowhead,
    102–108
  description of, 70–71
  observers, 69
  population, 71
Wicker, A., 6, 10, 15, 47, 48, 64, 67, 77, 92, 158,
    159, 160, 161, 162, 163, 164, 165
Williams, S., 18, 20
Winer, B., 12, 15
Winkel, G., 1, 15
Wohlwill, J., 1, 15
Wright, H., 9, 13, 21, 22, 32, 59, 70, 92, 119, 136,
    143, 153, 157, 165

Zeisel, J., 6, 10, 12, 15, 17, 20
Zlutnick, S., 7, 15